Meeting Christ in the Sacraments

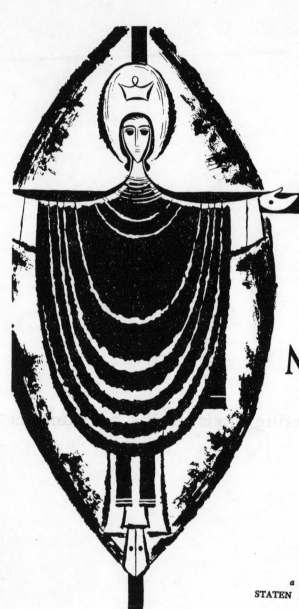

MEETING

alba house
a division of St. Paul Publications
STATEN ISLAND, NEW YORK 10314

COLMAN E. O'NEILL, O. P.

CHRIST IN THE

SACRAMENTS

First printing - October 1964
Second printing - December 1964
Third printing - September 1965

Nihil Obstat:

Anselm Moynihan, O.P., S.T.Lr.
John Cahill, O.P., S.T.Lr., S.T.D.
Rome, June 26, 1963

Imprimi Potest:

Louis C. Coffey, O.P., Prior provincialis
Dublin, July 12, 1963

Nihil Obstat:

Austin B. Vaughan, S.T.D.
Censor Librorum

Imprimatur:

✠ Francis Cardinal Spellman
Archbishop of New York
July 3, 1964

The Nihil Obstat and Imprimatur are official declarations that a book or pamphlet is free of doctrinal or moral error. No implication is contained therein that those who have granted the nihil obstat and imprimatur agree with the contents, opinions or statements expressed.

Library of Congress Catalog Card Number 64-20111

Copyright 1964 by Society of St. Paul, Staten Island, New York (10314)

Designed, printed and bound in the U.S.A. by the Pauline Fathers and Brothers

Alba House is staffed by the Pauline Fathers and Brothers of the Society of St. Paul, Staten Island, N.Y. All the operations going into the making of this book, from editing to binding, were carried out by the Fathers and Brothers as part of their publishing apostolate. The Society was founded to spread Christ's message by means of the press, radio, motion pictures and television.

Contents

ABBREVIATIONS

References to St. Thomas's *Summa theologiae* are given in the customary style, the numerals referring, in order, to: Part, question (q.) and article (a.); to these may be added:
ad 1 (etc.): reply to First (etc.) Objection of the article; c.: in the body of the article.

Denz.-S.: Denzinger-Schönmetzer, *Enchiridion Symbolorum*, ed. 32, 1963.

Vat. II Const.: The Second Ecumenical Council of the Vatican. Constitution on the Sacred Liturgy. (Promulgated 4th December, 1963.)

MD: Pius XII, Encyclical Letter, *Mediator Dei*, 20th November, 1947; English Catholic Truth Society ed.

HA: Pius XII, Encyclical Letter, *Haurietis Aquas*, 15th May, 1956; English Catholic Truth Society ed.

To My Mother and Father

Introduction

"Christ is always present in his Church, especially in her liturgical actions." "Christ always associates the Church with himself in this great work in which perfect honour is paid to God and men are sanctified." These two phrases from the *Constitution on Sacred Liturgy* of the Second Vatican Council (ch. 1, art. 7) formulate the theme of this book. They explain why "the liturgy is the summit towards which the activity of the Church is directed and, at the same time, the source from which all her vitality flows" (*ibid.*, art. 10). For the symbols of the liturgy provide the place where Christ and the faithful meet; and it is this meeting that gives meaning to all that is in the Church.

There is more to the Church than the liturgy; but there is nothing in the Church that does not depend on it. Through the liturgy, above all through the Blessed Eucharist, the saving action of God in Christ becomes effective in the Church. Christ, the Priest-Saviour, is active there, as he was on Calvary. The difference is that now he is present to draw men into the action of Calvary. This is the meeting between Christ and the Church in the liturgy, a meeting which issues in association.

It is this that liturgical instruction must make clear: in the liturgy the operation of Christ on Calvary becomes the cooperation of Christ and the Church. There is a true encounter, but one that is utterly different from the encounters which take place between man and man. All depends on Christ; though not all is done by Christ. The Church has her part to play; she must act as the Spouse of Christ, as the Body of Christ. These scriptural metaphors attempt to express one thing, which is almost inexpressible: that Christ comes in the sacraments to "draw all men to himself" (cf. *Jn.* 12:32), to make them active participants in the one great Act of Calvary which both symbolized and realized the gift of God to man and the loving response of man to God.

This is the challenge of the liturgy. For the Church that is summoned to meet Christ in the sacraments and to join him in his mystery is not an abstraction existing somehow apart from the individual faithful. True, within the Church, the individual is never alone; his personal deficiencies can always find support in the community of grace. But if the individual fails to grasp the implications for himself of his meeting with his Saviour, if he is not at least in some fashion aware of the demands that association with Christ in the liturgy imposes on him, if he is unappreciative of the immeasurable enrichment that this mysterious encounter with the Incarnate Word can bring him, then he is not taking seriously his obligations and privileges as an adult, responsible member of the Church.

It is the response of the individual faithful, within the community of the Church, that will measure the success of the Council's liturgical reforms. The formulation of laws simply indicates the pastoral concern of the bishops and provides means for helping the faithful. The major responsibility now lies on each individual believer. Whether or not local bishops consider it advisable to take advantage of their new faculty of modifying liturgical ritual, the Christian's task is clear. He must *find Christ* in the liturgy, the Christ who has the words of eternal life *(Jn.,*

6:69). And when he has found Christ and heard his words, he must make his own response to the Father, echoing the great Word that was spoken in love on Calvary.

The *Constitution on Sacred Liturgy* has underlined how urgently practical is the problem here outlined. It may appear oddly out-of-touch to turn to a thirteenth-century theologian, however venerable his memory, to find enlightenment on something that can make news headlines today. Yet the conviction of anyone who has followed the hard apprenticeship of reading St. Thomas cannot but be that, if only this theology were clearly presented in the style of the present day, it would of itself capture the enthusiastic assent of the faithful and provide for the vital movements of thought and action now at work in the Church the traditional intellectual orientation they so urgently need. The ritual of the liturgy may change; its essentials were given by Christ and were as real and compelling in the thirteenth and the fourth and the first century as they are today. The conciliar Fathers, St. Thomas, St. Augustine and the apostles are all at grips with the same mystery.

If St. Thomas is here chosen as the exponent of the traditional meditation of the Church on the liturgical mystery, it is not solely because of the writer's convictions concerning the perennial validity and relevance of Thomistic thought. I should like to think that these pages go some way to meeting the desire expressed by Pope John XXIII in his address to the Fifth International Thomistic Congress, September 16, 1960:

> Diligence in studying the works of St. Thomas, that is the first thing necessary. It is, accordingly, Our urgent desire that there should be a daily increase in the number of those who draw light and learning from the writings of the Angelic Doctor. Not only the clergy and those whose interest lies in specialized research, but those too who study the humanities should be included in this number. And among these We wish especially to see a larger representation of the younger generation, those engaged in Catholic Action and university graduates. The teaching of St. Thomas is like a hidden treasure;

Our earnest desire is that each day should see more of it uncovered, for this can only be to the supreme advantage of the Church. His writings must be published as widely as possible among the people, whether by way of formal instruction or in the language suited to the spirit and character of the present age. (*Acta Apostolicae Sedis* 52 (1960), p. 823.)

Recalling the last part of this quotation in his Apostolic Letter of March 7, 1963, *Dominicianus Ordo,* John XXIII added:

It is Our conviction that if the study of Aquinas' teaching is promoted with greater attention and enthusiasm the outcome will be that whatever decisions may be made by the Fathers of the Second Vatican Ecumenical Council will be more fruitfully put into effect. (*L'Osservatore Romano*, March 7, 1963.)

To this end, in what concerns the *Constitution on Liturgy,* the following pages may, I hope, in some part contribute. St. Thomas's teaching on the sacramental character as a participation in the priesthood of Christ is perhaps his major contribution to discussion of present-day liturgical problems; but it is above all in his theology of the Eucharist that he lays down the guidelines for an authentically liturgical Christian life.

*   *   *   *

The pages which follow were written as a series of twelve articles to provide background to the Council's discussions for *Doctrine and Life*, the Irish Dominican review, at the suggestion of the Editor. I should like to thank him for his permission to use these articles as the basis for the present work.

Mr. Michael Glazier of New York provided the encouragement necessary for the task of rewriting and expanding the articles and generously undertook the burden of acting for me with the publishers. Fr. Thomas C. Donlan, O.P., of Dubuque, Iowa, helped me too with his vast enthusiasm and his familiarity with the book-world in the United States. I am very grateful to both of these friendly guides. My thanks are also due to Fr. Anselm Moynihan, O.P., formerly my Prior in Rome, who read the typescript and helped me with his advice.

Fribourg, March 1, 1964.

1 The Priesthood of Christ

See the Church this way, the *Epistle to the Hebrews* suggests to us, see it for what it is, an epic adventure that calls for high endeavour if its goal is to be reached; see it as a great people on the march towards God, seeking a lasting city, a vast exodus of humanity, fleeing from the captivity of sin, stretching across the desert of time, weary sometimes of the journey, but urged on always by hope of coming to the land promised by God.

EXODUS

THE EXODUS OF ISRAEL

God is calling men to Himself, promising them rest: "We who have believed shall enter into rest" (*Heb.*, 4:3), the rest that is God's own in the still, unchanging contemplation and love of Himself (*ibid.*, v.4; cf. *Ps.*, 94:11).[1] The same call and

---

1. In quotations from **Hebrews** the Douai text has been modified in the light of the Jerusalem translation (Cerf, Paris, 1956) and that of Fr. C. Spicq, O.P., **L'Epitre aux Hébreux**, vol. II (Gabalda, Paris, 1953).

the same promise go out to the men of all ages, though not always with the clarity that they have been given in the Church of Christ. They take shape first in vague but compelling outline when God holds out to Adam and Eve the hope of a champion who will come to overthrow the power of Satan and, in association with a new mother of all the living, win for mankind the restoration of the happiness lost by sin (*Gen.*, 3:15-16). They are heard in the promises made to Abraham (*Gen.*, 17:1 f.) and to Moses (*Ex.*, 19:3 f.), taking on at this time a more material form which later revelation will show to have been symbolic of their true spiritual content but which represents a real, though provisional, phase in the realization of the plan of salvation implicit in the divine invitation to man. Across the desert and beyond the Jordan there awaits a land which will be given over to the political control of the Israelites. Moses, acting as God's spokesman and lawgiver, leads the captives out of slavery, instructs them in the terms of the Alliance established between God and themselves, and forms them into a homogeneous people, the chosen people of God. If they will lend ear to the voice of God, if they will obey His laws, He on His side will grant them His special favour (*Gen.*, 19:5).

THE SPIRITUAL EXODUS

But, as *Hebrews* recalls, many of those who took part in the exodus from Egypt provoked the Lord by their unbelief so that He swore in His anger: "No, they shall not enter into my rest"; and as a result those who betrayed the Alliance did not survive to enter the promised land; their corpses were left in the desert (*Heb.*, 3:11, 16-19; cf. *Num.*, 14:22-23, 29). Their failure to resist the temptations of the march is contrasted with the single-minded trust of those who, throughout the long history of Israel, read the call of God rightly. They observed the terms of the Alliance, confident that God would honour His promise to bring them into His perfect rest. Theirs was a spiritual exodus, a journey of self-discipline, a preparation for the moment when the promises would be fulfilled in all the perfection known only to God. Their great model was Abraham who, six hundred years before the Alliance of Sinai, obeyed the call of God and went out "towards a place which he was to receive for an inheritance; and he went out, not knowing whither he went" (*Heb.*, 11:8; cf. *Gen.*, 12:1-4). He was prepared to sacrifice Isaac, his only son, in whom the promises were to be fulfilled, "accounting that God is able to raise up even from the dead" (*Heb.*, 11:17 f.; cf. *Gen.*, 22:1-14). Like Abraham, those who followed his example, "so great a cloud of witnesses surrounding us" (*Heb.*, 12:1), "died according to faith, not having received the object of the promise, God providing some better thing for us that they should not come to perfection without us" (*Heb.*, 11:39-40).

THE NEW ALLIANCE AND THE NEW EXODUS

The Alliance entered into on Sinai was only provisional; it was destined to give place to a New Alliance drawn up in terms more suited to govern the relations between man and God. It is true that those who lived under the Law of Moses could penetrate to its heart and discover its authentic spiritual value; but they could do this only as individuals, the Law itself being inadequate to introduce them into the presence of God. For the Law was an external rule of life, graven on tables of stone; it demanded submission; it was a guide for those prepared to submit but it could not supply the means of submitting. The characteristic of the law of the New Alliance will be that it is interior, written in men's hearts: "for this is the alliance which I will contract with the house of Israel after those days, says the Lord: I will give my laws into their mind, and in their heart will I engrave them and I will be their God, and they shall be my people" (*Heb.*, 8:10; cf. *Jer.*, 31:33). Obedience to this law is not submission to regulations imposed from outside; it is rather the way of acting connatural to one who is of the same mind as the lawgiver. The law is no longer a constraint; it plots out the way of life adapted to one who has entered into interior union with God; in fact, this union with God itself constitutes the true law of the New Alliance, the written word being no more than its exterior reflection.

St. Paul, familiar as he was with the Old Law, takes delight in showing how its deficiencies are provided for in the New Alliance where union with Christ by faith takes its place. The Law was good; it was the Jews' "pedagogue in Christ" (*Gal.*, 3:24; cf. *Rom.*, 7:12), preparing them for the inward law of grace. It was valid and acceptable during the period of the first Alliance if used by men as a means of submission to God; but it was empty, made up of "weak and needy elements" (*Gal.*, 4:9), requiring something more than itself, requiring that men's hearts be touched directly by God if they were truly to approach Him. It is just this lack that is supplied by the New Law: "Man is not justified by the works of the Law, but by the faith of Jesus Christ" (*Gal.*, 2:16); and it was this faith in the future Messiah that saved some of the Jews, those who followed the example of Moses who "esteemed the reproach of Christ greater riches than the treasure of the Egyptians; for he looked unto the reward" (*Heb.*, 11:26).

Under the New Law the exodus remains. They are still fugitives, those whom the new Alliance gathers, setting a hope before them (*Heb.*, 6:18); but now there is a new leader who calls upon them to go with him outside the camp of the human city as exiles from the world of worldliness, seeking a lasting city that is to come (*Heb.*, 13:13-14). To hand on the New Law, the interior Law of grace, there is a new lawgiver "worthy of greater glory than Moses," for Moses was a servant in the house of God but Christ is the Son over his own house (*Heb.*, 3:3, 5-6). Christ is "mediator of a better Alliance which is established on better promises" (*Heb.*, 8:6). The march of those who follow Christ is a transformed exodus because the leader and lawgiver is no longer a mere image of Christ but Christ himself. The exodus, like the law, has become interiorized; it is a journey of the mind and the heart. The end of the march is not simply an earthly city now. The rest that God promises is the holy city of Jerusalem "coming down out of heaven from God" (*Apoc.*, 21:10) in which there is no Temple, for the whole city is a sanctuary: "the Lord God Almighty is the temple thereof, as is the Lamb" (*Apoc.*, 21:22). This sanctuary is nothing else but the life of the Blessed Trinity to which those who belong to Christ are called.

THE TEMPLE

At the end of each exodus there stands the Temple, the dwelling-place of God. The march is not just a nomadic migration; it is a pilgrimage of worshippers going up to the central place of worship, to Jerusalem, old or new. Moses, when the first Alliance was drawn up and when he received the tables of the Law on Mount Sinai prescribing the Israelites' obligations rising from the contract, was commanded by the Lord to organize a priesthood and to construct a tent to serve as a sanctuary for the worship of the new people as they made their way towards the permanent sanctuary. "See (says the Lord) that thou make all things according to the pattern which was shewn thee on the mountain" (*Heb.*, 8:5; cf. *Ex.*, 25:40). This was the glory of Jewish worship that it was modelled on the vision of the heavenly sanctuary granted to Moses. Its priests, fulfilling the prescriptions of the Law, could approach more closely the presence of God than those of any other people. But just as the Law was an external one only, warning the people of their duties but not itself strengthening their wills to obey it, so the official worship, being part of the Law, could not of itself satisfy the demands of God, nor could its priests enter truly into the presence of God (cf. *Gal.*, 3:11; *Rom.*, 3:20). For men enter the presence of God, not by offering ritual sacrifices, oblations, holocausts, victims for sin, but by doing His will (*Heb.*, 10:8-9; cf. *Ps.* 39:7). The Law and the liturgy it prescribed did not of themselves or necessarily imply the submission of man's will. The tent-sanctuary of the first exodus and the Temple of Jerusalem were nothing more than copies, formalized ritual evocations of the heavenly sanctuary where the divine will is done in the Love of the Blessed Trinity. "For having nothing but the shadow of the good things to come, not the substance of the realities, the Law is absolutely powerless, with its sacrifices, ever the same, offered perpetually from year to year, to render perfect those who approach God" (*Heb.*, 10:1).

The liturgy of the New Law also celebrates the worship of the Temple that stands at the goal of its exodus. But as with the Law itself, so with the worship: the empty symbolic forms of the old religion dissolve to give place to the reality which they foreshadowed. The worship of the New Law gives men access to the sanctuary where perfect homage is offered to God. This is because the priesthood of the New Law no longer has a purely ritual function; it is the priesthood of Christ and its powers are those of Christ himself, the Priest who ministers in the heavenly sanctuary.

THE PRIESTHOOD OF CHRIST

PRIEST OF THE HEAVENLY SANCTUARY

It is the Temple that gives meaning to the exodus. The sanctuary to be built in the earthly Jerusalem was to become the centre of the national life of the people welded together by Moses in the desert. Thinking along these lines, the author of the *Epistle to the Hebrews* interprets the Christian exodus in terms of the sanctuary of heaven and he draws on the ritual of the Jewish liturgy, particularly as it was carried out in the desert, for details with which to set up an analogy for expressing the Christian mystery.

The ninth chapter of the Epistle describes the sanctuary of the Israelites in the desert: a tent divided by a veil, on this side the Holy into which all the priests could enter to perform the daily sacrifices, on the other side the Holy of Holies, containing the ark of the covenant, the dwelling-place of God on earth. Only the high priest could enter the second sanctuary, and that on one day of the year, the Day of Expiations; nor could he enter unless he carried with him the blood of animals slain in sacrifice outside the tent. This blood he sprinkled round the ark in expiation of his own and the people's sins of ignorance (*Heb.*, 9:1-7; cf. *Ex.*, 25-26; *Lev.*, 16).

In terms of this ritual the Epistle presents an image of Christ the King entering the heavenly sanctuary as a priest. Risen from the dead, he crosses the heavens, "a tent not made by human hands, not of this creation" (*Heb.*, 9:11), that is, the place where God dwells, and he enters definitively the presence of God, the sanctuary (*Heb.*, 9:12). The blood he bears which wins him admission is not the blood of goats or calves but his own blood which has won for us eternal redemption (*ibid.*).

Christ has entered within the veil to the Holy of Holies into the presence of God (*Heb.*, 6:20; 9:3; 10:20). It is in terms of this comparison with the liturgy of Expiations that *Hebrews* lays more stress on Christ's bearing his blood into the presence of God than on the actual shedding on Calvary. The slaughter outside the tent was secondary in the Jewish ritual; what constituted the sacrifice was the sprinkling of blood in the Holy of Holies. "This is why Jesus also, that he might sanctify the people by his own blood, suffered outside the gate" of Jerusalem (*Heb.*, 13:12). Christians are come "to Jesus the mediator of the new Alliance and to the sprinkling of blood more eloquent than that of Abel" (*Heb.*, 2:24). Evidently, the metaphor is maintained here; what is expressed by the sprinkling of blood is the presence of Christ, body and soul, before the Father, the submission of his humanity to Him and the intercession which he makes for us in virtue of his sacrifice.

The drama of redemption is for *Hebrews* a great liturgical action celebrated by Christ whose mission is thus seen as essentially a priestly one. He comes into the world only so that he may return to the heavenly sanctuary as a priest who bears with him the blood which has been shed in sacrifice on earth. Now he may stand for ever, the high priest in the Holy of Holies, preserving unchangingly the culminating moment of the sacrifice offered for his people. This ritual of the new Expiations colours the whole existence of Christ. "As he enters the world he says: Sacrifice and oblation thou wouldst not; but a body thou hast fashioned for me. Holocausts and sacrifices for sin did not please thee. Then I said: Behold I come—for this is prescribed for me in the scroll of the book—to do thy will, o God" (*Heb.*, 10:5-7). Here is the heart of Christ's sacrifice; it is his obedience to the will of his Father which wins him admission to the heavenly sanctuary.

THE PATTERN OF OBEDIENCE

There is no other means of entering this sanctuary except obedience, for the sanctuary is nothing else than the sphere of those creatures who share in the life of the Blessed Trinity. Within the Trinity itself the divine will reigns supreme; the divine goodness dominates the entire activity of God; the Holy Spirit, who *is* God, is the seal of love set on the utter identification of Father and Son with their common goodness. This supreme harmony of the Blessed Trinity is the Pattern, glimpsed by Moses, to which all those who would enter into union with God must conform. It would be for God to deny His own nature if He were to admit to a share in His own life of knowledge and love of Himself any creature whose will was not fixed on the divine goodness. It is a necessary condition of the Alliance by which God calls man to enter into His rest that man should have God as the centre of his affections, for the rest that God offers consists in the satisfaction of man's desire to possess and enjoy God. That God should so be loved by man is a gift of God Himself; it is God sharing with man His own life, drawing man into His own happiness. These are two sides of one reality: God gives the gift of love; man loves and submits to God by a completely free act. Within the Trinity there is no submission, only love; when creatures are drawn into the life of the Trinity there must be submission to the Author of all that exists. When the Pattern of trinitarian harmony is reproduced in man it incorporates the new motif of obedience.

Christ comes on earth as the high priest who will lead his people into the heavenly sanctuary. It is not for the Father's sake that he comes, nor for his own. He is the Son, second Person of the Blessed Trinity, dwelling eternally with the Father and the Holy Spirit in the perfect harmony of God. It is man who must conform himself to the heavenly Pattern. Man, in his flesh and blood, involved in the strands of history, must, through union with God, through submission to Him, reproduce in human terms by human actions the supreme model of divine harmony. In the gift of grace granted to Adam mankind had the means to do this; but that grace was lost; the image of the Trinity was dimmed on earth; the will of God was no longer mirrored in men's actions; entry into the heavenly sanctuary was barred. Instead of the life of God being made over to man, the human race was held in the bondage of death. There was sin, the death which is precisely privation of divine life, and bodily death which is the effect and the image of sin (*Rom.*, 5:12). To restore the image of the Blessed Trinity, to make man's life once again a mirror of the divine will, men must be brought back into the presence of God, filled with His life, conformed to the heavenly Pattern.

So the Son took on our flesh and blood (*Heb.*, 2:14), became man in order that by his earthly life he might through his obedience reimpress on humanity the Pattern of submission to the divine will and thereby reopen the way for his new brethren into the heavenly sanctuary (*Heb.*, 2:11). No purely ritual reproduction of entry into the sanctuary, such as that enacted in the Jewish liturgy, could achieve true participation in the life of that most holy place. A true entry had to be made by an authentic act of human obedience. And since the sons of Adam had renounced their right to enter the sanctuary this act of obedience could be made only by one who, though human, held some other title to admission. This was Christ, true God as well as true man. He is "the brightness of the glory of the Father and the figure of His substance, who upholds the universe by His mighty word" (*Heb.*, 1:3). When the Word enters the world as man "He does not leave the right hand of the Father" (St. Thomas, *Verbum supernum*, Lauds hymn, Corpus Christi), and even as man he remains partly within the heavenly sanctuary; only his body stands outside. This must be explained; it is the key to Christ's priestly sacrifice.

WITHIN THE SANCTUARY

By reason of union with the Person of the Word the humanity of Christ is enriched in a quite unique fashion; the Word "dwelt among us full of grace and truth" (*Jn.*, 1:14). In her theological meditation on this perfect human nature, the Church has come to discern in it the dimensions of its fullness of grace and truth. Even while on earth Christ enjoyed in his human mind the beatific vision, reserved for other men for the future life; for this was God's own human mind and it is impossible to think that it should not attain the fullness of knowledge of God possible to a created being.

In addition, since God can be known indirectly as well as face to face, Christ's human mind could reach out to Him and to His plans for creatures through other mediums, less perfect than the beatific vision but providing new standpoints from which to contemplate the divine mysteries. Accordingly, Christ, even when he was on earth, had knowledge such as the angels have, infused, that is, into his mind by God. Finally, because he possessed the same faculties as other men, Christ could acquire knowledge in the way that we do, constructing ideas from the material provided by the senses.

The goodness of God, made manifest to Christ's human mind in all these ways, infallibly drew a response from his human will. For he was full of grace; grace was his by right; the sources of his human activity were purified and enriched by reason of his divine personality. His will was consequently fixed on God in constant loving submission. Here is the perfect reproduction of the Pattern of trinitarian harmony in a created nature. It is the supreme example of the introduction of a creature into the life of the Trinity. Not only as God, then, but even as man Christ never leaves the sanctuary of heaven. At the centre of his humanity he is always in the presence of God by knowledge and by love. This is true above all by reason of his beatific knowledge, his face-to-face vision of God. It is true also at the lower level of his infused and acquired knowledge where the response of his love for the goodness of God takes its colour from the indirect mode of this knowledge. It is the mystery of Christ's human psychology that, while the beatific vision with its full manifestation of the goodness of God calls forth necessarily the submission of the human will, the love that was directed by his infused and acquired knowledge was a love that could be withheld. The harmony with the Blessed Trinity enjoyed by Christ's human nature ruled out his ever actually denying such love; but the sovereign freedom of the human will is such that nothing can compel its love except goodness itself and God seen face-to-face, recognized as the only being who satisfies its infinite yearnings. While, then, Christ's submission to the divine will as known to him by infused and acquired knowledge placed him within the heavenly sanctuary, in union with God, it did so in such a way that he stood there freely, by his own human choice. In Christ humanity in its earthly condition has access to the presence of God, a means of making submission to Him. And because he is the Son, sent by the Father of mercy, to lead all mankind back into the sanctuary, the submission that he makes from the first moment of his earthly existence is one that has a universal significance. The unique reproduction of the Pattern of trinitarian harmony in Christ's humanity is established as the master-form which will be used to repeat the Pattern in the rest of mankind.

THE WAY OF ENTRY TO THE SANCTUARY

The fact that Christ's human nature belongs to the Son of God places it at the centre of human history. In the person of Christ the yearning of the sons of Adam for the restoration of the gift of divine sonship, lost by sin, is fulfilled in a fashion surpassing anything that might have been hoped for from the mercy of God. For Christ is the Son, the only-begotten of the Father. Accordingly the perfect, loving submission of Christ in his human nature to God is the supreme realization of the obedience which must be given by all those others who are called to be adopted sons of God. But Christ's obedience is more than an example to be imitated; it is too the means chosen by God in His loving mercy for reintroducing into the human race the possibility of other men submitting to Him in filial devotion. Raised out of the order of mere humanity, while remaining human, Christ concentrates in himself the whole of the human race. This does not mean that other men lose their individuality or their personal responsibility for their own lives; rather they have in Christ a chief, one who has entered into a transcendent union with God, one whose human actions sum up all that human action can ever be hoped to achieve for the sake of the love of God. Whatever disobedience to God may be found among men can be outweighed by the obedience of Christ if those who are guilty unite themselves to the humanity of Christ.

Union with Christ, this is the way of return to God. It makes possible the imitation of his obedience. As in the case of Christ's own humanity, the initiative lies with God. It is He who reproduces the Pattern in mankind. But the fact that He does this in other men through the humanity of Christ, in which is realized the supreme manifestation of obedience, means that He looks upon the human race as a whole which includes

Christ, and that accordingly He finds the human race as a whole worthy, prepared to receive His grace. This is the true sense in which we can speak of the merits of Christ being applicable to all men. We may sometimes think of this as though God were moved by Christ's actions to give His grace to men; but this is a too human way of thinking. God cannot change; His love for His creatures is not subject to the fluctuations, the giving and the withdrawing, which characterize human affections. Men, on the contrary, can change in their love for God; because they are free they can erect obstacles to divine love, prevent its transforming their souls. They can too advance in the love of God, prepare themselves, under the influence of His love for them, for greater gifts of His love. This is merit. God's gifts are granted freely, out of the abundance of His goodness; it is one of His gifts that man should be able to make himself worthy of further gifts and of the final gift of heaven. Christ's merit was such that he prepared the whole human race for receiving again after sin the gift of God's love and for growing in that love. Because of Christ's obedience mankind is now worthy of divine sonship. The sonship is actually bestowed when men come under the influence of Christ's humanity, when they are united to him, when the Pattern is impressed on them.

To be actually united with Christ in this fashion is for the individual a gift of divine liberality of which he personally cannot be worthy. But once given the union, then he is worthy because he shares in the worthiness of Christ. He is now in possession of the means to develop in himself the Pattern of submission, to impress it on all his action, and thereby to prepare himself for the fullness of divine gifts; but this will necessarily always be in union with Christ, benefitting from his universal act of obedience, appropriating by personal action his supreme worthiness.

It is because Christ remained by obedience within the sanctuary of the Blessed Trinity that he was able while on earth to win the right to draw all men after him into the presence of God. This is the bright centre of his priesthood which gave significance and value to whatever he did or suffered in the world. The pain of his passion and death did not of itself give pleasure to his heavenly Father; to interpret his priesthood in these terms would be to parody the sense of Christianity. The mystery of Christ is the mystery of God's dealing with man; it is a mystery of mutual love, and in Christ the Priest the two loves, divine and human, meet. This union in love could not remain interior, wholly spiritualized in Christ for he was truly man, come among men; and human action, human communication, must be in and through a body. But what gave his external actions significance was always the two loves that inspired them.

ENTRY BY SUFFERING

Yet Christ did suffer. In his body he stood outside the sanctuary; St. Paul says that he was "made a curse for us" (*Gal.*, 3:13; cf. *Rom.*, 8:3; *II Cor.*, 5:21; *Col.*, 2:14). Body and soul, he was indeed in personal union with the divine Son; but he deliberately prevented the glorification of body that would naturally have followed on that union. He enjoyed the beatific vision from the beginning of his human existence; this was enough to transform him in body in the way that the bodies of the saints will be transformed at the general resurrection. At his transfiguration he allowed momentarily the glory of his soul to change his body; but the mission assigned him by his Father forbade him to remain in this state. The vision gone, he tells his three disciples: "The son of man shall suffer from them" (*Matt.*, 17:12). His body was one that could suffer; and to this extent his soul, beatified though it was, could suffer too for it is the man who suffers, not just his body.

St. Thomas devotes a lengthy meditation in his *Summa theologiae* to the scandal of Christ's suffering (III, q. 46). He has no difficulty in showing that other ways of saving mankind were possible to God; but the way chosen was the only one perfectly adapted to the condition of the sons of Adam. The suffering of His Son was decreed by God, not for His own sake, but for man's.

It is characteristic of St. Thomas's view of the Incarnation—which for him is primarily a revelation to us of the way of *truth* to which we must respond, thereby entering into a personal relationship with God (III, Prol.)—that he sees the passion first of all as a form of divine teaching, a revelation of God's person. From it man can learn how much God loves him and so be moved to love in return; "in this consists the fullness of man's salvation" (III, q. 46, a. 3; cf. *Rom.*, 5:8-9).

In the suffering of Christ man will also find the supreme model of obedience and all the other virtues summoned up by the passion. Here we see the Pattern of loving submission being ·impressed on the body of Christ. Only by obedience can man enter the Holy of Holies; Christ could enter there in the fullness of his humanity, body as well as soul, only if he subjected his body to the trial decreed by his Father.

But the final and decisive reason for the passion lay in man's sinfulness. In his body Christ had to pay the price for the sin of men by submitting to death. "What the law could not do, in that the flesh rendered it powerless, God sending His own Son, with a flesh like to that of sin, and in view of sin, has condemned sin in the flesh" (*Rom.*, 8:3). The flesh of Christ was like to the flesh of sinful man precisely because it was not yet within the sanctuary; it was unglorified, subject to death; and death, of the body as well as of the soul, is the consequence of sin (cf. *Rom.*, 5:12). The obedience of Christ's will had to be expressed in his flesh, accepting death, the penalty of sin, if men were to be released from sin. The moment on Calvary was the supreme moment only because then the full implications of the interior sacrifice in the context of sinful humanity were accepted and fulfilled. When Christ's body is raised from death mankind has the certainty that death has been overcome, that the power of sin has been broken. And yet, as St. Thomas does not fail to insist, man's sin could have been absolved in other ways. Without violating the laws of justice, God could have condoned man's offence by an act of mercy (III, q. 46, a. 2, ad 3). In any event His mercy stands behind Christ's reparation for it was He who sent His Son, and this implies a basic condonation of sin. The true sense of Christ's sufferings, the need for his death, are to be sought in man. It was because God respects the dignity of the creature whom He has made to His own image that He sent His Son to die as man. It was man who was overcome by Satan and man, if he is to bear the responsibilities of his freedom, must pay in full the consequences of his fault. Because Christ suffered man can claim that humanity has met the debt of justice incurred by sin, an offence against God. "And that this should be so," writes St. Thomas, "is the result of even greater mercy on the part of God than if He had simply remitted sin without reparation being made by man. 'Thanks be to God who hath given *us* the victory through our Lord, Jesus Christ' " (III, q. 46, a. 3; a. 1, ad 3; cf. *J Cor.*, 15:57).

The master-Pattern of obedience now takes on new, bodily shape. It is transposed into terms of repentant humanity winning access once again to the heavenly sanctuary. To restore the Pattern in man and in human history Christ had to suffer death; only after this could he be raised up in body to the right hand of his Father and stand in the presence of God in his humanity, body as well as spirit. "We see Jesus, who was made for a moment lower than the angels, crowned with glory and honour because he has suffered death" (*Heb.*, 2:9). The risen Christ is glorified in body and soul so that now there is in the heavenly sanctuary a "spiritual body," united to the Word of life, a body which has become life-giving for men (cf. *J Cor.*, 15).

The Pattern reproduced bodily in the mysteries of Christ's life and death must be repeated in some fashion in the life of every man who will enter the heavenly sanctuary with Christ. Death and resurrection and glorification, affecting the individual in his whole being, spiritual and material, this is the new exodus, the flight from the captivity of sin under the leadership of Christ into the promised land where the temple is no longer a symbol of the meeting-place of God and man but is God Himself in whom mankind has its rest. We see this Pattern repeated for the first time and in a unique fashion in Mary, the mother and associate of Christ. Her compassion was the immediate reflection of Christ's passion. Her direct association with the bodily pasch of her son constituted her own exodus, brought to its fulfillment in her assumption.

THE NEW MEDIATOR

Moses, though he was the mediator of the Old Alliance, did not himself enter the promised land or see Jerusalem, the holy city. Christ, sent by the Father to establish the New Alliance, comes as a more perfect mediator, one who not only speaks for God and teaches His law but is able in addition to lead his people into the true sanctuary of holiness. He comes as a priest-mediator, offering the sacrifice of himself for sin, opening the way to life in the Blessed Trinity. His mediation, consequently, transcends that of Moses for the alliance which he negotiates is drawn up in terms of the saving love of God and the willing response of humanity. As sent by God he brings into the world the riches of divine truth and grace, in the first instance as his own exclusive attributes. In the name of mankind he offers his sacrifice as the expression of his filial acceptance of these gifts. In this priest the Alliance is not simply announced; it is achieved. Christ embodies the Alliance; others called to enter it must do so in him. Through him come grace and truth; through his sacrifice God's people express their filial acceptance of these gifts and their will to use them in imitation of their Priest.

The sacrifice of Christ, with which every man must be associated, is seen in *Hebrews* not primarily as an event of the past, something which happened on Calvary centuries ago, but as an abiding reality. We have "a great high-priest who has passed into the heavens" (*Heb.*, 4:14). The sacrifice of himself, the submission of his human will to the Father, will last for ever and the Precious Blood and the Body will remain for ever glorified by the resurrection from sacrificial death. He is our priest now in heaven, offering this sacrifice of himself, his Precious Blood, shed on Calvary, bearing witness to the completeness of his submission (*Heb.*, 10:12; cf. 8:3 f.). His presence within the sanctuary gives us certitude that his sacrifice has been accepted by the Father. The Jewish priests could offer only ritual, external sacrifices; their office was carried out in a sanctuary of this world (*Heb.*, 9:1 f.) and was terminated by death (*Heb.*, 7:32). The sacrifice of Christ, being primarily the sacrifice of his will, takes place in the presence of God in the heavenly sanctuary and is eternal. "He, by reason of the fact that he continues for ever, has an untransmittable priesthood. Whence it follows that he is able also to save in perfect fashion those who through him advance towards God, always living to make intercession in their favour" (*Heb.*, 7:24-25). He is a priest for ever, says St. Thomas, *quia est de veritate*: his is the true sacrifice of the will of which the bloody sacrifice was only the complement, necessary for a fully human expression of submission; whereas the Levitical priesthood was *de figura*: external, not of the will, an empty, ceremonial image of the true sacrifice (*Ad Heb.*, c. 5, lect. 1; Marietti ed., n. 252). Now that our High Priest officiates in the heavenly sanctuary, his blood speaks for us, eternal proof of his reparation for our sin; for if the blood of the Jewish sacrifices could obtain ritual cleansing for the people, "how much more shall the blood of Christ, who by an eternal spirit offered himself unspotted unto God, cleanse our consciences from dead works so that we may pay worship to the living God" (*Heb.*, 9:13-14)?

MEMBERS OF THE PRIEST

THE CHRISTIAN ENTERS THE SANCTUARY

The march of Christians is more than an exodus; it is a cultual pilgrimage; and this, we see now, not simply because it is directed towards the heavenly city of Jerusalem but because the leader of the marchers has already entered the sanctuary. This is the source of the certainty of the march, the certainty of arriving definitively beyond the veil in the Holy of Holies if we do not fall out of line. We hold fast the hope set before us and "in it we have as it were the anchor of our soul, sure as it is solid, and penetrating beyond the veil, there where our forerunner Jesus has entered for us, become for eternity a high priest according to the order of Melchisedech" (*Heb.*, 6:20).

The presence of Christ beyond the veil lends a special character to the Christian exodus. If our Priest has entered the sanctuary, we too, though we are still on the march, have in a certain sense entered with him. In the desert only the high priest of the Israelites was permitted to penetrate beyond the veil into the Holy of Holies. "The Holy Spirit signifies thus that the way into the sanctuary was not open while the former tabernacle was yet standing" (*Heb.*, 9:8). But Christ "by one oblation has perfected for ever those whom he sanctifies. Now, where sins are remitted there is no more oblation for sin. Having therefore, brethren, the assurance required for entering the sanctuary by the blood of Jesus, by this new and living way which he has opened for us through the veil—that is, his flesh—and a sovereign priest over the house of God, let us draw near, in the fullness of faith, our hearts cleansed from all stains of an evil conscience and our bodies washed with pure water" (*Heb.*, 9:14, 18-22). The veil of the Jewish temple was rent in two at the moment of Christ's death (*Matt.*, 27:50-51); the way into the presence of God is open to all His people through the flesh of Christ, a veil of the sanctuary which yields to faith. The hymn for Lauds on the feast of the Sacred Heart identifies the heart of Jesus as the new veil of the heavenly sanctuary, *scisso utilius*, more profitable than the veil that was torn. It also names the Sacred Heart the sanctuary of the New Alliance. The image envisages the Heart as enclosing us in the presence of God; by union with the love of Christ our Priest we are united with God (cf. *Apoc.*, 21:22: the temple is the Lord and the Lamb).

The "good things" Christ has won for us, the "heavenly realities" are "yet to come" (*Heb.*, 9:11; 10:1; cf. 2:5); and yet the faithful have already tasted them (*Heb.*, 6:5). The perfect rest, full entry into the sanctuary, is for the future; but the very fact that Christ, the Head of the body, has achieved the goal wins for his members a foretaste of that perfection. Just as Christ himself never left the sanctuary in the transcendence of his soul, though his body, animated by the same soul, was subject to time and death, so his members can share in the heavenly liturgy "in spirit and in truth" (*Jn.*, 4:23), entering into the presence of God by submision of will, even while the obscurity of faith and morality detain them as pilgrims. Heaven does not so much come after life as penetrate its every moment, for it is where God is. Faith gains entry there even as it forbids definitive possession. We see God, but indirectly; we know, but in part only (*J Cor.*, 13:12). We are "come to Mount Sion and to the city of the living God, the heavenly Jerusalem and to the company of many thousands of angels (. . .) and to God (. . .) and to the spirits of the just (. . .) and to Jesus" (*Heb.*, 12: 22-24). With our Head and Priest already in the sanctuary, we can go with confidence to the throne of grace (*Heb.*, 4:16).

THE ROYAL PRIESTHOOD OF THE FAITHFUL

When the first Alliance was drawn up, the Lord spoke to Moses on Mount Sinai and said: "Henceforward if you obey me and observe my alliance, you shall be my particular possession among all peoples (for all the earth is mine). And you shall be to me a priestly kingdom and a holy nation" (*Ex.*, 19:5-6). Bound to God by the Alliance, set apart from other nations, the Israelites were dedicated as a people to His worship and as such took on priestly dignity, again as a nation. With much greater force those who set out on the Christian exodus, united to Christ the Priest, entering through him the heavenly sanctuary, are called by St. Peter: "a chosen generation, a kingly priesthood, a holy nation, a purchased people" (*J Pet.*, 2:9). This priesthood must be understood against the background of the whole vast canvas of *Hebrews*.

All Christians form together a royal priesthood because they are members of Christ, King of creation and Priest of the New Alliance of grace. Every priesthood is defined in terms of the sacrifice which it offers (cf. *Heb.*, 8:3). There are some Christians, those who have received the sacrament of orders, who are denominated priests specifically and formally in relation to the sacrifice of the Mass, in which they play a very particular role as the ministers of Christ; these form a special class within the Christian community. The common priesthood of Christians, on the contrary, is denominated such in terms of the sacrifice of Christ as it is described in *Hebrews*. This is the heavenly sacrifice; "if he were on earth, he would not be a priest" because the earthly sacrifices were confided to the Levitical priesthood (*Heb.*, 8:4-5). This earthly priesthood, being provisional, is now abrogated and with it all earthly sacrifice not objectively incorporated into Christ's sacrifice (as is the Mass). The *only* sacrifice of the New Alliance is the heavenly sacrifice of Christ which he offered "once for all in offering himself (*Heb.*, 7:27) in the last age of the world" (*Heb.*, 9:26) so that he has "entered into the sanctuary once for all (. . .) with his own blood" (*Heb.*, 9:12). We have seen that this sacrifice incorporates the sacrifice of Calvary; we know too that it is brought on earth and made visible in the Mass; but the central element is the submission of Christ's will to the Father; it is this which makes it heavenly, winning admission to the presence of God, and which makes it eternal. It is in terms of this sacrifice, which was manifested on Calvary and which remains for ever, that all Christians form a kingly priesthood. This is their sacrifice since they are body of him who offers his own body. No matter what form the Christian's offering of Christ's sacrifice may take, and in particular when it takes the form of participation in the Mass, the central reality which gives meaning to whatever is being done will always be the union achieved with the submission of Christ's human will to his Father.

The history of the Christian exodus, of the Church, will recount the exploitation of Christ's eternal sacrifice. All the complex means given the Church for exploiting it—teaching authority, government, sacraments—are directed to one end: to unite the wills of Christians to that of Christ in submission to the Father (cf. *Heb.*, 13:15, 21). To submit to the Father so that our actions will mirror the life of the Blessed Trinity, this is the sacrifice of our priesthood. It is sometimes called a spiritual priesthood because it is directed towards this spiritual sacrifice, and, in fact, St. Peter devotes the whole of his first Epistle to developing the practical means of fulfilling its moral demands. But it cannot be a purely spiritual priesthood because man is not a spiritual being, nor is Christ's body a mere appearance. We cannot unite ourselves to our High Priest in heaven—we cannot, that is, exercise our priesthood—by purely spiritual means. For this reason we have the Church, with all its external apparatus of law, teaching authority and liturgy, through which we can come into bodily contact with our Mediator-Priest to receive from him, in the human fashion that the Incarnation implies, the law of grace and the word of life and so participate in his sacrifice. Mary, standing at the foot of the cross, could see and touch the body of her son; through it she received grace and knowledge of God; through it also she offered the sacrifice of her will in union with Christ. The Christian comes into contact with the same body of Christ in and through the Church; and it is for the same reason: to draw from it grace and truth and to offer it together with Christ and Mary as the token of interior participation in the sacrifice of Christ's will.

PRIESTS IN THE DESERT

Though we are able, by living the life of the Church, to share in the heavenly liturgy of Christ we remain, while the present life lasts, always on the march. This is the characteristic of the Christian exodus. The visible reality of the Church constitutes the new flesh of Christ through which he sanctifies the world and through which the world finds entry into his heavenly worship; but at the same time and for precisely the same reason the visible Church is the exterior, temporal form assumed by those who believe in Christ and who are still seeking full union with him. The Church, because she belongs both to Christ and to his members, belongs both to heaven and to earth. While then we are indeed "strangers and pilgrims" (*Heb.*, 11:13, *J Pet.*, 2:11), not having in the desert of the world a lasting city (*Heb.*, 13:13), while we suffer all the trials of migrants in a strange country (*Heb.*, 12:1 f.; 13:12 f.), this represents only our share in the heavenly aspect of the Church. We must not think that we have abandoned the earthly city; that is the other aspect of the Church. The Christian in renouncing Satan has fled from the captivity of Egypt; but he must be a priest in the desert; this is his dwelling-place even though he lives nomad-fashion in a tent, recognizing that his true home is the new Jerusalem. The Pattern of the Blessed Trinity has been revealed once on earth in the associated mysteries of Christ and Mary. It must be revealed again in Christians on another plane of history in the complex cross-currents of the earthly city. This is the meaning of the priesthood of the faithful, the fullness of the priesthood of Christ. If we are to grasp its full implications we must look more closely at the nature of the Church and try to discover how this institution forms the area of living union between Christ and his members. How is Christ's mission brought to fulfillment through the Church? How are we to understand that what the Church does Christ is doing? Why does life in Christ necessarily imply life in the Church? All these questions may be resolved into one dominating query: how does God send out through the Church His invitation to men to enter into His rest, and how is it that man can make his response to that call only through the Church?

2 Christ is Active in the Church

Stephen, the first to lay down his life in imitation of Christ, looking up to heaven at the moment of his condemnation, "saw the glory of God, and Jesus standing on the right hand of God. And he said: Behold I see the heavens opened and the son of man standing on the right hand of God" (*Acts*, 7:55).

This vision, coming at the moment when the Pattern of Christ's obedience was being reproduced for the first time in the body of one of his followers, brings into dramatic focus the teaching of the apostles on the mystery which had entered into their lives. Their preaching centered on the risen Christ who had entered bodily beyond the veil into the Holy of Holies, into the presence of God. "Ye men of Israel hear these words (...): Neither was he left in hell, neither did his flesh see corruption. This Jesus hath God raised again, whereof all we are witnesses. Being exalted therefore by the right hand of God, he has received of the Father the Holy Spirit, the object of the promise, and hath poured him forth. It is this that you see and hear" (*Acts*, 2:22, 31-33).

THE EXALTATION OF CHRIST

SENDING OF THE SPIRIT

The humiliation of the Son of God who took on human nature and in it became obedient even to the death of the cross has led to his exaltation so that now, in his human nature, he is the Lord (*Phil.*, 2:8-11) since he has entered into the full and perfect exercise of his royal power (cf. *Acts*, 5:31; *Rom.*, 1:4; *Eph.*, 1:20-23; *Col.*, 1:18-20; *Apoc.*, 1:5; etc.). This is the meaning of his ascension. It makes him in his humanity a "life-giving spirit" (*I Cor.*, 15:45). In his glorified humanity he now sends down the Spirit upon the Church. His bodily submission and consequently glorification have drawn his human soul and body into participation in the action by which God gives His own life to men. The humanity which even in the years in Palestine could transmit the power of God to heal men's physical and spiritual sickness is now imbued definitively with the power of the Holy Spirit to sanctify men.

St. Thomas takes a thoroughly realistic view of this power of the heavenly Christ; that is to say, he understands it to belong to Christ in all the reaches of his humanity. It could quite well be said that Christ sends down the Spirit in virtue simply of his intercession for men in heaven. We would think then of the Spirit being sent by the two divine Persons, Father and Son, in response to, or on the occasion of the human intercession of Christ. But for St. Thomas this is not enough; it does not take full account of the dignity accorded Christ's humanity when it was united personally to the divine Son or of the significance to be attributed to the saving actions performed by the Son in his human nature. The Incarnation, with all that it implies in terms of the utter humanization of the action of God in the world of grace, was not just a passing interlude in the story of the divine love for men. It has established the permanent characteristic of the Christian economy. The reproduction of trinitarian harmony in mankind is now achieved through the supreme example of human conformity to the Pattern. The humanity of Christ in all its reality, physical as well as spiritual, has become the instrument through which the grace-giving Spirit is sent into the world.

Though connected with the name of St. Thomas and his followers, this understanding of the mystery of the heavenly Christ is scriptural in its origin. The Spirit belonged to Christ throughout his life, as was manifested by the descent of the dove at his baptism (*John*, 1:33); nevertheless Christ was not fully to give the Spirit until he was glorified (*John*, 7:39; 16:7-8; 20:22. It is assumed here that Christ ascended to the glory of heaven on Easter day, what is known as the ascension being the last of a series of appearances to his disciples; cf. *John* 20:17 and recent exegesis). It is only when his corruptible flesh has been glorified and has thus been brought through the full cycle of suffering, death and resurrection that it is adapted to the function of serving as the instrument through which the Word of life, and with Him the other Persons of the Trinity, restore divine life to the rest of mankind. This idea of grace coming to men not only through Christ's mind (where he designates those who will benefit from it) but also through the material reality of his body is central to St. Thomas's understanding of the Incarnation and of the sacramental Church. We shall see later (in Chapter Four) how he develops it.

VICTORY OVER DEATH

In Christ's power to send the Spirit into the world lies the completeness of his triumph over death and over sin. Not only has he risen himself, but in his risen humanity he is now the source of all supernatural life: ultimately of the resurrection to life everlasting of all the faithful, but already of spiritual resurrection from sin (*J Cor.*, 15; cf. *Summa* theol., III, q. 56, aa. 1 and 2). The sense of the preaching of the apostles is that all humanity is transformed by the resurrection and glorification of Christ. Because the Head is risen, the whole body of the faithful is in a sense risen. The universal cause of all resurrection, the scholastic theologians will put it, has been placed. It is not that sin, original and personal, and death have ceased to be realities for the faithful, nor that moral effort is not required of the Christian if he is to enjoy heaven. We are not deprived of responsibility because we become members of Christ; we retain our liberty to use or abuse. But because Christ is risen and has entered into the sanctuary of heaven the way of resurrection lies open for us and every step that we make has already been made for us by Christ; we have only to make the step for ourselves. This perhaps sounds like deliberate paradox; but it is in fact the mystery of Christian grace. The gift of grace and the further gift of using grace well have been won for us by Christ; and that inevitably means that they have been assigned to each one of us individually in the eternal design of God; yet our liberty and consequent responsibility remain untouched. The paradox of grace and liberty lies beyond theological controversy; though if we wish to be faithful to St. Thomas we will say that the springs of true liberty lie in grace. For the apostles, seized with the primitive simplicity of the faith, the central message of their preaching was that the risen Christ sends down the Spirit, won for men on Calvary, to extend to all the faithful the glory which is now his in body as well as soul.

CHRIST'S ACTIVITY IN THE CHURCH

The Church is the place on earth to which the Spirit is sent; and, because it is Christ in his humanity who sends the Spirit, Christ is active in the Church. This simple statement synthesizes a whole array of particular statements that can be made about the Church. It singles out the dominant theme which coordinates all the various elements which go to make up the complex reality which is the Church; and each of these elements must be analyzed in itself if the full sense of the whole is to be discovered. The first and most important thing to grasp is that Christ is active in the Church in two distinct though related ways.

He is active in the individuals who belong to the Church, because he sends the Spirit into them as a new principle of life; and this is the central reality of the Church towards which are directed all the other elements of its structure.

He is active also in the juridic or institutional functions of the Church, not sending the Spirit to dwell in them, for the Spirit dwells only in individual men, but subordinating them to his own action of sending the Spirit, so that the Church, in exercising these functions, co-operates with the human Christ in this sending. This second mode of Christ's activity in the Church takes on very many different forms and necessitates a quite complex structure in the Church, which will appear throughout the succeeding chapters. For the moment it is sufficient to develop in general terms the two basic forms of Christ's activity in the Church. The details can be filled in only after the broad outlines have been grasped.

CHRIST IN THE FAITHFUL

Without Christ man is subject to death and to all those evil tendencies of a nature disrupted by sin which St. Paul calls "the flesh" (*Rom.*, 7:5, 14, 24; etc.). The death of Christ "in the likeness of sinful flesh" frees man from this subjection. For this death achieves what no other could; it constitutes full acceptance by one of the human race of the consequences of sin. The complete abasement of the divine Son in his human nature redresses the infinite evil of mankind's rejection of adoptive sonship. As a result of the Son's obedience, the flesh is henceforward stripped of its dominion over those who belong to Christ; having removed the obstacle to divine sonship, Christ can share his sinlessness with all men (cf. *Rom.*, 8:3). The risen Christ sends down his Spirit to make men "spiritual" like himself, no longer under the dominion of the flesh. With the Spirit dwelling in them the faithful "are not in the flesh, but in the spirit" (*Rom.*, 8:9).

It is of paramount importance, if the relevance of Christianity to life in the world is to be grasped, that the sense of this "spiritual" life be properly interpreted. St. Paul does not contrast the spirit with the body, as though to imply that Christ provides some form of impossible escape from our human condition with its involvement in material reality. The Christian revolution is based on the opposition between spirit and "flesh," between a completely human form of life, involving body as well as soul, led under the inspiration of the Holy Spirit, and a life that is controlled by the corrupt instincts of a nature disturbed by sin. The faithful have within them a principle of "spiritual" life in this sense so that, though they still walk in the flesh, subject to temptation and destined for physical death, they do not walk according to the flesh (cf. *II Cor.*, 10:3; *Rom.*, 8:10; 5:12). Rather they reproduce Christ in themselves by their faith (*Gal.*, 2:20). This is the work of the Holy Spirit sent by the risen Christ. It may be useful to put this combined activity of Christ and the Spirit in terms of an image. The sun, shining through a stained-glass window, throws on the ground an image of the glass. The Holy Spirit, coming to man through the humanity of Christ, reproduces in man the image of Christ risen from the dead. By the power of this Spirit and led by Him, the faithful live according to the "spirit," that is, not according to the "flesh," even in their bodily actions. By virtuous action their whole being, including their bodies, is drawn progressively under the influence of the spirit and into the sphere of the Holy Spirit. The natural consequence will be the vision of God and bodily resurrection (*Rom.*, 8:11).

There is in effect only one resurrection-ascension, that of Christ, the first-born Son. The resurrection and glorification of the justified is simply an explicitation and a manifestation of the inner meaning and power of that one event. Only the Son can go to the Father in the heavenly sanctuary: "No man hath ascended into heaven but he that descended from heaven, the son of man who is in heaven" (*Jn.*, 3:13). If men go too it is because they are sons in the Son, loving the Father in the power of that Spirit in whom Christ loves his Father. "The Spirit himself giveth testimony to our spirit that we are the sons of God. And if sons, heirs also; heirs indeed of God and joint-heirs with Christ" (*Rom.*, 8:16, 17).

United to Christ by the Spirit we have access to the Father (*Eph.*, 2:18). We participate in the heavenly liturgy conducted by Christ now that he has passed wholly beyond the veil, bearing his blood. All that belongs to Christian life and Christian morality must be interpreted in terms of this union with the heavenly sacrifice of Christ. The fact that the faithful can join in his sacrifice is itself a result of his sacrifice so that it is proper to say that Christ offers his own sacrifice by a double title: in his own person and in his mystical person. There is one sacrifice and one priest. Those who receive the Spirit from him share thereby in his priesthood. When they offer, it is still he who offers in and through them, even while their offering is in the highest degree personal and responsible. Christ is active in the Church in every person who belongs to it. There are obviously to be distinguished variations of intensity in this action of Christ. The sinner can share only very imperfectly in Christ's priestly activity in the Church community; but even here, while faith, a gift of Christ, remains, there is submission of the human intellect to the word of God; and the remnant of good will which this implies effects a distant sharing in Christ's sacrifice. This is inadequate to win the principal fruits of the sacrifice but it provides the basis for a new intervention of divine mercy leading the sinner back into the fullness of filial submission.

There is a danger that those who like to call themselves practical Christians would be tempted to dismiss these ideas as nothing more than poetic speculations of theologians who have lost contact with the struggle involved in keeping the commandments. But St. Paul had to deal with men who were unjust, fornicators, idolators, perverts, liars and thieves and the rest (cf. *1 Cor.*, 6:9 f.; *Gal.*, 5:19 f.; *Eph.*, 4-6; etc.). It was for people like these that he formulated his teaching and to them, in all their plight of sin, he applied it. It was something more than a far-off ideal he was setting before his converts. He was explaining to them the plain facts of Christian life. The real meaning of the most modest effort to follow Christ sincerely as well as of heroic conquest of the flesh is to be found in the resurrection of Christ from the dead. The mystery and the power of that resurrection is being gradually unfolded in the life and the struggles of every Christian. The Church in which the faithful are gathered is humanity rising from the grave of sin with Christ and entering with him into the presence of God. It is Christ rising from the dead in his members.

CHRIST IN THE WORSHIP OF THE CHURCH

It is natural that those on earth united with the heavenly Christ should express in ritual the fact and significance of their union. It is true that every good action of a Christian is an expression of his union with Christ and participation in his heavenly worship. But the community character of resurrection or salvation in Christ requires communal expression. This need to come together for worship can be explained purely in terms of man's social character but the new association that mankind has entered into with Christ the unique Priest provides a higher motive and a more compelling necessity for a public liturgy. The charity which binds together the faithful and joins them to Christ seeks naturally for symbolic gestures which will give visible form to a union which is radically spiritual. Christ has in fact provided for this need by establishing his Church.

At its most fundamental the Church, like Christ, is a teacher of truth. The Church is the authorized guardian and proponent of the truth of revelation, the truth of Christ, which must be accepted by faith under the impulse of the Holy Spirit and which provides that understanding of God's dealing with man which is necessary if there is to be a human response to the divine invitation. It is clear that when we consider the Church in this way our point of view has swung away from our previous consideration of the Church as the assembly of the faithful. It is the same society that we are looking at but now the institutional or organizational function has come to the foreground. As the basic office of teaching indicates, the visible Church is the vehicle by means of which Christ exercises his saving activity on those who believe in him. This second form of Christ's activity in the Church, directed towards the development of his interior activity within the faithful, affects every function of the visible Church, not excluding that of the laity. The precise form that it takes at the various levels of ecclesiastical society will be considered in connection with the sacraments of orders, baptism and confirmation. For the moment we wish to concentrate on one function of the visible Church, that of liturgical worship. This is in fact a privileged area in the activity of the Church because Christ intervenes in it and is active through it in a quite exceptional way. But the best approach for grasping the significance for the faithful of this activity of Christ is not to consider it in isolation as a heavenly intervention in the life of the Church but to attempt to assign it its place in a scheme of life which is dominated by interior union with God and by the moral effort which this entails. If this line of thought is followed the continuity which exists between the interior activity of Christ and his intervention in the visible actions of the Church will become apparent and the danger will be avoided of thinking that liturgical participation and the benefits it brings can in some way compensate for lack of co-operation with the inner promptings of the Holy Spirit.

CHRISTIAN WORSHIP

EXPRESSION OF FAITH

As members of human society and of the mystical body the faithful have an innate inclination towards corporate worship. Accordingly, as a natural outgrowth of its status as a juridically-based community of faith the Church conducts a liturgy, understood in the widest sense of all external community actions of worship. The fact that the individual believer is confronted with an established ritual conducted by ordained priests should not obscure the other fact that this ritual, whatever else may be its significance, serves also, and indeed in the first instance, as a bodily manifestation of corporate spiritual union with Christ. It is the public expression given to the hidden activity of Christ the Priest in his members. Considering public worship from this side, from the side of the faithful, there is no essential *religious* distinction between liturgy in the narrow sense and so-called "popular" community devotions, though obviously there exist profound differences in the extent of ecclesiastical approval, in historical origins and, as is painfully evident, in cultural values, whether humanistic or Christian. Those united by faith to the heavenly liturgy of Christ find in these ceremonies—ranging from the Stations of the Cross to the ceremonial of a pontifical Mass—a tangible instrument for evoking active participation by faith in his worship of the Father. This is not to say that the ritual prayers and ceremonies are purely psychological gadgets designed to trigger or activate interior union with Christ. They do have this function; but when the members of the congregation take part in the manner prescribed for them in the public action the whole ritual becomes a genuine external act of religion. That is to say, public worship, if the people are really worshipping, constitutes the adequately human form of participation in the heavenly liturgy of Christ. The body itself, the words it speaks and the actions it performs, are drawn into the sanctified sphere of union with Christ.

It is worthwhile making it clear that a Catholic plumber by repairing a pipe may also exercise his share in Christ's priesthood and participate in the heavenly liturgy. This is clearly not quite the same thing as taking part in the Church's public worship; but the difference, from the point of view of personal expression in external activity, is one of emphasis; for there is no legitimate action which cannot be performed for the love of God and thereby be incorporated into Christ's sacrifice, directed towards the Father. It is simply that the ceremonial of the Church, evolved in the course of her history and considered purely as a symbolic expression of faith, is concerned immediately only with submission to the Father, whereas Christian secular activity has in addition a temporal significance and value. In the current theological jargon, one provides "vertical" contact with God, the other "horizontal." The ritual of the Church is concerned immediately only with "vertical" worship. The central virtue called into play is religion, working under the prompting of faith, hope and charity; and religion is concerned directly with the homage which must be paid to God by man. Christian secular activity, on the contrary, calls to the front other moral virtues, though the basic religious attitude remains constant.

The comparative simplicity of direct or "vertical" worship, withdrawn as it is from immediate involvement in the often distressing complexities of Christian behaviour in everyday life, can be deceptive. Enthusiasm for the parish choir does not always go hand in hand with regard for the rights in justice of business or social associates. One of the first requisites for an authentic liturgical spirituality is a realization that the two planes of worship differ only in emphasis and cannot be thought of as in any fashion mutually independent or exclusive. Implicit in "vertical" worship is the resolve to develop "horizontally," in daily life, the priesthood of Christ active in each of his members. Likewise, the outward forms of "vertical" worship are coloured by "horizontal," historical and cultural, factors. The ceremonial of the Church reflects the temporal interests of Catholics at different periods. Traces of former anti-Semitism, for example, have been removed from the Holy Week liturgy only in the past few years. In particular, popular devotions, as distinct from the official worship of the Church, are a valuable indication of the level of secular and theological culture achieved by the mass of the clergy and faithful.

THE PROBLEM OF CHRISTIAN WORSHIP

By approaching the worship of the Church from below, seeing it as the expression of the faithful's union with God in Christ, it is possible to discover the central problem confronting it. Only if the difficulty is appreciated will the solution provided by Christ be fully valued. It has just been pointed out that the bodily actions involved in taking part in, for example, the Stations of the Cross are just as much genuine external acts of religion as are the prescribed movements and responses of the congregation at Mass. Such acts are at the same time expressive of faith in Christ and endowed with an intrinsic moral value as bodily actions inspired by the virtue of religion. But the principal act of this virtue, the offering of sacrifice, and the associated rites of participation in the fruits of sacrifice raise a special difficulty in the Christian religion.

It might appear that the central and unique character of the sacrifice of Christ involves as an inevitable consequence the exclusion of genuine external sacrifice from the Church on earth. The all-sufficiency of Christ's sacrifice seems to require that it can be offered by Christ's members only by faith, that is, spiritually. It appears to have taken out of men's hands the possibility of offering a true external sacrifice of their own on earth; and this is what is meant by genuine sacrifice for, as always, religious actions are adequately human only when they involve the body. Many non-Catholics have argued along these lines. The most that can be done, they are convinced, is to recall the memory of Christ's sacrifice on Calvary by a purely symbolic ritual devoid of any meaning other than that attached to it by faith. This is a genuine insight into the primacy of Christ's redemptive sacrifice and, if properly interpreted, reveals the basic religious attitude that must be adopted by the faithful; for it is beyond question that faith, in one way or another, provides man's primary bond with Christ and his sacrifice. But the question is whether Christ has opened up to faith a mode of union which transcends the possibilities of faith itself.

The problem arises again when the distribution of the fruits of Christ's sacrifice are considered. The fact that Christ has ascended bodily into heaven and from there sends down on his members the Spirit to awaken grace in their hearts might suggest once more that our only contact with our Priest-Mediator can be through faith, accepting his word as preached by the Church and opening our hearts to the influence of the invisible Spirit. If ceremonies should be used in the Church evocative of the gifts of grace made us by Christ, it appears inevitable, however vividly they announce or present the mystery, that they should be nothing more than stimulants to faith, activating our spiritual submission to Christ and in this way prompting us to merit grace for ourselves.

If these two suppositions about sacrifice and its fruits were correct, our effective entry into the heavenly sanctuary with Christ would retain during our time on earth an exclusively spiritual character in these principal acts of our religion. Our ceremonial of worship being purely an expression of faith in the saving work of Christ, there would be no essential difference between our condition as Christians and that of the pre-Christian Jews who kept faith in the future Messiah. They could already share by faith in the sacrifice of Christ and could win grace in virtue of their acceptance of that sacrifice; for they believed in the word of God and submitted implicitly to all that it contained. The resurrection-ascension of Christ would not have significantly altered the nature of Christian worship.

It could be argued that such a situation would not be out of harmony with our present condition, risen from sin in spirit but subject to the law of death in our bodies and striving by moral effort to bring these mortal bodies under the rule of the spirit. The body of Christ has entered beyond the veil, as has that of Mary, but these are the first fruits of resurrection; others will follow, "every one in his own order" (*J Cor.*, 15:23). To seek for any kind of bodily participation in Christ's heavenly sacrifice, to think it possible that our liturgy could be any more than an expression of our faith in Christ's mediation, seems to be a patent confusion of our present imperfect union with Christ and the future union that we hope for in heaven. How is it conceivable that the material things which we use in the Church as a visible sign of our involvement in Christ's unique sacrifice should in reality be the very things which Christ offered on Calvary and which still act in heaven as the visible expression of his eternal submission to his Father? How can we presume to think that the ceremonies in which we proclaim our faith in Christ as the source of all grace should themselves, material things that they are coming into physical contact with our bodies, convey to us the fruits won by Christ's sacrifice? That all these material things can stimulate our faith and so are an essential element of our religion is quite clear; but that leaves them as simple adjuncts to faith required by our bodily condition; how can we go further and imagine that our sacrificial ritual is something more than a memorial of Calvary, that it is in fact a true, visible sacifice? And what is true of this central ceremony of the liturgy is true also of the ceremonies which surround it. They can help our faith; but since the unique Victim of the sacrifice is beyond our grasp it seems pointless to expect that use of material symbols of the Victim should have any power of themselves to communicate to us the grace won for us by Christ.

It may be thought that this point is being laboured since it is quite clear to all Catholics that the Mass is a sacrifice and that the sacraments do give grace. But it is just these things which are quite clear to us and that we take for granted that need to be examined closely. Our very familiarity with the sacramental system not only closes our eyes to its truly extraordinary character but in addition, because we concentrate on the salient fact of its intrinsic efficacy, tends to draw our attention away from its basic structure which is that of an expression of faith in Christ. This is to be insisted on, not just because it is theologically precise, but above all because it indicates the fundamental religious attitude required of those taking part in the liturgy. This point will be treated more fully in the chapter on baptism. For the moment it is sufficient to recognize the considerable element of truth contained in the "faith alone" approach to liturgy. It must be conceded to this position that it lays bare the precise dilemma of the Christian life which is constituted by a kind of ecstasy, a drawing out of the spirit towards God while the body remains enmeshed in temporal affairs. There is in fact an orthodox school of Catholic spirituality, firmly based on a line of thought traditional in the Church, which stresses just this aspect of Christianity. If its formula, *agere contra*—which might be translated "repress purely natural instincts"—embodies an over-simplified view of Christian morality, not to say a misunderstanding of certain of its specific values, it nevertheless expresses quite vividly a psychological truth (and in this lies whatever value it has). The Christian feels himself divided between two worlds and cannot but be conscious, unless he is either a saint or very superficial, that his hold on Christ and on heaven is not shared by his whole being. To put it in terms of the Christian mystery: our resurrection is at present only provisional, or better, it is a resurrection in slow motion; it awaits definitive completion at the return of Christ.

CHRIST'S SOLUTION TO THE PROBLEM

The arguments of "faith alone" are the arguments of human reason. Faith itself tells us that Christ has found a way to overcome the limitations of our present condition. He has devised a means by which we may enter bodily into the heavenly sanctuary while still on earth, so that we may be united to his sacrifice in body as well as spirit even before the final resurrection. We cannot be treated like angels, nor are we called on to deny the values of the body, even when we are endowed with the supernatural life given by the Holy Spirit. The spiritual effort involved in holding to Christ by naked faith would be more than supernatural; it would be superhuman in the sense that it would be incompatible with our nature. It is something that might have been possible had our flesh not been weakened by sin, but not now that we are banished from the earthly paradise.

It is the risen body of Christ which opens the way for our bodily entry beyond the veil even now. The glorified body of Christ: this is the distinctive mark, the treasure of the New Testament. Our entry in body consists in bodily contact with his body—bodily communion we should say if the phrase had not a particular connotation, whereas here the sense is quite general. Because the Church can lay hold on the body of Christ she has in her possession the Victim that was offered on Calvary, the visible thing which Christ sacrificed which is the channel through which the fruits of the sacrifice are distributed.

The body of Christ comes to us in our liturgy. At the principal ceremonies, the sacraments, in which we as a community express our faith in Christ, a point of insertion is provided in the earthly ritual for the entry of his body. Or we may say, the sacraments *give body* to Christ in the Church. Mary gave the Word a body with which he lived and died in Palestine and which is now raised up to heaven. The Church fulfills a like function. Her sacramental ceremonies give Christ a new bodily form on earth; not a new body, for he has only one; but an extension to his body, or better, a transposition of his body into a new dimension. The ritual actions which constitute the essential parts of the sacramental ceremonial and the materials employed in these actions provide the means by which the risen Christ is bodily present and bodily active in the Church. The economy of incarnation is here brought a stage further than in Palestine. *External expressions of faith* in the Incarnation become themselves the material of incarnation. They are not united personally to the Word as is the human nature given by Mary. But they are linked to the humanity of Christ not merely by faith —as even the Stations of the Cross or the recitation of the Rosary are—but really and objectively in a fashion that transcends the realm of symbolism and is brought about through the infinite power of God.

SACRAMENTS OF FAITH

There are accordingly two poles which determine the nature of the sacraments: on the side of the Church, an act of faith in Christ, externalized by ceremony; on the side of Christ, an entering into the ceremony to act in the Church. It is essential to grasp the nature of these two constitutive elements and to see their mutual dependence. The entry of Christ into the ceremonial is a natural, though wholly gratuitous, development of the sign of faith. In the Mass the Church enacts a ritual evocation of the sacrifice of Christ so that the faithful may participate by faith in Christ's heavenly worship and consequently in Calvary. The bodily entry of Christ into this ritual incorporates it really into his worship. The heavenly liturgy is now actually being conducted *in and through the Church ceremony,* in and through, that is to say, the community expression of spiritual participation in that liturgy. The Church ritual is at once transformed; the memorial of Calvary has become the very sacrifice of Christ. In the other sacraments the Church performs signs of faith in the sanctifying power of Christ's heavenly liturgy and applies them to an individual, praying that he may benefit from them. The bodily entry of Christ into this ritual makes of it the actual means by which the Spirit of grace descends on the recipient.

A certain deliberate ambiguity has been preserved in the preceding paragraphs in order to bring out the unitary theme of the sacraments: bodily contact with the body of Christ. But it is clear that not every sacrament embodies or contains Christ in the way the Eucharist does. In it there is true and complete bodily presence. The others make present the activity of Christ sanctifying the faithful through his body. The distinction between the two kinds of sacrament as regards bodily contact is one of degree only. The complete humanity of Christ, glorified body as well as soul, is active in all the sacraments. In all of them the faithful are brought into direct physical participation in the heavenly liturgy. Their spiritual participation by faith in this worship is the natural presupposition and concomitant of the bodily participation made possible with the entry of Christ into the ritual action.

The individual shape of the various sacramental actions performed by the Church is of capital importance. Just as Mary gave to the Word his humanity and thereby determined the individual characteristics of that humanity, so the ritual performed by the Church determines the fashion in which Christ is made present in the liturgical assembly. In the measured terms of scholastic theology: the sacraments effect what they signify (and now that this phrase has been introduced it must not be made an excuse for the mental laziness of eliminating from view all that has been said about the necessity for faith in the community's use of the sacraments). There are two distinct kinds of sacramental action, corresponding to two phases of Christ's heavenly worship. One kind is constituted by the Mass alone, which signifies immediately *the sacrifice* of Christ, offered to the Father. All the other sacraments, including Holy Communion, belong to the second class. These signify *the effects* of Christ's heavenly worship. By using both kinds of sacrament the faithful participate to the full, in the measure permitted by their present state, in the heavenly liturgy. We must form here the image of the Whole Christ, the Head in glory, the members on earth, united in worship of the Father. All worship redounds to the benefit of the worshipper for we can give nothing to God, cannot add in the slightest to the glory which He possesses from eternity: "If thou do justly, what shalt thou give him, or what shall he receive of thy hand?" (*Job.*, 35:7). By submitting to God, the creature places himself in his rightful position in the scheme of reality, the place best suited to him. When we apply this to the worship of the Whole Christ a certain modification is called for since individual worship is here assumed into community worship and, moreover, the worship of the Head is communicated to the members. Accordingly, the worship of Christ in heaven benefits the Whole Christ worshipping in and with him. It can bring no further perfection to the Head; the effect is all for his members. The sacramental system of the Church is wholly centered on the heavenly worship of Christ. It brings the two phases of this worship among men so that they are able to offer a true external sacrifice and to receive from the hand of Christ, acting through the material elements of the sacraments, the grace which gives them the dignity of sons of God.

THE CHURCH OF THE WORD

The sacramental ceremonial of the Church has therefore a two-fold significance and validity. It is an expression of the faith of the Church; and at the same time it is the visible sign of the active presence of Christ and of the divine love which sanctifies man. The initiative here only apparently lies with the Church.

In fact it is Christ who has given the Church the sacraments; it is he who has given the power to the Church to perform ceremonies which will procure his saving presence. From Christ is derived the ministerial power required for the validity of the sacraments, the power which will ensure his active intervention in the liturgy. In the case of all the sacraments, including marriage, this power constitutes one element of the mission given by Christ to his Church. The words pronounced by the minister in each of the sacraments are words which are pronounced in the name of Christ; the minister's actions are performed in the name of Christ. When the faithful call upon their ordained ministers to perform the sacramental ceremonies they are responding by faith to the invitation of Christ.

From this may be seen how the sacraments find their place within the framework of the primary function of the Church which is that of acting as the spokesman of the word of Christ. The sacraments belong to the same category as the preaching of the word. Non-Catholics speak of them as the visible word as opposed to the audible word. Once again this represents a genuine insight into the mystery of the Church. Certainly the sacraments transcend the realm of preaching, but they still retain its characteristic features. They constitute with preaching and with the holy Scriptures the continued proposal of the word of Christ within the Church, which calls for the response of faith. The word proclaimed by the Church, if received by faith, brings into being in the world the body of Christ. Here lies the ambiguity which divides Catholics from other Christians. How are we to understand the "body" of Christ? Is it the mystical body, the congregation of the faithful? The answer from both sides is yes. But in the case of the sacraments is it also the physical body of Christ, brought into the world by the power of the word in order to build up the mystical body? It is this that non-Catholics deny and that Catholics affirm. The difference is clearcut, but perhaps it is not radical. The Church does not deny the primacy of the word and of the response of faith; she maintains rather that the mystery of the word has depths unsounded by Protestant theology. Christ has given the Church more than his voice; he gives himself, his full humanity, his body which brought healing to the sick and the sinners of Palestine, and which, now that it is glorified in heaven, is the channel of being and life for his mystical body.

Christ is active in the Church, not only in the spiritual life of the faithful, awakened by the preaching of his word, but also in the material ritual of the liturgy. Subjectively and objectively, as the community of the faithful and as the juridical society of salvation, the Church is alive with the life of Christ. The unifying motif, the purpose of all that is in the Church, is the submission to the Father perfected in the heavenly sacrifice of Christ. In this sacrifice the faithful participate by every action springing from the Spirit, from their spiritual priesthood. The Mass *is* this sacrifice. The other sacraments bring the fruits of the sacrifice, richer than any that the Church could merit for herself; fruits which, when received and interiorised by the faithful, turn back to their Author and introduce the faithful once again, but now with greater intensity, into the one sacrifice. That the Church may carry forward the work of redemption, notes the Second Vatican Council:

> Christ is always present in his Church, especially in her liturgical actions. He is present in the sacrifice of the Mass, both in the person of the minister, "the same now offering, through the ministry of priests, who then offered himself on the cross," and especially under the eucharistic species. He is present by his power in the sacraments, so that when a man baptizes it is Christ himself who baptizes. He is present in his word, since it is he himself who speaks when the Sacred Scriptures are read in the Church. He is present, finally, when the Church prays and sings, for he promised: "Where two or three are gathered together in my name, there am I in the midst of them" (*Matt.*, 18:20). (Vat. II Const., ch. 1, art. 7.)

Christ our Priest has entered in body beyond the veil. The sacraments of his body are the new veil through which the faithful may enter with him in body into the Holy of Holies. Christians are not escaping from the market-place into the sanctuary. They are preparing themselves to bring the holiness of the sanctuary into the daily life of human society. United with the physical body of Christ they are his mystical body, involved by their own bodily condition in the affairs of this world. Through them Christ is active in the world.

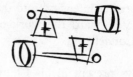

3 The Mysteries of Christ and the Sacraments

Nicodemus, the cautious, uncommitted intellectual, comes to Christ by night and hears the message of rebirth in water and the Holy Spirit. He is unconvinced: "How can these things be done?" (John, 3:9). Christ's reply mingles reproof with prophecy: "Art thou a master in Israel and knowest not these things? ... As Moses lifted up the serpent in the desert, so must the son of man be lifted up. That whosoever believeth in him may not perish, but may have life everlasting" (John 3:10-15). The raising up of Christ is one of the leading ideas of St. John's Gospel: "I, if I be lifted up from the earth, will draw all things to myself" (John 12:32). This Christ said signifying what death he should die (v.33); and this gospel reaches its dramatic climax when the lance of the Roman soldier pierces the side of Christ raised on the cross. The physical thrust of the weapon, opening the way to the Sacred Heart, crystallizes the conflict between Christ and the world which is the theme of St. John. It forms the denouement of the drama of Light and Darkness, the synthesis of the dialectic of belief and unbelief, the victory of Christ achieved through defeat. "These things were done that the Scripture might be fulfilled: 'You shall not break a bone of him.' And again another Scripture saith: 'They shall look on him whom they pierced'" (*John*, 19:34-37). The reference to the ritual preparation of the Paschal lamb (*Ex.*, 12:48) reveals the raising upon the cross as the sacrifice which liberates the people of God from captivity. The blood of the lamb which preserved the Israelites from destruction appears again, flowing from the side of Christ. But the raising up of Christ goes beyond the squalor of Calvary and the mockery of the Jews and Gentiles; it is brought to its appointed fulfillment in the ascension and glorification which can be seen only by the eyes of faith (cf. *John*, 7:38, 39). It is when Christ the Priest enters into the Holy of Holies after his exodus from death to life, when he is enthroned as Lord, the giver of the Spirit, that he truly draws all things to himself. As the new Moses he gathers the chosen people about him. His two-fold activity in the Church, through the material structure and within men's hearts, draws the faithful after him through the mysteries of his Pasch.

RENEWAL OF THE MYSTERIES

THE NEW MOSES

This is what the master in Israel should have known or at least should have recognized when preached to him. The Jewish people were waiting for a messiah who would take the place of Moses, the historic founder and law-giver of the nation. A promise had been made them through Moses himself: "I will raise them up a prophet out of the midst of their brethren, like to thee" (*Deut.*, 18:18; cf. *Acts*, 3:22-23). On the basis of this promise the people looked for a prophet who would renew the marvels of the first exodus, one who would lead them out of captivity and re-establish them as a nation. That most of them interpreted the mission of their future saviour in terms of political independence and social well-being is strikingly revealed in their reaction to Christ when he provides food miraculously for the crowds. "This is of a truth the Prophet that is to come into the world"; and the next day, anxious to secure a constant supply of bread, they slyly remind Christ that Moses gave the

Israelites bread from heaven (*John,* 6:30-31). These crude notions of a messianic age of material plenty could be excused in the unlearned masses, but the teacher in Israel should have known that the coming of the new Moses would be marked by a spiritual restoration of the chosen people, by an outpouring of the Spirit upon men.

The preaching of the apostles to the Jews centred on this spiritual fulfillment of the promises made to the nation and was filled with almost a delirium of joy at recognizing in the death and resurrection-ascension of Christ the second and true exodus (cf. *Acts,* 3:22-26). "You are the children of the prophets and of the testament which God made to our fathers, saying to Abraham: 'And in thy seed shall all the kindreds of the earth be blessed.' To you first God raising up his son, hath sent him to bless you" (vv. 25-26). The glorified Christ had himself returned to speak to his disciples to make clear to them the connection between his suffering and his glory: "Ought not the Christ to have suffered these things, and so to enter into his glory?" (*Luke,* 24:26). By his passion and death he has won the redemption of all men; the blood which he bears into the heavenly sanctuary is his title to pouring out the Spirit on them (*Heb.* 9:12; etc.).

Under the leadership of this new Moses the people will indeed experience from the hand of God a renewal of the wonders of the exodus but not in the material form of the first redemption of the Israelites from slavery in Egypt. That central episode of Jewish history is now seen to have been a mime, played in history, foreshadowing the reality of the true exodus, that of Christ and his members from the world of sin to the presence of God. The words Stephen addresses to his judges speak of Moses but it is to Christ that they refer: "This Moses whom they refused ... brought them out, doing wonders and signs in the land of Egypt and in the Red Sea and in the desert forty years" (*Acts,* 7:35-36). The people who follow the new Moses on his exodus must go by the way of his mysteries, the mysteries of his death and resurrection, if they wish to receive the gifts of God. The only way for the Israelites to reach the promised land was to follow Moses through the waters of the Red Sea, through the desert, across the Jordan. The only way for men to follow Christ is by passing through the mysteries of death and resurrection. The Pattern of the Passover, the Pattern of submission to the Blessed Trinity, impressed on the humanity of Christ, must be repeated in each member of Christ. It is towards this that Christ's activity in the Church is directed. The word that the Church preaches is the call to men to follow Christ along this path; but it is more than a word of invitation or encouragement or warning; it is a word endowed with the divine power which alone can reproduce the Pattern in mankind. The power of the Spirit which is in the word of preaching and in the word of the sacraments draws men into the mysteries of Christ.

THE MYSTERIES IN THE CHURCH

It will be seen, then, that the mysteries of Christ play the central role in the life of the Church. Not only do they establish the Pattern to which the faithful must conform but as well—and this is the reason why there must be conformation—they are the source of life in Christ. St. Paul expresses this dependence in terms of the descent of Christians from the second Adam. "The first man, Adam, was of the earth, earthly.... Such as is the earthly, such also are the earthly" (*1 Cor.*, 15:47-48). "We have borne the image of the earthly" (v. 49), inheriting original sin from him by a necessary law of corrupt nature. But the "second Adam," Christ, has been made into a "life-giving spirit" by his resurrection and glorification. "Such as is the heavenly, such also are they that are heavenly" (vv. 45, 48). By a necessity comparable to that of inheriting sin from the first man those who belong to Christ will rise again in body, achieving perfect configuration to his mysteries: "As we have borne the image of the earthly we shall bear also the image of the heavenly" (v. 49). The resurrection of Christ, the consummation of his Passover—implying therefore all the values of his sacrificial death—is the cause of the resurrection of the body at the last day (cf. *Summa theol.*, III, q. 56, a. 1). The risen Christ "will reform the body of our lowness, made like to his glorious body" (*Phil.*, 3:21; cf. *1 Cor.*, 15:54-55).

A necessary preliminary to final conformation is configuration to the mysteries of Christ in the present life. If the body is to be glorified at the resurrection the person must have merited glory. If he is to merit while on earth he must have been cleansed of original sin and must have followed the law of Christ. Though expressed in negative form, cleansing from sin is something positive; restoration of the sinner can be achieved only by grace. The new divine life which grace brings denominates the whole process: we rise to a new life; consequently we die to the old life of sin. St. Paul again links this moral event with the historical events of Christ's Passover. "Know ye not that all we who are baptized into Christ Jesus are baptized into his death. We are therefore buried together with him by baptism into death (to sin); that as Christ is risen from the dead by the glory of the Father, so we also may walk in newness of life" (*Rom.*, 6:3, 4; cf. *Col.*, 2:12; *II Cor.*, 5:14). "Christ rising again from the dead, dieth now no more, death shall no more have dominion over him. For in that he died to sin he dieth once; but in that he liveth he liveth unto God. So do you also reckon that you are dead to sin, but alive unto God in Christ Jesus our Lord" (*Rom.*, 6:9-11; cf. *Gal.*, 3:27).

PRESENCE OF THE MYSTERIES

In recent years the traditional teaching on the role of Christ's mysteries in the life of the Church has been the subject of animated discussion. The sixth chapter of *Romans*, in particular the verses just quoted, is of particular significance for it raises the problem of the precise connection between the sacraments and the historical mysteries of Christ's life, death and resurrection. The most vivid solution—the one that sparked the discussion—is that proposed by the late Dom Odo Casel, a Benedictine of Maria Laach, in Germany, for whom the words of St. Paul could only mean that the actual death and resurrection of Christ were *made present* by the baptismal ceremony, not indeed in their historical reality but "sacramentally." To illustrate what he meant he drew a parallel between baptism and the Mass on the one hand and the Eucharist on the other. Just as the body of Christ exists in its natural reality in one place, heaven, and yet is present sacramentally in all the tabernacles of the world, so, he explained, the mysteries of Christ's Passover, though taking place at a particular moment of history, are made present in the sacramental ceremonies.

This theory has fascinated theologians for several years. Very few of them have been able to accept it but they have found in it a stimulus to research. The reasons for not accepting the theory as it stands are many, most of them concerned with the interpretation of the scriptural and patristic texts which were Dom Casel's favourite sources; but the principal reason, shorn of its technicalities, is the commonsense one that what is past is past and cannot be made present again. The example of the Eucharist is held to be irrelevant since there is an essential difference between sacramental presence of something which is locally distant and presence of an event now past. Very far, however, from adopting a purely negative attitude to this opinion, theologians have recognized unanimously that it embodies a very profound insight into the sacramental system, even though Dom Casel's own reflection on his insight is held to be unacceptable. Thomists have re-read the pages of St. Thomas and his commentators with fresh eyes and have rediscovered themes which had been forgotten. The question is still very far from settled but no consideration of the sacraments is complete unless some approach to the problem is made.[1]

A guide to discussion, which does not commit itself to any detailed solution, is provided by Pius XII in *Mediator Dei*:

> The liturgical year, animated throughout by the devotion of the Church, is no cold and lifeless representation of past events, no mere historical record. It is Christ himself, living on in his Church, and still pursuing that path of boundless mercy which, "going about and doing good" (*Acts*, 10:38), he began to tread during his life on earth. This he did in order that the souls of men might come into contact with his mysteries and, so to speak, live by them. And these mysteries are still now constantly present and active, not in the vague and incomprehensible way

---

1. The matter cannot be dealt with here in adequate detail. For a fuller account cf. "The mysteries of Christ and the sacraments," **The Thomist**, XXV (1962), pp. 1-53.

which certain recent writers describe, but as Catholic doctrine teaches us. The Doctors of the Church tell us that the mysteries of Christ's life are at the same time most excellent models of virtue for us to imitate and also sources of divine grace for us by reason of the merits and intercession of the Redeemer. They live on in their effects in us, since each of them is, according to its nature and in its own way, the cause of our salvation. (CTSE ed., § 176)

While these comments are to be found in the section of the encyclical concerned with the liturgical year, and therefore with something which is of ecclesiastical origin, their phraseology is quite general so that there appears to be no doubt that they are intended to apply to the sacraments as well, particularly as it is in this regard that recent writers have been proposing extravagant ideas. Christ's mysteries, for Pius XII, are relevant to present Christian life because they are *models* of virtue, *sources* of grace in dependence on the merits and intercession of Christ, and because they are *reflected* in their effects in us. The solution proposed in the present chapter remains within the bounds laid down here.

THE MYSTERIES: MODELS OF JUSTIFICATION AND HOLINESS

UNION WITH CHRIST

We can best get a clear idea of what things are by examining what they do. For this reason it is important to focus attention on the nature of the conformation to Christ achieved by use of the sacraments. This is what the sacraments are for and it constitutes accordingly the central connection between them and the mysteries of Christ. Though other connections may be discovered to be indicated or suggested in revelation, these will be interpreted in terms of their function in promoting the conformation of the faithful to Christ in his mysteries.

It is clear that this conformation does not require that the faithful sustain the same suffering and death as Christ, nor does it necessarily involve bearing any kind of physical suffering. The conformation is at its deepest level a moral one: a renunciation of sin (death to sin) and a following of the law of Christ (resurrection).

To say this is quite out of fashion nowadays. Recent biblical theology has insisted that our union with Christ, our conformity to his mysteries, is not purely "ethical" but involves a "vital union" with Christ. The distinction is in itself a valid one; but when applied to the doctrine of the mystical body its significance must be carefully weighed if we are not to allow our thinking to be dominated by metaphors. If by a purely ethical union is meant one consisting solely in unaided human effort to keep the law of Christ, then it is of course true that union with Christ means more; without the grace of the Holy Spirit it is impossible to follow Christ. But if the idea of ethical union is extended to include moral effort based on grace and the conformation to Christ's mysteries which this can achieve, then there is no distinction between it and "vital union." Though there are undoubted advantages in making it clear that moral effort involves a community of life with Christ, it would be extremely dangerous for Catholic practice if the impression were allowed to win ground that there exists some kind of union with Christ which is in any fashion independent of moral commitment. A more detailed analysis of what is meant by "vital union" with Christ—an analysis that biblical theology of its nature is incapable of making —reveals that the tradition represented by, for example, *The Imitation of Christ* (with its stress on personal effort) is no more than superficially in conflict with Pauline theology. Whatever be the exact conditions of the Christian's vital union with Christ, any Catholic who has learned his catechism knows what constitutes its essential element, though the unusual terminology might cause him to hesitate before saying so. It is by sanctifying grace that man enters into the fullness of earthly union with God. The historical circumstances in which grace comes to us in the Christian dispensation are of the highest importance, and the role Christ plays establishes certain special relations between him and the Christian; but the central reality which gives meaning to the rest is grace.

UNION BY GRACE

Now the significance of grace lies primarily in the moral order. It makes us sharers in the divine nature (cf. *II Peter*, 1:4), reproduces in us the image of God, brings about the indwelling of the Blessed Trinity, and thus pertains to the mystery of God; but it does this in such fashion that it raises up the essence and faculties of the creature so that he can *act* in a divine fashion, knowing and loving God supernaturally. If "in Christ" is substituted for "supernaturally" here, so introducing all the overtones of the scriptural phrase, the essential meaning is in no way altered. New perspectives will certainly be opened up. More explicit reference will be made to the fact that Christ has disposed the whole human race to receive grace (reparation and merit), that it is Christ in his humanity who sends the Spirit of grace, and that grace makes man like Christ and subordinates him to Christ. But none of these circumstances, all of which have their origin in contingent historical events freely willed or permitted by God, brings any essential modification to grace; it remains what it is, namely, a principle of supernatural action rooted in God. The idea of vital union with Christ may be closer to what is expressly formulated in the Scriptures than this statement summing up the reflection of scholastic theologians; but the present question offers an ideal example of how much the Church needs systematic theology if the concrete, "existential" formulas of the Scriptures are to be given clear and unambiguous expression.

It is not being asserted that the conceptual clarity of scholasticism should take the place of biblical thought and imagery. Such a statement makes nonsense to a theologian for he realizes that he cannot attempt to think within the limits of his science unless he draws constantly on revelation. What is necessary is that the Scriptures be read within the context of the living Church; and this means that, without renouncing in any way the sense of biblical mystery, the pages of Scripture should be read within the light of the teaching and of the intellectual heritage of the Church. As far as the present question is concerned this requires that the notion of vital union with Christ and all that it involves be under no circumstances contrasted with moral action

and its principles. The uneasy sense of ambiguity aroused by
some exegetes' accounts of the mystical body can be traced
to this partially unresolved duality. Faith and baptism are not
fully coordinated in their writings so that priority as a means of
union with Christ is given to the sacrament. A distinction is
called for here. If it is understood that the priority of baptism is
that of an efficient cause in relation to its effect then there is no
objection to the conclusion. But if what is meant is that baptism
is prior to faith as formally constituting union with Christ then
we are faced with a form of sacramental mysticism, based on
supra-ethical union with God, which contains the seed of profound error. While union with Christ is certainly not purely
moral in the sense that union among members of a benevolent
society is, equally certainly it is a union which is essentially
moral or ethical in its orientation. The only bond between the
members of the friendly society is their common interest, whereas
the Church is united by factors deriving from divine life shared
by mankind. To conform to the Christian ethic, to "imitate
Christ" in the superficial sense in which the phrase is sometimes
used of following his example, is possible only within the context
of "vital union" with Christ and with the three divine Persons.
To act as a Christian one must be united to the body of Christ,
both mystical and physical. But the scriptural *metaphors* of the
vine and the body must not be allowed to obscure the fact that
the branches and the members are individuals, endowed with
liberty, responsible for their own conduct. The Holy Spirit does
establish a vital union between Christ and the Christian; but
it is a union of persons who retain separate existences, and on
the side of the Christian its effect is, in the last analysis, to be
measured in terms of virtuous action and its abiding principle,
sanctifying grace.

MORAL RE-ENACTMENT OF THE MYSTERIES

The re-enactment of the mysteries of Christ brought about
by the sacraments in their recipients is quite simply the development of the life of grace in the individual. St. Paul, as we have
seen, establishes a connection between this development and the

Pasch of Christ, which is at once the cause and the model of spiritual regeneration. St. Augustine denominates this reproduction in the Christian of the Pattern set by Christ's death and resurrection the "sacramental exemplary causality" of the mysteries of Christ (*De Trinitate,* L. IV, cap. 3). "Sacramental" has a wide sense here. St. Augustine is thinking, not of the seven sacraments, but of what we now call typology. What happened to Christ on the plane of external, historical event, happens to the member of Christ within his soul: physical death and resurrection are paralleled by moral renovation (cf. St. Thomas, *Compendium theologiae,* c. 239; Marietti ed., n. 514).

THE MYSTERIES: SOURCES OF GRACE

St Paul's image of the second Adam transmitting the life of resurrection to his members indicates that the mysteries of Christ, like the sin of the first Adam, influence those who belong to him. The argument of *1 Corinthians,* Ch. 15, rests on the proposition that Christ's resurrection is the cause of the Christian's bodily resurrection; and *Romans,* Ch. 6, postulates a like dependence in the case of the Christian's spiritual resurrection. This two-fold causality is attached by St. Paul to the final events of Christ's earthly mission and to his definitive entry into heaven, all of these being grouped together as the single redemptive mystery of the Pasch or Passover of Christ. That we are not to understand this in an exclusive sense, as though the other mysteries of Christ's life from the Annunciation onwards were not saving mysteries, is made clear in the passage from *Mediator Dei* already quoted. "Each of them is, according to its nature and in its own way, the cause of our salvation." But the Pasch of Christ enjoys a primacy here because it is the divinely appointed consummation of Christ's mission. The other mysteries of Christ's life have saving efficacy in so far as they are subordinated to the principal mystery, all of them having been lived by Christ as preparation for, and in the same spirit of obedience as, the death and resurrection-ascension. The task of the theologian is to define precisely what is implied in the causality of the mysteries.

REPARATION AND MERIT

One element is clear and belongs to the ordinary teaching of the Church. By his sacrificial death Christ made reparation for sin and merited grace and glory for all men. The sacraments, as belonging to the scheme of things devised by Christ for giving effect in individuals to what he won by his death, draw their efficacy therefore from the passion. If they procure forgiveness of sin or strengthen union with God it is in virtue of Christ's reparation and merit. It will be noticed that the resurrection-ascension plays no part here, the reason being that reparation and merit are possible only to one who has not reached the goal of his journey to God. Christ's bodily separation from God, the curse of sin in his flesh, lasts up to the moment of his death and this marks the end of the period in which he could merit.

We should try to see the dependence of the sacraments on Christ's reparation and merit in the context of the whole mystery. It is an over-simplification if we think of redemption as a kind of spiritual banking system with Christ depositing a sum of capital in the treasury of heaven and with the sacraments as blank cheques drawn on this account. This may do as a pre-liminary scheme of thought but it imposes human, not to say mechanistic, categories on the mystery of salvation which is a mystery of persons, divine and human. Christ did not redeem man-kind in the vague; he redeemed individual men. Moreover, because he enjoyed the beatific vision and infused knowledge even during his passion, he was conscious in his human mind of each individual man for whom his sacrifice was being offered. He applied his reparation and his merit to each and every indi-vidual of the human race; and again, he did not do this in any general, confused way but rather designated the measure in which each member of the human race would benefit from his offering. There was nothing arbitrary about this. Christ knew the eternal design of God for every human person and he obeyed the prescriptions of this design, assigning to each one the degree of fellowship in his own sacrifice established from eternity. The mystery of Christ, it is clear, must be inserted in this way in the mystery of predestination. This is not the place to enter into a discussion of this latter, all-embracing mystery. It must suffice to recall the teaching of the Church which maintains both the gratuitousness of divine election and human liberty. The Council of Quiersy, held in the year 853, formulates this teaching: "That some are saved is the gift of Him who saves them; that some perish is the fault of those who perish." In apportioning the fruits of his passion in accordance with the divine plan, Christ designated also the means by which they would take effect in individuals. This implies, among other things, that Christ was conscious while hanging on the cross of every Mass that would be offered in the Church and of every sacrament that would be administered. Without prejudice to the liberty of any individual he appointed the exact benefit that each would draw from each sacrament received and from each Mass attended. At first sight this may appear exaggerated, for our human knowledge cannot cope with the mass of details which go to make up the unfolding in time of the eternal saving plan of God; in fact it indicates the extraordinary fullness of Christ's human knowledge consisting as it did in the vision of God and in divinely-infused ideas as well as in experimental knowledge like our own.

THE MYSTERIES SANCTIFY

When we say, then, that the sacraments draw their efficacy from the passion of Christ we must understand that this means that Christ, as he lived the mystery of his suffering, decreed that the sacrament which I receive on this particular day, twenty centuries after the event of Calvary, should forgive the sins of which I am at this moment guilty and should bring me the grace allotted me by God from eternity for today. It must be insisted once again that the individual's liberty is untouched by this, for human liberty too is part of God's design; and consequently the obligation lies on the individual to receive the sacraments with the greatest fervour possible. But what is happening is that the mysteries of Christ are here and now producing their predetermined effect in a particular member of Christ. We must be careful not to let purely human analogies distort our understanding of the mystery. It is inadequate to think of Christ on the cross as though he were a dying man making dispositions for the distribution of his property to his heirs. A last will and testament does no more than express the desires of the dead person; it has no intrinsic power to procure the execution of these desires. The act of Christ's will, on the contrary, formulated as he hung on the cross, is efficacious. It can actually put into effect what it prescribes; for it is in perfect conformity with the divine will and is the created means established for executing God's plan of salvation. The sacraments, consequently, are the instruments chosen by Christ for giving effect to the dispositions of his human will. They are the prolongation of Christ as he existed in the act of redeeming men through his earthly mysteries. They do for individuals of succeeding ages what the body of Christ did for Mary as she stood at the foot of the cross. They are the signs of faith which embody Christ in the Church.

It must also be taken into account that the acts of Christ's will which are governed by his beatific and his infused knowledge are not subject to the time which measures material things and the form of knowledge with which we are familiar. Our thoughts change rapidly from moment to moment, keeping time with the impressions we receive from our senses. It would take us too far afield to analyze closely the form of duration belonging to Christ's two higher knowledges. It is sufficient here to state that both of them, each in its own way, can be fixed unchangingly on a single object so that the self-same act of thought is held throughout the normal succession of events which continue to take place on the plane of corporeal reality. The significance of this for Christ's mission is that the identical acts of mind and will which were his on Calvary are maintained now that he is in heaven. This is specially noteworthy in the case of his infused knowledge. Its object, which is primarily the mystery of redemption, is revealed to Christ, not in the divine simplicity according to which he already knows it in his vision of God, but in a fashion connatural to a created mind so that he has direct knowledge of the details of the plan of salvation. It has already been pointed out that Christ's meritorious activity was carried out under the direction of his infused and acquired knowledge. And, whereas his acquired knowledge is subject to the law of time just as much as our own is, his infused knowledge and the obedience of will deriving from it can be maintained unchangingly in his mind throughout all the mysteries of his life on earth and on into his heavenly mystery. The moment of death cuts short the possibility of further merit but the identical interior act which gave meaning to the exterior sufferings of Christ and which is therefore the principal act by which mankind was saved can still exist at this moment in the mind of our High Priest in heaven.[2]

In suggesting that this act is in fact preserved in Christ we go beyond what is explicitly contained in revelation; but one of the procedures of theology is to seek for the connection between the different revealed mysteries; and the teaching of the Church on the sacraments, especially in what concerns the relation between Calvary and the Mass, can best be explained on the hypothesis that Christ's saving act is still maintained in heaven. Since, then, within Christ's mind is certainly preserved the self-same act of beatific vision which he enjoyed through his life on earth, and since there are in addition good reasons for saying that his saving act is preserved, it will be seen that the same moment of thought includes for Christ both Calvary and the whole history of the Church. It is by one and the same act that he determines on Calvary the measure in which individuals are to benefit from his sacrifice and that he now determines in heaven the efficacy of the sacramental means of distributing his benefits. For Christ, holding in his mind his redemptive act, there is no succession from Calvary to the present day. Certainly the external actions of Calvary, the suffering and the visible sacrifice, are past and the history of the Church moves forward through time; but Christ's mind moves to another rhythm as does that of God and that of the angels.

No excuse is offered for this excursion into very difficult theological thinking. It is worth while to take some trouble to understand what has been said because it can lead the way to a most fruitful sense of the mystery of the sacraments. So far, in fact, from Christ making a deposit of good works with God which the Church can draw on to give value to the sacraments,

---

2. This suggestion has been made by W. Barden, O.P., **What happens at Mass**, Alba House, 1963, pp. 110-113; Dublin, 1960, pp. 83-86. I must record how much I am indebted to Fr. Barden for his inspired teaching of the Third Part of the Summa theologiae.

he is instead constantly, from the first moment of the Incarna-. tion, on Calvary, now in heaven, offering his life and death for each individual man and is directing that the sacrament which I now receive should grant me fellowship in his sacrifice. The mysteries of Christ are not simply events of the past which have pleased God in virtue of which the Church can make a claim on divine favour. To receive a sacrament is to enter into communion with the act which made the events of Christ's life saving mysteries and which enfolds the whole mystery of the Church. To assist at Mass or to receive a sacrament fruitfully is to be drawn into union with Christ's saving act, accepting its benefits and making one's own its God-centred worship. Christ's primary, interior mystery is unaffected by time; the sacraments incorporate us into it.

THE MYSTERIES: DIRECT CAUSES OF GRACE

It will have appeared from what has already been said that the sacraments constitute a new mystery of Christ, additional to the mysteries of his earthly life and of his passing to perfect life. But this mystery is additional only in the sense that the sacraments apply to the individual Christian the reparation and merit of the earthly mysteries and the intercession of the heavenly mystery so as to produce in him a likeness, at the level of moral activity, to the historical mysteries. The scholastic theologians would say that it is additional as far as men are concerned, not as regards Christ; in their neat shorthand: *quoad nos, non quoad se*. The sacraments are the means by which men of succeeding ages are incorporated into the unique mystery of Christ, into his supreme act of worship. We must be careful, however, not to over-spiritualize the mysteries of Christ; we would be guilty of this were we to concentrate exclusively on that abiding interior act of charity and religious obedience of his which is the human root of our salvation. It was because of this act that his physical sufferings and death were redemptive; nevertheless, he redeemed us by these exterior actions. They were necessary for an act of redemption which was integrally human, involving body as well as soul. Keeping in mind, then, all that has been said about Christ in his mysteries applying to us the merits of his passion through the sacraments, we must still ask whether the exterior actions of Christ have any influence on us.

ST. THOMAS'S TEACHING

It is clear that in so far as Christ's exterior actions were reparatory and meritorious their efficacy is communicated to us by way of Christ's interior act of worship; for they form a unified principle of merit with this interior act. It must not be forgotten, however, that Christ's merit does no more than dispose the human race for grace. Grace itself is a gift of God. It is not inconceivable that by receiving the sacraments we should have communicated to us the worthiness of Christ so that God would find us prepared to receive grace directly from Him. There are theologians who think of the sacraments in this way. They speak of them as pleading the merits of Christ so that God is "moved" to give grace to their recipients. We have seen that this is not St. Thomas's teaching and have also suggested that the theory does not do justice to the scriptural account of the way in which the Incarnate Word gives physical and spiritual healing. For St. Thomas the physical body of Christ is the instrument which, by the power of God, gives effect to Christ's redemptive act. That is to say, not merely were the bodily actions of Christ meritorious; they also bring to men the grace for which they have disposed them. St. Thomas calls this the "efficient (instrumental) causality" of the mysteries of Christ as opposed to their efficacy by way of merit. He is to be found attributing the justification of the sinner to the efficient causality of the resurrection (*Summa theol.*, III, q. 56, a. 2), to that of the passion (*ibid.*, q. 48, a. 6), and of the death (*ibid.*, q. 50, a. 6), as well as of the passion and resurrection together (*ibid.*, q. 56, a. 2, ad 4), and indeed of all the actions and sufferings of Christ (*ibid.*, q. 48, a. 6; q. 56, a. 1, and 3).

INTERPRETATIONS OF ST. THOMAS

It ought to be a little difficult to grasp exactly how St. Thomas envisages this efficient causality of the mysteries of Christ because Thomists are not agreed among themselves on this. The idea of such causality is quite clear to them and they have no

difficulty in showing how it was exercised in Christ's miracles
when the touch of his hand or a mere word could bring to the
sufferer the healing power of God. It may be necessary to repeat
once again that for St. Thomas these miracles were brought
about by the physical action of Christ, not by its own power,
but by reason of the divine power using the action as an instrument, somewhat in the fashion in which a writer uses a pen to
produce intelligible signs on paper. Where Thomists disagree
is in their interpretation of St. Thomas's attribution of direct
instrumental causality of grace to the mysteries of Christ. Does
he mean that the past earthly mysteries through divine power
produce grace now, two thousand years after the event, when
a person receives a sacrament? Or should it be said that he
understands Christ in heaven, who has passed through his
earthly mysteries, to be the direct cause of grace? The question
concerns the exterior, bodily aspect of the earthly mysteries, not
their interior aspect, for it is accepted by all that Christ's interior
redemptive act is preserved in heaven.

There is a certain attraction in the solution which attributes
present-day production of grace to the past exterior actions and
sufferings of Christ. It permits us to say that when we receive
a sacrament we come into contact not simply with the central
element of Christ's mysteries, the interior act of worship maintained in heaven, but with the passion and resurrection in their
visible, historical reality. It is as though God were using these
events as a tool with which to shape the Christian to the likeness of Christ. The passion and resurrection in their integral
reality, comprising bodily as well as spiritual elements, would
be impressing on the Christian the Pattern of submission to the
Blessed Trinity. They would be the seal in the hand of God
reproducing themselves in Christ's members. This is the teaching
of some of the most eminent modern Thomists; but it represents
a departure from the interpretation given by the leading commentators of St. Thomas from the fifteenth century to the present
day.

According to the traditional explanation St. Thomas understands efficient instrumental production of grace to be exercised
by the humanity of the heavenly Christ. The visible, historical
mysteries are involved only in so far as they have affected Christ's

humanity. In the phrase of Cardinal Cajetan, the early-sixteenth century commentator on the *Summa theologiae*, the risen humanity of Christ with its scars is the channel through which grace comes directly to us. At first sight this explanation may appear to do less than justice to the expressions of St. Thomas in which he speaks of the mysteries themselves acting on us by efficient causality; but there are several good reasons why it should not be abandoned, at least until the proponents of the new theory have provided satisfactory solutions to the serious difficulties which are to be found in their position.

DIFFICULTIES IN THE NEW INTERPRETATION

In the first place it is by no means clear how the new theory is to be reconciled with the scriptural image of the risen Christ, established as Lord at the right hand of the Father, and become by reason of his ascension the source of the Spirit of grace. Certainly the apostolic preaching looked up to the glorified Christ as to the centre of the life of the Church and the whole theme of *Hebrews*, as we have seen, is that our High Priest has entered definitively into the Holy of Holies and from there distributes the graces won for us by his intercession. That Christ in heaven preserves the principal, interior act of his earthly priesthood and his earthly mysteries appears to be established; but to limit, as the new theory seems to do, the heavenly activity of Christ to intercession and to appeal backwards into history to locate the instrument used by God in the external mysteries of Christ's life calls for a new and quite unexpected interpretation of the Scriptures. Some confusion may have arisen from translations of *Romans*, 6:9. The Douai version has: "Christ rising again from the dead, dieth now no more" which is taken directly from the Vulgate: *Christus resurgens ex mortuis iam non moritur.* Taken out of the context of St. Paul's theological vision of the heavenly Christ, this phrase might suggest that it is Christ in the act of rising from the grave who is the source of Christian life and resurrection, and this would accord admirably with the new theory. In fact the Greek text has *Christos egertheis.* Here the verb is transitive, not intransitive as in translations, and the participle is past (aorist) passive, not present. This idea cannot be expressed with the Latin verb *resurgo* which lacks such a participle. The English should properly read: "Christ, having been raised from the dead, dieth now no more"; and, this being so, the phrase suggests the traditional idea of Christ in heaven as the source of new life.

There is too a metaphysical difficulty about the notion of Christ's past external actions being used by God as instruments to produce grace in men today. To appreciate the objection fully it is required that a close analysis be made of instrumental causality. This is impossible here; but it may be said briefly that when God uses a creature to produce effects of which He alone is capable He infuses a created power into His instrument, thereby raising up the native powers of the instrument so as to make them adequate to the task assigned them. The writer does something like this to his pen. When Christ performed miracles his gesture or his voice were raised in the fashion described so that through them divine power was applied to a sick person. What is to be noticed about the power lent to the creature by God is that it is not a permanent enrichment of the creature's faculties; it is a power flowing from God through the creature and attaining the object in which the supernatural effect is to be produced. Accordingly it is of the nature of this divine power that it be infused into the created instrument only at the moment when the effect is actually being produced; just as a pen will make intelligible signs only while it is actually being applied to paper by the writer. What this comes to is that the human actions of Christ when he was on earth, while they were certainly used instrumentally by God, could only be so used to produce supernatural effects contemporaneous with Christ at any given moment. This, at least, is the view of traditional Thomism. It has not yet been proved that God can use Christ's mysteries in their historical reality as instruments which would produce grace after their visible, external element has passed. The proponents of the new theory appeal to the eternity of God to whom all succeeding ages are uniformly present; but this is to overlook the situation of God's created instrument and of the created power with which He elevates the instrument, both of which are strictly limited by temporal conditions. The fact that time has no relevance where God is concerned means that it is in virtue of one and the same divine decree, efficacious by the very fact of being placed, that He raises Christ from the grave and all Christians from sin. Indeed, the whole Christian mystery is encompassed by this unique divine decree, present to God from eternity, identified with the divine being. All this is part of the common theology. The innovation introduced by the upholders of the new theory consists in their extending to a creature, involved in the succession of time by reason of materiality, the supra-temporal conditions of God. To put in a nut-shell our objection to their proposal: it is a new form of Dom Casel's theory of the presence of the mysteries, differing from it only in so far as the escape from the laws of time is attached to the instrumental power elevating the mysteries instead of to the external mysteries themselves.

ACTION OF THE GLORIFIED CHRIST

According to traditional Thomism the earthly mysteries of Christ are the direct causes of grace, and are consequently active in the sacraments, to the degree that they remain in the glorified Christ. The interior aspect of the mysteries, Christ's act of worship, is preserved unchanged, measured by a time other than that which rules material things. The exterior aspect, the bodily actions and sufferings of Christ, remains in so far as it is the same body now in heaven, marked with the Pattern of physical submission to the Father, which suffered on earth. It should be noted, if St. Thomas's way of speaking of the influence of the mysteries is to be understood, that the experiences to which Christ's body was subjected on earth may be said to have imparted to his humanity a certain instrumental power. This is distinct from the power given the humanity by God when He uses it as an instrument in the production of grace; it is not directed towards an immediate effect; it is rather a preparation of Christ's humanity for actual use by God.

Something similar is to be found in the sacraments. Before the materials used are actually employed in the action of sanctifying the recipient they must be consecrated for their function. The materials of sacraments which Christ himself used—the baptism received from John and the Eucharist—are thereby consecrated once for all. St. Thomas repeats the affirmation of the Fathers that the waters of the world have been sanctified by the contact of Christ's body with the Jordan. Likewise bread and wine have received their preliminary sanctification, making them suitable for the Eucharist, because Christ used them at the Last Supper. The materials of the other sacraments require a blessing from the Church before they are used in the sacramental ritual. St. Thomas makes the following comment on this sacramental law; its relevance to the mysteries of Christ will be apparent:

> Just as an instrument acquires its instrumental power in two ways, namely, when it receives the form of instrument and when it is moved by the principal agent, so also the material of a sacrament requires a two-fold sanctification, by one of which it becomes suitable material for the sacrament, while by the other it is applied to the effect (III, q. 72, a. 3, ad 2).

The case of Christ is not quite the same as that of the material used in the sacraments. His humanity was already consecrated as an instrument of God by the Incarnation itself for, being united in person to the Word, it is thereby suited to be used as an instrument by the Blessed Trinity. But a certain preparation is required for this humanity to become an apt instrument for raising men from sin to the life of grace and heavenly glory. If it is to impress the Pattern of submission to God on mankind Christ's humanity must first receive the Pattern itself. This was precisely the function of the historical mysteries of Christ. By reason of them his glorified humanity is constituted an instrument adapted to bring men salvation. In this sense they impart instrumental power to Christ; but a further instrumental power must be infused into the glorified humanity if it is actually to produce grace in men living in the world subject to time.

In brief, the historical mysteries of Christ are on two counts the direct causes of the grace which they have merited and which is given in the sacraments. The interior act of worship which made them saving mysteries remains actually in the glorified Christ. The exterior aspect of the mysteries adapted Christ's humanity to the function of bringing grace to sinful man. Consequently, the intercession offered for humanity by Christ in heaven, which is the self-same act of worship that was his on earth, is raised up by divine power so that it is capable of producing in men the grace for which it pleads. Since this intercession designates the individuals to whom grace is to be given, it directs, by the very fact of being offered, the divine power to the individuals specified. And since Christ acts in the fullness of his humanity, the divine power comes to men at the appointed time through his glorified body, marked as it is with the Pattern of his life, death and resurrection-ascension. Accordingly, the sacraments bring their recipients into direct contact with the life-giving humanity of the heavenly Christ in whose soul the earthly mysteries live on and in whose body their sanctifying Pattern remains. At the moment of reception, Christ is thinking of the recipient, turning his redemptive love upon him, and reaching out to sanctify him.

RE-PRESENTATION OF THE MYSTERIES

There is still another, a fourth, way in which the sacraments are linked to the mysteries of Christ. Consideration of the three other ways has shown the sacraments as extensions of Christ's humanity, bringing to men the saving power of his mysteries. In this sense we have said that the sacraments give body to Christ, supplying him with material things, in spatial and temporal contact with ourselves, so that he can use them as instruments through which to sanctify us. But it has also been pointed out that this new "body" is provided for Christ by ceremonies conducted in the Church and that the character of each of these ceremonies determines the fashion in which Christ intervenes in the life of the faithful. The sacraments, in other words, are basically liturgical actions of the Church, expressive of her worship. The fact that Christ uses these actions means that they are transformed, not that their fundamental structure is violated. The connection of the sacraments with the mysteries of Christ which we are about to consider is one which derives from this fundamental structure; its examination is most illuminating, for it brings us to the heart of the sacramental idea.

EFFICACIOUS SYMBOLISM OF THE SACRAMENTS

When we examine the external ritual of the sacraments we find that two of them at least refer very clearly to the mystery of Christ's Passover. St. Paul sees in the ceremonial of baptism by immersion a re-evocation of the death and resurrection of Christ as the catechumen descends into the grave of water and rises from it (*Rom.*, 6:4). In the Mass also the ritual recalls the sacrifice of Christ. The body is separated from the blood and the priest offers. The ceremonies of these two sacraments are symbolic of the principal historical mystery of Christ. Those who follow Dom Casel base their argument on this fact. The sacraments, they reason, give reality to what they signify; but they signify the death and resurrection of Christ; therefore the death and resurrection—and indeed all the mysteries from the Incarnation to the Return of Christ—are made sacramentally but really present in the Mass, in baptism, and, by analogy, in the other sacraments also.

This argument displays an expert piece of theological sleight-of-hand and has dazzled many a poetically-inclined student of theology. Apart from the radical objection already seen that what the conclusion asserts is impossible of realization, there is the scriptural difficulty that the New Testament in other places attributes different symbolism to baptism. It is a bath which purifies (*Eph.*, 5:26; *Heb.*, 10:22), a rebirth, the water being a womb (*John*, 3:5; *Titus*, 3:5), an illumination (*Heb.*, 6:4; 10:32). Nor has it ever been explained how exactly the mysteries of Christ are symbolized in the remaining five sacraments. Marriage certainly symbolizes the mystery of Christ's union with the Church; but this is not an historical event, though it is manifested in history. Nor, finally, is it in any way apparent what use it would be to have the mysteries of Christ made present in the sacraments in the fashion proposed by the school of Maria Laach. That we should be baptized into the actual death of Christ and into his act of resurrection does sound very impressive; but what can it possibly mean? There is no denying that the sacraments are a mystery; but the mystery which surrounds this account of their symbolism is almost entirely of human making.

Traditional theology suggests a more sober though no less exalted approach. The principle that the sacraments give reality to what they signify (*efficiunt quod figurant*) is restricted to the signification of the effect produced in the Church. In sacraments other than the Eucharist this means the effect produced in the recipient, that is, moral renewal of the mysteries. The Eucharist is a special case which will be considered more fully in a later chapter. It realizes within the Church not the historical event of Calvary but Christ's sacrificial offering of his body and blood in view of associating the faithful with the sacrifice. Nevertheless it would be to miss the richness of sacramental symbolism if it were to be restricted to signification of the effect. The precision brought by systematic theology to our understanding of one aspect of the sacraments is not all that there is to be said; nor indeed (though critics of scholastic "conceptualization" do not always give credit for this) is that all that systematic theology has to say. The symbolism of the liturgy extends beyond the central area of efficacious signification; and it may be readily agreed that for this reason the sacraments are not intended to appeal only to the intellect. Their symbolism awakens all kinds of resonances in the religious sensibility of the faithful. In this more shadowy, outer sphere the vaguely-formulated sense aroused in the recipient of being plunged into the death of Christ and of rising with him from the grave towards the Father can have its value; this depends very largely on individual temperament and culture. While acknowledging this and similar symbolic richness in the sacraments, we cannot base our theological analysis on such a foundation; it is too shifting, too subjective.

FOCAL POINT OF SACRAMENTAL SYMBOLISM

St. Thomas brings order to Christian experience of sacramental symbolism with his well-known classification comprising three "directions" of significations. The sacraments, he explains, signify our sanctification and since three factors contribute to sanctification these will all be signified by the ritual. Consequently the sacraments are signs of a past event, the passion of Christ, which causes our salvation (by way of reparation, merit and efficient causality), of a present reality, grace and the virtues, produced in us by the passion and procuring formally our sanctification, and of a future state, eternal life, towards which present sanctification is directed. At first sight this three-fold symbolism is a little confusing, much as if a traffic signal were to show red, green and amber all at the same time. There is, however, nothing ambiguous about sacramental signification, St. Thomas adds, because the three signs are not disparate; two of them enter the ritual in subordination to the third. The sacraments signify primarily the application of Christ's saving work to the individual recipient (III, q. 61, a. 3; ad 1; cf. a. 2). This means that the symbolism is centred, not on the historical mysteries, nor on the future consummation of the whole mystery, but on the recipient who is being incorporated as a morally responsible individual into the mystery as it exists today. The historical perspectives, both past and future, of this present event are connoted in the symbolism exclusively in so far as they bear some relation to the recipient. This explains the scriptural variants regarding the symbolism of baptism. It is incorporation into the death of Christ in the measure that it is a washing, a rebirth, an illumination. Christ's historical mysteries enter the symbolism in subordination to the sanctification of the individual, that is to say, they are signified as causes, as model and as consummation. The Mass itself fits into this general scheme of sacramentalism. The passion as such, considered as the unique act of redemption performed by Christ on earth, is not made present; it is signified as sanctifying the faithful, the Mass being a memorial meal. The fact that the central, efficacious symbol is in this case sacrificial means that the Mass is a true sacrifice but, as will be more fully explained in another chapter, the purpose of this is to associate the faithful in Christ's unique sacrifice still offered in heaven and given new visible expression on the altar.

THE QUESTION OF PRESENCE

The problem which remains to be solved is whether this indirect signification of the historical mysteries, common to all the sacraments, procures in any fashion a presence of the mysteries. For the sake of clarity it may be recalled that we are concerned now with what belongs to the sacraments purely as acts constituted by Church worship so that the presence of the mysteries we are enquiring about is something distinct from what is achieved by the active intervention of Christ in the liturgical ceremony, an intervention which, as we have seen, obtains the application of the mysteries to the faithful and the incorporation of the faithful into the mystery. We are thinking of the fact that the sacraments signify all this and consequently have their own reality as signs distinct from their function as direct causes of grace, though normative of the latter.[3] This may appear to be a question of no more than marginal interest once the active intervention of the Christ of the mysteries has been established. Any purely symbolic representation of the mysteries may seem in comparison with this of very slight importance. In fact the question is fundamental because it is concerned with the basic structure of the sacraments, what they are in themselves before they become the instruments of Christ's saving humanity. This structure they preserve even when Christ intervenes and we must try to understand it if we are to grasp how the coming of Christ with his gifts is coordinated with the life of the faithful in the Church.

THE FAITH OF THE CHURCH

Sacraments are essentially signs or expressions of faith. Although it is through a sacrament, baptism, that the individual is introduced into the society of the Church and of the mystical body, nevertheless if we consider the Church as a whole faith is seen to hold the primacy. Since what is meant here by the faith

---

3. Not all theologians make this distinction between sacrament as sign and sacrament as cause. They insist that the sacraments cause by signifying. It is true that signs exercise causality but it is confined to the order of knowledge and is defined technically as extrinsic formal (exemplary) causality to which is added final causality when the sign is employed to move a person to action. That is to say a sign imparts knowledge and may be used to express a command or request. On the contrary, when we speak of the sacraments as causes we are referring to their efficient causality deriving from the use made of them by God and Christ and directed towards producing grace and other extra-mental effects of the sacraments. For St. Thomas, if this efficient causality is not admitted, the sacraments are reduced to simple signs (III, q. 62, a. 1).

of the Church is the theological virtue which exists in the faithful who form the community of the Church, it might be argued that it derives from baptism, received either actually or in desire; in which case the sacrament must be said to be primary since it is the cause of faith. But while this is true as far as the present community of the Church is concerned, it is not so for the earthly community in its full temporal extent which includes Our Lady and the apostles. Before the Church administered baptism she possessed faith received by the first believers directly from Christ without the intervention of a sacrament. Our Lady and the apostles formed the nucleus of the Church; it was to this primitive community that the sacraments were given so that through them the saving humanity of Christ might be applied to men even after it had been raised up to heaven. The present Church rests on the foundation of the original community, and this not solely by reason of hierarchic powers handed down through the apostolic succession but also by reason of the faith which accepted the word of God in the flesh of Christ.

If the Church lacked faith there could not be any sacraments because the sacraments are signs of faith. There are of course very many other signs of faith. We might say, for example, that a parish church is a sign of the faith of the parishioners. But there is this essential difference between signs of this kind and the sacraments, that a church or anything similar is built of bricks and mortar and other materials and consequently has an existence of its own quite apart from its function as sign. But the sacraments have no existence except as signs of faith. Faith enters into their intimate structure and without it they are not sacraments but simply water, oil and the rest. It is not a question of the faith of the individual minister or recipient because even if these are unbelievers the validity of the sacrament is not prejudiced; the sacrament if administered properly is a true one even though the recipient draws no benefit from it. The faith which makes the liturgical ritual a sacrament is the faith of the Church, the community of believers, and this faith is called on whenever a sacrament is administered. The reason is that each sacrament is a sign of the application of the saving power of Christ's mysteries to an individual. But how is it to be made a sign? It was Christ who first established the relation of signification between the ceremonial of the sacraments and the execution of the divine mystery of salvation. It was he who said, for example, that washing with water and the use of certain words would signify the cleansing from sin actually being effected by means of the visible ritual. But how is the ceremony of baptism being carried out in the Church today to be made to signify this? Obviously only if the Church whose ceremony it is is acting in response to Christ's command issued when he instituted the sacrament. This act of obedience establishes that the Church's ceremony is one of those designated by Christ as a sign of redemption-in-realization. This particular ceremony is therefore actually constituted a sign of the mystery of salvation by Christ's act of institution made effective here and now by the obedience of the Church. Nor is this an isolated act of obedience; it forms part of the supernatural mission of the Church and as such it implies the faith of the Church. By faith the Church responds to the promises of Christ made when he directed that the sacraments should be administered.[4] Though bearing immediately on Christ's act of institution, this act of faith implies acceptance of the whole mystery of Christ, of all that is included in that one master decree of God the object of which is the salvation and eternal glory of men through the mysteries of Christ, through the Church itself, and through the sacraments. The sacrament is the sign of this faith. The focal point of the sign varies from sacrament to sacrament, being fixed by the precise efficacious signification which determines the effect of each.

IN THE CONTEXT OF FAITH

The most important consequence of all this is that it is within the context of the faith of the Church that the sacraments exist. Faith gives them their being as sacraments and establishes their basic connection with the mysteries of Christ. Nor is this sur-

---

4. Cf. St. Thomas, **Commentary on Fourth Book of the Sentences**, dist. 1, q. 1, a. 4, sol. 3: "The principal and adequate agent bringing man into the state of justification is God as the efficient cause and the passion of Christ as the meritorious cause. To this agent a sacrament is connected by the faith of the Church which establishes the connection between instrument and principal cause and between sign and what is signified."

prising. The primary demand that Christ makes on men, his primary gift, is faith in himself as the one sent by God to save us. We must believe that his mysteries are the cause of our salvation; this is the beginning of our moral conformation to his mysteries, the basis of our vital union with him. Now, faith, of its nature, is indifferent to the passage of time; it can attain the historical mysteries of Christ in all their actuality as they existed two thousand years ago and can reach forward to the return of Christ at the end of the present world. It can make these mysteries present today as objects of thought and love. It can give life to the formalized symbolism of liturgical action so that the descent of a catechumen into the font—or even the pouring of water on his head—can re-present the mysteries of Christ. It may be objected that this is a purely mental re-presentation externalized by symbols. But that fails to take account of the difference between simple recalling of past events and the gift of faith. Our present salvation depends on mental acceptance of the mysteries of Christ as the source of grace under God. By professing our faith in the past mysteries we are united to Christ in his present and supreme mystery, the resurrection-ascension, the giving of the Spirit. The present mystery is not a new mystery, distinct from the others; it is the final achievement of the one mystery of Christ's Passover. By faith—the Church's which may and ought to include his own if he is capable of it—the catechumen performs the symbolic evocation of Christ's death and resurrection not as an actor in a passion play, concerned with recalling the historical event, but as one being involved in the event in so far as it concerns himself. It is precisely the passion-as-applied to an individual that is made present in baptism and the other sacraments by the faith of the Church. The whole community of the Church makes that submission to Christ which is the foundation of individual redemption. It will be seen that the sacraments, purely as acts of worship, establish that essential connection with the mysteries of Christ without which salvation is impossible. It is quite true that, of itself, such a community action cannot ensure the gift of grace to one who is incapable of personal faith; and consequently, were it not for the intervention of Christ, the most that it could achieve for an infant would be to recommend him to the mercy of God. But in the case of an adult who enters by faith into the common act of worship being offered in his favour there is at once for him contact with the mysteries of Christ and personal fellowship in them; in making this contact by faith he is assisted by the worship of all the members of the Church. The personal intervention of Christ, active through the visible elements of the liturgical action, brings a direct, bodily contact with the mysteries as they are preserved in the glorified Christ. This is a new and wholly gratuitous addition to the mental contact achieved by faith and it brings with it a richness of grace unattainable to faith alone; yet it is fully in harmony with the contact of faith. It intensifies, makes corporeal, the union of faith. Faith is led beyond itself, finding opened to it a way to Christ and to his mysteries that it could never have opened for itself. Christ, who was worshipped from afar, comes near and touches the believer; and at his touch power goes out from him.

FAITH IS CENTRAL

When the word of God takes root in man's mind it calls forth the response of faith. For the word of revelation is a living word which not merely affirms truth but has the power to lay hold on the sources of human understanding and have them assent to truth. Man is now involved in the mystery of God, called effectively to share in God's own life. This is only the beginning of a progressive assimilation of the creature into God, a process which will never eliminate the abyss which separates the two but which, nevertheless, will reach its climax in the creature's possession of God through an act of direct perception. Only God can draw man into this union with Himself; and the only way in which He can do so is by revealing Himself to man and by moving man to receive His revelation, first by faith, finally by vision. For such is the life of God into which man is drawn, a life of knowledge of Himself which is necessarily accompanied by love for Himself as the supreme good. It is possible for God to draw man into this union only because He has made man in His own image, endowed with the spiritual faculties of intellect and will.

The life of faith, leading to vision, and the mystery of grace constitute the necessary conditions for man's entry into participation in God's intimate life. These conditions are necessary in a way that the mystery of Christ is not. Given God's supremely free decision to associate men in His own happiness, the nature of things requires that He extends His favour to man in such fashion that man is raised up by created grace, operating through faith and later vision, to a level where by his own action he can, under the impulse of God, reach out for God by personal acts of intellect and will. The mystery of Christ has no necessary place in this scheme. If, as is the case, God freely wills the Incarnation and the Church for man's salvation, in order to supply the means, that is, for man to receive grace and faith, then these new mysteries will find their place within the scheme of essential relations between God and man established by the nature of God and man. This is why faith is central in the Christian life, not baptism or any other sacrament. This is why grace as a participation in the divine nature is the foundation of the Christian life, while the conformation which it gives to Christ is a contingent addition following on sin and on the historical mysteries of redemption.

The central position of faith makes it the point of reference for co-ordinating the various connections we have discovered between the sacraments and Christ's mysteries. The renewal in the Church of the wonders of the exodus takes place in time. The relation between the Leader and his followers is basically one of faith which is indifferent to time and can reach back to the earthly phase of the mystery of Christ, upwards to the risen Christ and forwards to the repose of the whole Christ. The sacraments express this faith. Through the faith of the Church in the earthly mysteries the merit and reparation of Christ are brought to bear on the individual faithful. The risen Christ makes use of this liturgical action to produce in the recipient who is playing his due part in the act of worship a conformation to the mysteries which is impressed in the intimate sources of the believer's moral activity. The power of the risen Christ which will ultimately draw all the elect into the fullness of his resurrection is, as it were, filtered through the sacramental rite, producing in the recipient only a partial likeness to the glory of Christ.

The faith of the Church directs each of the sacraments, in accordance with the central efficacious signification given each by Christ, towards a different aspect of the resurrection-power of the mysteries.

Resurrection for the Christian is living faith. As this faith grows through moral effort and through the use of the sacraments Christian resurrection grows with it, building up the earthly body of the risen Christ by the power of the risen Christ, realizing the fullness of Christ (cf. *Eph.*, 4:13). It is not Christ who must die and rise again in the sacraments; it is upon us that the Pattern must be impressed. Our faith is in a risen Saviour who raises us now secretly but who will return to "reform the body of our lowness, made like to the body of his glory" (*Phil.*, 3:21).

4 The Church as Sacrament of Christ

God's design to save His people is achieved through Christ. The humanity of the Word made flesh manifests this design within the world and at the same time is the means of accomplishing it. All the words and actions of Christ reveal to us what God is doing in the world in order to bring us into His rest. These same words and actions put into effect the divine plan of redemption; they bring among men the saving action of God. They do this in the various ways already seen. They teach us about God's loving, active care for us, announcing the gospel of salvation so that we may respond to it from the depths of our freedom. They make reparation for our sins and render mankind worthy to receive grace. They shape Christ's own humanity as it proceeds through the mysteries of his Pasch, forming his flesh so that it may be used as the apt instrument through which God gives us the grace that reproduces the mysteries within us. Christ's words and actions are the sign or symbol of God's action in the world; but they are an efficacious sign, achieving what they signify. Because of this, Christ's humanity may be said to be the sacrament of the God who saves us.

We are accustomed to thinking only of the seven major liturgical ceremonies as sacraments. This is a convention of language amply justified by the technical sense which the Church has attached to the term. But it is suggestive to take note that the characteristics which account for the seven sacraments being so named reappear in more or less modified form in all the material realities connected with the Incarnation. Nowhere is this more true than in the humanity of Christ himself. Here materiality is impregnated with the saving power of God; and this is sacramentalism: sign and source of grace. Indeed, the characteristics of a sacrament are realized in Christ more perfectly than in the rites of the liturgy. They are sacraments because they derive from Christ. This does not mean simply that he instituted the sacraments. More important still is the fact that they are modelled on him. Christ's humanity is the symbol and source of saving grace because it is the humanity of the Word of God who exists in it and acts in it in order to redeem us. The sacraments are signs of grace because they recreate in liturgical actions the saving actions of Christ in his humanity. They are causes of grace because Christ acts through them. And just as Christ is the source of their significance and of their efficacy, so he realizes their characteristics at a higher level and in a more excellent way. He is the original and foundational sacrament of Christianity; his actions, which reveal the saving design of God, have efficacy of themselves to procure salvation, for they are the human actions of God. The seven rites of the liturgy are sacraments only because they are related to the foundational sacrament and share in its symbolism and its efficacy. If we bear in mind their relative status, we may say that they are sacraments only because they transpose the humanity of Christ into terms of Church ceremonial.

Not only the seven sacraments but the whole visible Church, because of its relation to Christ, realizes in its own way the characteristics which justify it being named a sacrament (cf. Vat. II Const., ch. 1, art. 5). But once we leave the area of the seven we must pay particular attention to the modifications which affect the sacramentalism of the Church. The visible Church, clergy and laity, the society, endowed with the means of salvation, and formed by the body of faithful, is the manifestation in the world of the redemption achieved by Christ. With her four marks of holiness, unity, universality and apostolic succession, the Church is the sign, raised up among the nations, of Christian redemption. She is more than an empty symbol; she is an efficacious sign of salvation; she plays a part, in subordination to Christ, in realizing the salvation of the world. It is true that her sacramentalism reaches a peak of intensity in the seven great sacraments which achieve what they signify because Christ himself, the heavenly High Priest exercises his saving action in and through the very reality of these major signs by which the Church proclaims her faith in him. Here the sign of Christ made by the Church becomes the sign of Christ actually intervening in the action of the Church and giving his gifts through the liturgical rite itself. Though this fullness of efficacious symbolism is not attained outside the privileged area of the seven major sacraments, there is still an active presence of Christ throughout the whole visible structure of the Church. The words that the Church uses to express the teaching of Christ and to formulate her directives are more than human words. The power of Christ accompanies them so that, while they are not themselves direct carriers of grace, they promote the realization of the mystery of Christ in the world.

In one sense or another, whoever or whatever belongs to the visible Church shares in her sacramental presentation of Christ to the world. This is the thesis of the present chapter. That it is true of the clerical hierarchy is not difficult to show. But our purpose is to show also that it is true of those who are inserted into the visible Church by the sacraments of baptism and confirmation. As we shall explain, there are very different functions in the Church assigned to those who receive the sacraments of initiation and to those who are ordained; moreover, baptism and confirmation have each their own significance. Nevertheless, each one who belongs to the Church, whatever function he fulfills, has some part in putting into effect the mystery of salvation through the official acts of the Church. Our explanation of this assertion extends through the chapters on baptism, liturgical activity and confirmation. As a basis for the whole exposition we must investigate more closely the sacramental nature of the Church. In the present chapter this will be followed by an enquiry into the various means by which individuals are inserted into the sacramental Church. The way will then be clear to develop the specific form of insertion achieved by each of the sacraments of orders, baptism and confirmation. By reason of the specially close connection between the nature of the Church and the sacrament of orders, the present chapter will close with a brief examination of this sacrament.

THE SACRAMENTAL STRUCTURE OF THE CHURCH

CHRIST'S PHYSICAL BODY AS SACRAMENT OF SALVATION

We can be a little more specific than we have been about designating the humanity of Christ as the sacrament of God's saving action. It is in fact his body which constitutes the foundational sacrament of Christianity. A sign must be visible or audible; and it is only Christ's body and his bodily actions which can be seen or heard. Christ's body in its human activity finds its true significance beyond the sacred humanity in the divine mystery of redemption itself. "That which was from the beginning," writes St. John, "which we have heard, which we have seen with our eyes, which we have looked upon, and our hands have touched, of the Word of life, (. . .) that which we have seen and have heard, we declare unto you, that you also may have fellowship with us, and our fellowship may be with the Father, and with his Son Jesus Christ" (J Jn., 1:1-3). St. John too tells us that the apostles "saw his glory" (Jn., 1:14), the glory manifesting the presence of God (cf. Ex., 24:16), upon whom no man can look and yet live (cf. Ex., 33:20), made flesh in Christ. It is this presence of the God of the Alliance in tangible form that makes the body of Christ the sacrament on which the Church is founded.

The body of Christ was the sacrament of redemption while Christ was on earth; it retains its sacramentality now that Christ is glorified. On earth the divine mystery of redemption was carried out by Christ in his humanity; and, just as any man's external actions execute and make known his intentions, so Christ's body, in its actions and in what it suffered, signified or made known the hidden movements of Christ's soul by which he freely obeyed the command of his Father offering his life for our redemption. The physical body of Christ, as we see it with the eye of faith, passing through the earthly mysteries, is consequently the sacrament of the whole mystery of redemption in both its divine origin and its human realization. Now that Christ is glorified in heaven and has become the source of the Spirit, his body remains for the eye of faith the sacrament of salvation. Endowed with the power of the three Persons of the Blessed Trinity, the body is the direct cause of our sanctification. As sign and cause, the body of Christ is the basic sacrament of salvation.

THE FULLNESS OF CHRIST'S BODY

There is a suggestion in St. Paul that the Church, the mystical body, is the "fullness" or completion of the physical body of Christ. God "has established (the risen Christ) over all as Head of the Church which is his body, the fullness of him who is filled all in all" (*Eph.*, 1:22-23). Though the interpretation of this passage is a matter for discussion, the sense widely accepted is that Christ attains the fullness of his stature as Head of the Church by uniting to himself the body formed by his members. That this "mystical" body is intimately connected with the physical body of Christ appears when St. Paul speaks of the union of Jews and Gentiles, both reconciled to God "in one body by the cross" (*Eph.*, 2:16). According to some exegetes the crucified body of Christ is here in the foreground of St. Paul's thought; it is in this physical body that the two peoples are become fellow-members (cf. *Eph.*, 3:6; 4:11-16; *Col.*, 2:19). When St. Paul speaks of the eucharistic body there is no longer any ambiguity, though now the idea of "fullness" or completion does not appear so clearly. It is because they eat the body of Christ that the faithful form one body (*J Cor.*, 10:17).

While there may be some hesitation about the precise meaning of St. Paul, there can be no doubt that for Thomists the concept of the Church as the fullness of the physical body of Christ is rich in significance. For St. Thomas, as we have seen, the physical body plays a central role in the life of the Church. As sacrament of salvation it is the source from which the Holy

Spirit is sent to men. It is the unique channel of salvation, impressed with the Pattern of obedience and used by the three divine Persons to give grace; consequently it is the immediate origin of the mystical body. The mystical body derives its perfection from the physical body; it constitutes, as it is built up, the progressive realization of what Christ won for men in his physical body. In this sense there is no difficulty about saying that the Church is the fullness or completion of the physical body. It is a fullness that will be perfect only when Christ returns in body to raise the bodies of the dead. Since, however, the mystical body on earth is a visible society formed of both an interior, spiritual reality and a complex external structure, the sense in which each of these two elements may be said to contribute to the fullness of the physical body must be more closely investigated. From this will emerge more clearly how the Church is the sacrament of Christ and, in particular, the significance of the external structure will be brought to light. In order to express their connection with the physical body of Christ we speak of the spiritual life of the Church as "fullness of resurrection" and of the visible form and functions of the Church as "fullness in structure."

FULLNESS OF RESURRECTION

The perfection of the mystical body, as has just been suggested, will be achieved when the risen Christ returns and "the body of our lowness" is "made like to his glorious body" (cf. *Phil.*, 3:21). But conformation to the personal body of Christ goes deeper than simple physical glorification of the bodies of the just at the general resurrection; the member's life of grace and glory also contributes to the fullness of Christ's body. This is to be understood in the light of what has been said in the preceding chapter concerning the members' moral conformation to the mysteries of Christ. These historical events of Christ's flesh are reproduced in the spiritual life of the faithful. The Pattern of the Blessed Trinity—the return of man from the world of sin to submission to the Father—which marks the glorified body of Christ, risen from the grave bearing the wounds of the passion, must be laid on the personal life of the individuals who belong to the mystical body of Christ. The physical sufferings, death and resurrection take on their full significance—are completed or "filled"—only when they achieve man's moral restoration, the prelude to his bodily resurrection. Our first conclusion, then, is that the spiritual and bodily resurrection of all Christians constitutes the fullness of Christ's physical body; and indeed this is the principal significance of the idea, for it is to this fullness of resurrection that the whole mystery of Christ is directed.

FULLNESS IN STRUCTURE

To speak of the Church, as it is on earth and as it will be in heaven, as the fullness of Christ's bodily resurrection is to interpret the fullness in terms of the effect achieved by the mysteries of Christ's earthly and heavenly existence. It is, accordingly, a way of expressing the relation which exists between Christ's body and the community of the faithful and which is founded on grace. But there is more to the Church than the assembly of Christians who rise with Christ and by the power of Christ. It is a visible, organized society on earth, endowed with means of building up the assembly of the faithful. As such it is still formed by individual human beings, but considered now as each of them has in the external structure of the Church a particular place to which are attached prescribed community functions. Under this aspect, too, the Church may be considered as the fullness of the physical body of Christ. Now we are concentrating our attention, not on the interior resurrection of grace, but on the manner in which the visible Church cooperates with Christ as he gives grace and all the other gifts connected with grace.

Not all the functions pertaining to the members of the visible Church are of the same kind. There are distinct groups in the Church, bishops, priests and laity, subordinated one to the other, as far as official function goes, in strict hierarchic order. Yet, while there is this very clearly defined diversity, all of the groups do belong to the visible structure of the Church and each of them has an official status there.

Now, we have already seen that Christ is active in the

Church, building up his mystical body, through the activities of the external structure, through, that is, the official actions of those who hold a place in this structure. He is active as a corporeal being in the Church through the medium of these official actions, sending his Spirit to his members.

His activity through the institutional structure of the Church takes on a variety of forms in harmony with the variety of functions of those who belong to the structure; but it is an activity which extends throughout the entire structure, from pope to layman. What is common, as a result, to all functions is that they are all, directly or indirectly, concerned with the giving of the Spirit. The diversity of functions must be examined more closely if we are to define the precise fashion in which each group in the Church cooperates with Christ in his sending of the Spirit. It will have to be made clear, in particular, that the baptized cooperate officially only in those Church actions which bring the Spirit to themselves. Nevertheless, in virtue of the common characteristic of all official functions a striking resemblance may be discerned between the physical body of Christ and the institutional structure of the mystical body on earth. Only when his body was glorified could Christ give the Spirit as sovereign Lord. In this function of the risen Christ the Church, as juridical society coming from God, shares.

This is the second element in our understanding of the Church as the fullness of the physical body of Christ. The visible Church is filled with the Spirit in a fashion comparable to the heavenly body of Christ, and this by reason of the fact that the official actions of the Church are the fullness or completion of Christ's body as it is used by God as the instrument of sanctification. This is the fruit of Christ's merit; for, by suffering in his body, Christ has merited, not only the glorification of his own body and the interior conformation of men to the mysteries of his humanity, but also the power belonging to his physical and mystical body to give the Spirit (cf. *Summa theol.*, III, q. 19, aa. 3, 4).

This mystery of the communication of the Spirit to the visible Church was manifested on the day of Pentecost. The Church of Pentecost is henceforward the sacrament of Christ, the heavenly

High Priest. When we have examined these two ideas our consideration of the visible structure of the Church will be complete.

PENTECOST

The significance of Pentecost, when Christ sent down the Spirit in public fashion on the apostles, lies in the assimilation just described of the visible structure of the Church to the glorified body of Christ. The Spirit descends on the apostles, not primarily to dwell in their souls by grace, but to endue them, in their official capacity, with the power won for his body by Christ. The role of the official Church in the mystery of salvation, its mission, is explained to the apostles by our Lord himself in Jerusalem after the resurrection when he opens their understanding of the Scriptures: "Thus it is written that the Christ should suffer and should rise again from the dead the third day. And that repentance and the remission of sins should be preached in his name unto all nations, beginning at Jerusalem. You are witnesses of these things. For my part, I shall send upon you what my Father has promised. Stay you then in the city till you be endued with power from on high" (*Lk.*, 24:46-49; cf. *Acts*, 1:8). The apostolic Church must bear witness to the passing of Christ to his Father and must preach its moral implications for men; the words of the apostles will draw power from the Spirit. The preaching of the apostles and their successors will share in the sacramental nature of the Church. Their teaching will be a re-presentation of the mysteries of Christ and will tell of the mystery of salvation. The ministry of the word will be efficacious in reproducing the mysteries in men's lives and so the mystery will be realized.

At a private ceremony the risen Christ had already given the Spirit for the remission of sins: "As the Father hath sent me, I also send you. When he said this he breathed on them; and he said to them: Receive ye the Holy Ghost" (*Jn.*, 21:23). Pentecost is a public and more general re-enactment of this scene, the sound like that of a great wind replacing the breath of Christ; it is the breathing forth of the Spirit from the body of Christ into the earthly fullness of the body. Peter makes this

specific claim in the first apostolic preaching: "This Jesus hath
God raised again; of this we all are witnesses. And now, exalted
by the right hand of God, he has received from the Father the
Holy Spirit, the object of the promise, and he has poured It
forth. It is this that you see and hear" (*Acts*, 2:32-33). The
extraordinary manifestations of the first Pentecost reveal the
presence of the Spirit in the visible Church. At the centre of the
Church's activity, in the seven major sacramental actions, not
only is the mystery of Christ preached, not only does the gift
of the Spirit accompany the word of the Church; the action of
the Church itself gives the Spirit directly. In the words of the
Second Vatican Council:

> Just as Christ was sent by the Father, so he too sent the
> Apostles, filled with the Holy Spirit. Preaching the Gospel
> to every creature, they were to proclaim that the Son of
> God, by his death and resurrection, had freed us from
> the power of Satan and from death, and brought us over
> into the kingdom of his Father. But he sent them to do
> more than this. They were also to put into action the
> work of salvation which they had proclaimed, by means
> of the sacrifice and the sacraments, around which the en-
> tire liturgical life revolves. (Vat. II Const., ch. 1, art. 6.)

The event of Pentecost indicates that the Spirit dwells in the
Church's structure primarily by reason of the apostolic succession. It is the sacrament of orders which inserts individuals into
the structure of the Church in such a way that they become
carriers of the Spirit for other men. But the sacraments of baptism and confirmation insert their recipients into the same structure, each of them giving in its own way a function in the
Church of Pentecost. In each case it is a function which is related to the giving of the Spirit. Baptism enables the faithful to
receive the Spirit from the ordained priesthood; confirmation
associates the faithful in a certain manner with the giving of
the Spirit to others. At the present stage of our inquiry these
ideas are only beginning to take shape; our purpose is to build
them up, step by step. Our next step is to draw together the

various notions so far explained in this chapter and unify them in a single notion which is central to St. Thomas's sacramental theology.

SACRAMENT OF CHRIST THE PRIEST

Though individual members may be sinners, if we consider the institutional Church as she comes from Pentecost we see that she is "without stain or wrinkle" (cf. *Eph.*, 5:27). She is a "glorious Church" (ibid.) because, though holiness has not yet taken definitive possession of her members, she shares through her official functions in the glory of the personal body of Christ, cooperating with him in the sending of the Spirit.

By the same token she shares in the priesthood of Christ. To say that the Church participates in this priesthood is only another way of saying that she is the fullness of his body; and, just as there is a two-fold dimension to the fullness, so her participation in Christ's priesthood is realized at the two levels of grace and of visible structure. As has been explained in Chpater One, all who possess sanctifying grace share in Christ's priesthood because by faith they offer through him the sacrifice of Calvary. But, in addition to this, the visible Church participates in the priesthood of Christ because those who are inserted into her by baptism, confirmation and orders have official functions in the exercise of which they cooperate with Christ the High Priest who sends his Spirit into the world. Participation by grace is the fruit of Christ's priestly activity; participation by official function is cooperation in the priestly activity itself. It is important to grasp, first of all in these general terms, the nature of official participation in Christ's priesthood; otherwise it is impossible to understand St. Thomas's teaching on the key reality of the sacramental system, the sacramental character. For he describes all three characters precisely as participations in the priesthood of Christ.

We have stressed so much the role played by the physical body of Christ in the life of the Church in order to bring to light the fact that by exercising her official participation in Christ's priesthood the Church brings the faithful into contact with his body. Union with Christ, as St. Thomas repeats again and again, is achieved through faith and use of the sacraments. These are not two arbitrarily associated bonds with the Redeemer. They constitute the normal conditions of encounter between human beings. Men cannot communicate with each other by purely spiritual intercourse. Their most subtle ideas and their most intimate affections must be given corporeal expression in words and gestures and common activity if they are to be made known to others. God has become man so that men may be able to encounter Him in this human fashion. The Christian's union with Christ is not purely spiritual; on the contrary, it is human; and this necessarily implies that, while faith is at its heart, bodily contact is essential to its fullness. While Christ was on earth men could meet him as they met other men. They could encounter him as their Redeemer if they had faith in the words which he spoke with his human voice or in the touch of his human hand. Now that he is ascended into heaven faith remains the spiritual link with him but the corporeal contact is still essential. If there are no human words spoken, there is nothing for faith to believe; it has no truth to assent to. If the believer cannot stretch out his hand to touch Christ's body to be healed by the contact then the Incarnation, with all its humanization of man's encounter with the God of holiness, affects his life only imperfectly. The Church with her official functions brings this necessary complement to the union with Christ by faith. Her official participation in the priesthood of Christ makes possible for the believer corporeal contact with the unique High Priest.

We must, accordingly, look on the visible Church as the sacrament of Christ the Priest. The official actions of her ordained ministers, the ministry of the word and of the sacraments, present Christ in bodily fashion to the faith of the members. The heavenly Priest, whose physical body was the sacrament of God on earth, finds a new corporeal shape in the actions of his ministers in the Church. He speaks through these actions and permits men to touch him through them. They are the way of entry to the basic sacrament, his glorious body. While the functions of the confirmed are in some ways similar to those of the ordained, the official actions of the baptized are directed towards coming into bodily contact with the High Priest presented to them in the actions of the clergy.

For those who live as believers in the Church on earth bodily contact with Christ is, accordingly, one stage removed from the kind of contact which they can establish with their fellowmen. The secret of liturgical participation is the realization that the ceremonial sacrament of Christ presented in the liturgy is as real and as significant as the bodily presence of those we meet in our daily life. It is, to be sure, only a temporary measure, adapted to the state of faith in which we do not see God face to face. When Christ returns in body there will no longer be need for ceremonial representation. His physical body will be the immediate instrument of God, infusing the light of glory, the perfection of faith, into the saints who will be reintegrated as corporeal beings.

We have said above that the spiritual and bodily resurrection of Christ's members constitutes the primary significance of the idea that the Church is the fullness of Christ's physical body. Likewise, and for the same reason, the participation in Christ's priesthood given by grace is more important in the context of the whole mystery of redemption than the participation given by official function. In the more restricted area of the life of the Church on earth official participation plays an essential role in establishing corporeal contact with Christ; but its purpose is to increase participation by grace. The Church is for the baptized; which means of course that it is for the clergy also, but only because they also are numbered among the baptized. The official participation in Christ's priesthood enjoyed by the baptized themselves and by the clergy is directed towards perfecting union with God by grace. The functions exercised by the baptized in virtue of their membership of the visible Church are, accordingly, most intimately bound up with their spiritual union with Christ. Their official participation in Christ's priesthood is an extension of their participation by grace. Because they have received the sacrament of baptism their life as believers can find expression and can be enriched by their participation in the activity of the visible Church; and this is true above all of their participation in the seven sacraments. For them, as for the clergy, the performance of a public official act will preserve its validity even if carried out with minimal self-commitment; but it can and ought to be made a genuine external act of personal worship.

On the side of Christ, especially in the sacraments, this interiorization is always assured when the official Church action is performed validly. The religious value of his priestly intercession is infallibly introduced into the action of the Church, taking on the particular signification expressed by it. In the Mass the sacrificial ceremony of the Church is expressive of the worship of the heavenly Priest. The sacrifice that he can no longer offer of his glorified body is made possible for him by means of the sacramental body of the Eucharist. In the other sacraments the sanctifying ceremony of the Church symbolizes and contains the sanctifying power of Christ's worship transmitted through his body. In both the Mass and the other sacraments the ceremony is expressive of the worship of the faithful. The sacramental system as a whole, embracing Mass and sacraments, is, consequently, the worship of the whole Christ, Head and members.

Mass and sacraments each grasp a distinct phase of Christ's single act of heavenly worship. In conformity with the symbolism of each, the Mass brings into the Church the God-ward movement of sacrifice, the sacraments realize within the Church the man-ward movement of sanctification which is the fruit of Christ's worship. Both Mass and sacraments, that is to say, are sacraments, or efficacious symbols, of Christ's worship. At the same time they are acts of Church worship. Head and members are, accordingly, united in a common system of external worship. At this centre of her liturgy the visible Church is the sacrament of Christ the High Priest worshipping the Father in union with his members.

INSERTION INTO THE STRUCTURE OF THE CHURCH

Though the members of the Church are obviously visible because they are men and women, this does not constitute the visibility of the Church. The Church is visible in virtue of her public acts and, in a special way, in the Eucharist. Her basic visibility as an organized society derives from the administration of three sacraments: baptism, confirmation and orders. These three structural sacraments give grace but this is an interior gift; their contribution to the visibility of the Church depends on the sacramental ceremonies themselves and on the activities in which the individual engages as a result. Moreover, in order to take part in the official activity of the Church a special power is needed. This is the sacramental character given by the structural sacraments.

THE SACRAMENTAL CHARACTERS

It will be recalled that sacramental acts of the Church have been defined as actions which symbolize or manifest faith. It may not be immediately apparent why any special power distinct from faith itself existing in a normal human being should be needed to take part in such acts. There is a certain amount of truth behind this doubt. Any individual who possesses faith can manifest the virtue externally by a bodily action, for example by a genuflection before the Blessed Sacrament; and this calls for no special power beyond control of one's own movements. A new power is needed, however, for taking part in sacramental actions, those, that is, that pertain to the seven major sacraments; for these are no ordinary manifestations of individual faith; they are community actions of the Church which engage the intervention of Christ himself and realize in the world the divine plan of salvation. They are signs of faith in Christ actually applying his saving action to the faithful through the signs themselves. To take part in such actions of the Church a person must belong to the Church, must form part of that great sacrament of Christ in the world. He must be able to make a bodily protestation of faith which constitutes part of the visible structure of the Church. The externalization of faith must be visibly or sacramentally in the Church and of the Church. It is destined to signify not simply personal faith but the faith of the Church and as a consequence the divine decree of salvation here and now active through the humanity of Christ and through the official act of the Church.

THE CHARACTER AND CHRISTIAN WORSHIP

His teaching on the sacramental character forms one of the richest veins in St. Thomas's sacramental theology; subsequent theologians have so far mined only the surface. The analogy he uses to lead his readers to an understanding of the character is taken from the former custom of branding a soldier with the mark of the captain of the army. This served as a sign that the soldier was assigned to the performance of military duties. His actions on the battle-field would now be placed at the service of his captain, the one responsible for the military undertaking in its entirety. The character is like the military brand because it assigns an individual to the performance of actions which form part of a much broader enterprise being conducted under a single chieftain. The enterprise is the application to mankind of the fruits of Christ's priestly worship. The character assigns individuals to participation in the acts, primarily of worship, which belong to the visible Church and which depend on Christ's universal act of worship (cf. *Summa theol.*, III, q. 63, a. 3, ad 2 - a reply which brings into focus the broad lines of St. Thomas's exposition in the first part of this question). There is, however, a major difference between the military brand and the sacramental character. The soldier has the basic equipment for serving in the army in his own natural powers of mind and body, whereas one who takes part in ecclesial activity will be called on to receive divine gifts or, if he has a position of authority, hand these gifts on to others. This means that the Christian must be given a new, supernatural power, making him capable of such association with Christ's priestly action in the Church.

THE KEY TO ST. THOMAS'S TEACHING ON THE CHARACTERS

So much of St. Thomas's teaching may be said to be generally accepted by theologians. Where very many of them depart from him—unintentionally, for it is their purpose to reproduce his doctrine—is in the way they understand his terming the character a power or faculty (III, q. 63, a. 2). The temptation is to explain this at once as a power of giving grace through the sacraments, on the side of the minister, and as a power of receiving sacramental grace, on the side of the recipient. Now, while this interpretation encounters no great difficulties in the case of the minister, it is far from illuminating when applied to the recipient. The fact that St. Thomas describes the character required in the recipient as a "passive power" (ibid.) is fastened upon and it is usually said hurriedly that this is a power for receiving grace and other effects of the sacraments. But why should the recipient need a special power for receiving grace or any other effect from the sacraments? The soul by itself, the created image of God, is as adapted as any creature can be for receiving grace and whatever other supernatural gifts God gives; no additional power is needed for this. The trouble with this explanation is that it misses the subtlety of St. Thomas's teaching and as a consequence can find no real meaning in several of the things that he says.

He is very careful to point out that the characters are not immediately concerned with giving or receiving grace. "The character disposes the soul directly and immediately for performing those actions which belong to divine worship"; grace is a consequence of this, required if such actions are to be performed worthily (III, q. 63, a. 4, ad 1). The question then is: what kind of actions are envisaged if it is not the giving and receiving of grace? St. Thomas supplies the answer in one of the most illuminating—and most ignored—replies of his sacramental tract: "The character is directed towards what belongs to divine worship. Now this is one kind of manifestation of faith by external signs. Accordingly, the character must be found in the intellect where faith resides" (ibid., ad 4). This is the key to St. Thomas's teaching on the character, whether of orders, confirmation or baptism; and it is not surprising that he explains the sacramental character in terms of his definition of sacraments as signs of faith. The characters are not in themselves powers of giving or receiving grace. They are powers of manifesting faith by external signs which are the special property of the visible Church on earth, which, as a consequence, are signs of the mystery of Christ here and now active in the signs, and which, as a further consequence, give grace and whatever other effects divine Providence has decreed.

THE CHARACTER: AN INSTRUMENTAL POWER

It is because the signs constructed by the Church are simultaneously signs of divine intervention that St. Thomas adds a qualification to his description of the characters as powers or faculties of acting. The Church by herself is not responsible for the full significance of her actions; and this applies in the first place to her major sacramental actions. She does not possess within herself the authority to give grace; that is the prerogative of God. If, then, her sacramental actions do in fact contain the saving action of Christ, through whom God gives His gifts, it is only because she serves Christ, because she supplies the ceremonial "body" through which he acts. Accordingly, says St. Thomas, those who bear the character—and he makes no distinction here between the three characters—serve God as ministers, they are His instruments. The characters are "instrumental powers"; they can act only because God has decreed that the manifestations of faith for which they are responsible will be the signs and carriers of His grace (III, q. 63, a. 2). It must be observed here, so as to avoid possible confusion, that St. Thomas is not using the word "minister" in this place in the specialized sense of minister or administrator of the sacraments. Likewise, he is not using the word "instrument" in the strict sense that he will employ when he is explaining that the minister of a sacrament is an instrumental cause of grace subordinated to the humanity of Christ. Here the sense of the two words is much more general; all three characters are envisaged, as well as actions which the Church performs outside the major sacraments. What St. Thomas has in mind is the contribution which all those who belong to the visible Church make to the external activity of the Church. All such actions will be sacramental in the broad sense, signifying, that is, as does the Church, the mystery of redemption; some of them will be sacramental in the strict sense.

VISIBLE SACRAMENT AND CHARACTER: MEMBERSHIP OF THE CHURCH

It is worth while to pay some attention to the diverse roles played by the visible sacramental ceremony of the three structural sacraments and by the characters which they give. It is sometimes said that for St. Thomas the baptismal character incorporates a person into the Church. This is not altogether accurate and could lead to misunderstanding of St. Thomas's sacramental theology as well as to confusion about what constitutes membership of the Church. A brief summary of St. Thomas's teaching on membership—which would have to be exposed in full if an adequate presentation of his position were called for [1]—is to be found in *Summa theologiae*, III, q. 69, a. 5, ad 1:

> Adults who already have saving belief in Christ (*credentes in Christum*) are incorporated into him mentally. When later they are baptized they are incorporated into him in a certain bodily fashion, that is to say, by means of the visible sacrament; and unless it was in their intention to receive the visible sacrament they could not be incorporated even mentally.

The very clear notion that St. Thomas had of the visibility of the mystical body is apparent in this quotation. The very possibility of membership of Christ is bound up inextricably with external membership of the Church achieved through the visible sacrament, that is, the ceremony, of baptism. The Church is the unique fundamental sacrament of Christ on earth, so that if a person is to be a member of Christ his membership must be made visible, corporeal, by adherence to this institution. This is an inherent demand in Christian grace; accordingly, if a person receives grace before submitting to baptism, he is by that very fact related to the visible sacrament by means of an intention, either explicit or implicit, to receive it. That this is not to be described as wholly invisible membership of the Church will be explained more fully when the Blessed Eucharist is discussed. What is relevant at the moment is that the immediate and specific factor in bodily or sacramental incorporation is the visible cere-

---

1. Cf. Members of the Church: "Mystici corporis" and St. Thomas, "The American Ecclesiastical Review" 148 (1963), pp. 113-128, 167-184; St. Thomas on the membership of the Church, "The Thomist" 26 (1963), pp. 88-140.

mony of baptism, as is in accord with the nature of the Church as a sign of Christ in the world. One must be *seen* to adhere to Christ. In similar fashion it is the visible ceremony of confirmation and orders which grants to an individual a special office in the visible Church. In all three sacraments the character has another function. It gives the power necessary to fulfill the duties which follow upon incorporation or granting of office in the visible Church. It is for action, whereas the visible sacrament is for insertion, in one way or another, into the visible structure of the Church.

THE CHARACTER: A PARTICIPATION IN THE PRIESTHOOD OF CHRIST

In the light of what has been said it is now possible to appreciate more fully what St. Thomas means when he describes the sacramental character as a participation in the priesthood of Christ (III, q. 63, a. 3). Possession of a character—of baptism, confirmation or orders—gives its bearer a new kind of participation in this priesthood, distinct from that given by grace, though in harmony with it, and referred immediately to the external, bodily activity of Christ the Priest in so far as this is exercised in and through the Church. The activities corresponding to each of the three characters are quite distinct; but from their common point of reference they derive, each in its own way, a priestly quality.

One who bears a character forms part of the visible sign or sacrament of Christ in the world, the visible Church. The baptized, the confirmed, the ordained, each group with its own function, form the visible fullness of the physical body of Christ for, like it, they give visible, tangible evidence to the world of the holiness of Christ and in different ways serve to conduct the saving power of his body into the world. Their own personal actions deriving from grace should infuse into the life of human secular society the reality of the divine life which they hold from Christ. But since they are not simply individuals, attempting with greater or less success, to live a virtuous life, but in addition are inserted into the visible fabric of the institutional Church which is filled with the Pentecostal Spirit of Christ, they constitute a sign raised up in the world of the sanctifying power of Christ the heavenly Priest.

There are essential differences between the modes of signification of Christ's priestly action which belong to the actions performed in virtue of each of the three characters; these will be dealt with in detail when each of the structural sacraments is considered. In general it may be said here that the actions of a baptized person, on the one hand, differ from those of one who is confirmed and even more from those of one who is ordained, on the other hand, by the fact that the latter signify the application, sacramental or otherwise, of Christ's priestly action to others, whereas the former co-operate in signifying sacramental application of Christ's action to the person of the baptized individual himself.

Further, just as the activity of Christ's physical body is not simply a sign of Christ's interior priestly holiness but is also the means through which Christ communicates his holiness to his members, so too those who bear the character of Christ have some part in directing the saving action of Christ towards the one who benefits from it. Once again, the baptized person directly influences only himself by his part in this action as it is exercised in the sacraments; the confirmed and the ordained, in very different ways, can influence others.

THE VISIBILITY OF THE CHURCH

We are now in a position to see the framework of the visibility of the Church. It is brought into being by the external sacrament, the visible ceremony, of baptism, confirmation and orders. As a living organism, it has distinctive actions which bring it into visible contact with the world. The basic power from which these actions spring is the sacramental character in its three forms. The official actions of the baptized, the confirmed and the ordained do not, however, simply make known the presence of the Church in the world; they form the visible sign of Christ's activity within and through the Church. They show the Church to be one, holy, and catholic, not simply because of the qualities of the earthly community—in which imperfections are to be found at any moment of history—but much more by reason of the fact that these actions are sacraments, in the broad or strict sense, of Christ, ever active in the apostolic Church as the source of unity and holiness and as the saviour of all men.

There is one action of the Church which surpasses all the others in making visible the community of the faithful and Christ. From it results a stable reality within the Church, the Blessed Eucharist, a sign of unity, holiness, universality, which contains the body of Christ. This is the centre of visibility of the Church to which the visible, apostolic head on earth directs mankind by his teaching.

It should be noted finally that the description of "sacrament of Christ" applied to the Church grasps only the visible reality. The Church is more than this, including the life of grace which is transmitted and expressed by the sacramental structure. For this reason the description suggested by St. Paul, that of "fullness of the physical body" of Christ, is more adequate, on condition that it be understood in the fashion outlined above. That is to say, it must be seen to refer to the reproduction of the mysteries of Christ in the moral life of Christians as well as to the sacramental role which the visible Church plays in relation to Christ's physical body, the visible source of all gifts given by God to the Church. A description is not a definition. To define the Church a formula would have to be found expressing the essential nature as well as the extrinsic causes, namely, the causes which bring the Church into being and give it increase, and the goal towards which the Church is moving. Theologians are still searching for a formula which will do all this. The difficulty in their task arises from the obscurity attaching to the first element which would have to express the precise relationship between the invisible and the visible aspects of the Church.

THE PRIESTHOOD OF ORDERS

Now that the basic structure of the visible Church can be seen, a further investigation is called for. The three structural sacraments insert individuals into the visible Church in a clearly defined order. In the official activity in which they participate in virtue of their characters, the baptized and the confirmed are subordinate to the clerical hierarchy. Actions exercised in virtue of the character of orders play a determining role in all the activity of the visible Church. If baptism and marriage are excepted, no sacrament can be administered without the intervention of the clergy; and since authorization is required for the celebration of marriage, and baptism is normally administered by a priest, it is in fact only in exceptional circumstances that the hierarchy does not explicitly· control the use of the sacraments. The nature of the actions flowing from possession of the characters of confirmation and baptism will be considered when these sacraments are discussed. Here something must be said of the function of the character of orders.

GIVING THE SPIRIT: WORD AND SACRAMENTS

The two modes of giving the Spirit which are inherent in the hierarchy, administration of the sacraments and the preaching of the word, may be seen exercised in the infant Church as described in the *Acts of the Apostles.* "Do penance, and be baptized every one of you in the name of Jesus Christ, for the remission of your sins; and you shall receive the gift of the Holy Ghost" is the conclusion of the apostolic preaching (*Acts*, 2:38). The Spirit-bearing character of the new Church was manifested through the extraordinary phenomena of the charisms, the speaking with tongues, the power of prophecy and miracles, and the rest, which were given to the apostles and to their converts (cf. *Acts*, 2:4; 10:46; 11:15; 9:6; *J Cor.*, 12:1 f.). These were extraordinary in the sense that they did not constitute the primary gift of the Spirit;·they served to manifest the essential power of the apostles and their helpers to give the Spirit into men's souls. When the apostles baptize (*Acts*, 2:38) or impose hands (ibid., 8:16; 19:6) the interior gift of the Spirit is rendered visible by charismatic gifts. Even before baptism Cornelius and his companions receive the gift of tongues while Peter is speaking the word to them (*Acts*, 10:44 f; cf. 2:33). Besides this demonstrated power of the sacraments and of preaching to give the Spirit the whole legislative organization of the Church is carried out under the influence of the Spirit (cf. *Acts*, 8:29; 8:40; 10:44-47; 11:12-16; 15:28; etc.).

THE BISHOP

The key-stone of the earthly structure of the Church is the body of bishops in union with the pope, the successors of the apostles. The bishop represents in the Church Christ as founder of the Church. By his consecration he contracts a relation with the Church, based on the character of orders, in virtue of which he has by divine right the power of maintaining the structure of the Church by preaching the faith and giving office in the Church through conferment of the sacraments of orders and confirmation. He wears a ring because he is wedded to the Church, taking the place on earth of Christ the heavenly Spouse. Or if we use the 'metaphor of the body to describe the Church, the bishop in his official capacity is on the side of the Head, representing Christ on earth. He can use his divinely-given powers of preaching and building the Church if the pope as supreme vicar of Christ assigns him a group of the faithful as his subjects, thereby conveying to him (in restricted or unrestricted form) divinely-given jurisdiction (cf. Encyc. *Mystici corporis*, CTSE ed. § 40).

The bishop's function in his diocese is to build the Church by transmitting the body of revealed teaching left by the apostles, the eye-witnesses of the mysteries of Christ, by preserving the sacramental life of the Church through the sacrament of orders, by giving the basic powers to exercise official functions in the Church through the sacraments of orders and confirmation, by permitting the actual use of such powers through delegation or appointment to certain positions, by preserving unity through directives. The bishop has the fullness of the priesthood of orders, combining all these sacramental and hierarchical powers, with the limitation imposed by the necessity of receiving subjects from the pope and with them the divinely-given power of government or jurisdiction.

PRIESTS AND DEACONS

The office of priest or deacon is to be understood as a participation in that of the bishop; these two share in the fullness of the priesthood possessed by the bishop. By ordination the priest has divinely-given sacramental power in virtue of his character to administer the sacraments reserved to him. By ordination too the priest, and this time the deacon also, contract a hierarchical relation to the order of bishops arising from the new position in the visible structure of the Church given by the sacrament. It is important for lay apostles and for congregations of teaching brothers or sisters to understand that the hierarchical position occupied by priests and deacons gives them a special aptitude to assist the order of bishops in the office of teaching the faith, which they can exercise when one invested with the appropriate jurisdiction delegates the necessary authority. This aptitude has nothing to do with natural ability; it arises from the nature of the Church as a hierarchical society. The fact that the sacrament of orders places priests and deacons in this special relation to the episcopal teaching office means that their co-operation with the bishops is essentially distinct from that of a lay person, even if the latter should be delegated to carry out a task similar to that entrusted to a priest or deacon (cf. Pius XII, Address to Second World Congress of Lay Apostles, 5th October, 1957). Accordingly it is false to say that priests are ordained to administer the sacraments and that the teaching of the faith should be left to religious congregations founded for this purpose. It is another thing to suggest to the prudent consideration of the bishops that teaching congregations train their members to be specially efficient in such work.

The power of forgiving sins is a sacramental one, belonging, that is, to the character of priestly orders. Nevertheless in order to exercise this power a priest must receive authority over penitents because this sacramental function involves the exercise of jurisdiction. Priests who hold certain offices in a diocese —parish priests for example or vicars general—or in exempt religious orders receive this authority with their office; others must obtain delegated authority from the superior of the penitents.

While by divine right only a bishop is the ordinary minister of confirmation, an act of papal jurisdiction can supply for the lack of hierarchical power in a simple priest so that he may validly exercise the power given by his character to administer this sacrament. Such jurisdiction is in fact given to priests of the Eastern Church and, in certain circumstances, to priests who have the care of souls (as the saying goes) in the Western Church. It used be given to cardinals who were not bishops; but such a case no longer arises since Pope John XXIII decreed that all cardinals should be consecrated. Some few theologians suggest that with similar delegation priests could administer priestly ordination and the lower orders. The opinion is based on an argument of analogy with administration of confirmation and a supposed granting of such power to Cistercian abbots in the fifteenth century; but the exact nature of this privilege is not clear so that most theologians reject the idea as far as major orders are concerned.

By his character the priest is deputed and empowered to conduct the sacramental liturgy of the Church in subordination to the bishop and in the person of Christ the Head of the mystical body. When the limitations of his power and the restrictions on its use are taken into consideration it is seen that his principal sacramental function is concerned with the Blessed Eucharist. Even when he holds no jurisdiction or other delegated power this function remains. By virtue of his ordination, then, he is expressly designated as one who acts in the person of Christ the Head at Mass; whatever other activities, sacramental or pastoral, are assigned him, they all centre on this.

SACRAMENT OF CHRIST THE HEAD

The official liturgical actions of bishops and priests constitute the precise element of the visible Church which is the sacrament of Christ sanctifying his members. For these actions to be valid there is required, besides possession of the appropriate character, an intention on the part of the individual minister in virtue of which he makes over his performance of the ritual to the Church. This means that the minister must sincerely will that his action be the one prescribed by the true Church; or, as it is usually put, he must intend to do what the Church does. An extreme case can be envisaged where the minister has lost faith in the sacraments of the Church. This will not affect the validity of his action if he intends to perform the ceremony prescribed by the Church. The value of considering this extreme eventuality is that it clarifies the exact nature of the minister's function. Because he is willing to act for the Church he places his external action at the disposal of the Church. His action is not that of an individual; it serves as a sign of the faith of the whole Church in the mysteries of Christ and in their saving power. As we have seen, this is what is required for the making of a sacrament. It is not something that the minister does by himself; it is an act of the whole Church and for this reason it is always an act of authentic worship.

If the minister did not possess the requisite character his intention of supplying the visible element of the Church's act of worship would be without effect. Here is seen the application to the priestly character of what has been said about characters in general. The character gives validity to the minister's intention of serving the Church. Accordingly, the formal or precise purpose of the character is not to enable the minister to give grace; it is to make the minister's action a sign of Church worship. A confirmation of this is that the minister's character is called into play even when a sacrament is received by a person who is not prepared for grace. Equally, when the priest pronounces the words of consecration at Mass there is no question of giving grace. In all the sacraments what the minister does in the first place is provide the visible action expressive of the faith of the Church.

We may now proceed a step further. In the very act of performing such a sign, and again in virtue of his character, the minister is the symbol or sacrament of Christ at this moment acting through him to produce the effect of the sacrament in a recipient who is duly participating in the action, or to consecrate the eucharistic species. Again this statement is an application of the general notion of the sacramental character. St. Thomas calls it an instrumental power because its· act is possible only on condition that Christ himself enters the Church's act of worship. The action placed by the minister in virtue of his character signifies at one and the same time the faith of the Church and the saving intervention of Christ. The character gives the minister's actions a quality which properly belongs to the actions of the personal body of Christ. That glorious body is the visible sign of the redemptive charity of Christ and of the love of the Blessed Trinity for men. It is also the instrument—and hence the efficacious sign or sacrament—through which those two loves implant in men's hearts the love of sons for God and bestow all the other gifts of the Spirit. The minister of Christ is drawn into union with this body, becoming in his turn symbol and instrument of the love of God and of Christ for men. The supreme act of the priest is the repeating of the words of Christ: This is my body. Here again he is the sacrament of Christ, now offering his body; but he does more than symbolize a bodily action of Christ, more than direct the physical touch of Christ to an individual; he makes present in the Church the Body itself, the sacramental Victim.

It will be noticed that a reservation has been made indicating that the minister's becoming a sacrament of Christ actually operative is conditioned by the behaviour of the recipient. This obviously does not apply to the consecration of the Blessed Eucharist; but it introduces a most important factor affecting the other sacraments. If an adult recipient has no intention of receiving a sacrament then the whole action is null; there is no sacrament. If there is an intention but no further participation on the part of the recipient then the sacrament, though valid, can at best be only partially effective; and this affects the extent to which the minister is the sacrament of Christ. This is a first hint of the essential role played by the faithful in the liturgy. It will be developed in the chapter on the liturgical activity of the faithful.

THE CENTRES OF LITURGICAL LIFE

The fact that the simple priest shares in the priesthood of the bishop has certain consequences regarding the place in which the liturgy is celebrated. The bishop is the central figure in the liturgical life of his diocese because he represents Christ as builder of the mystical body. It is he who must be approached by candidates for orders and ideally by those for confirmation. He must consecrate the oils used in anointing of the sick and in ceremonial baptism as well as the chrism for confirmation. He too consecrates the building in which the liturgy is celebrated, the altar, and the sacred vessels used. All this indicates that the bishop is "the governor (*princeps*) of the whole organization of the Church" (*Summa theol.*, III, q. 82, a. 1, ad 4). His cathedral is the central place of worship in the diocese. It should not be allowed to become a merely symbolic centre. At least on occasions when the bishop is performing ceremonies reserved to himself the people should be gathered round him. Since the whole diocese obviously cannot attend each parish should have its representatives, not only the parish priest but lay people as well.

Similarly the parish church is the centre of the liturgical life of the parish; and again it should not be foreign territory to the parishioners, particularly when ceremonies reserved to the parochial clergy are being celebrated or on the principal feasts.[2]

For pastoral reasons it is normal for the bishop to delegate priests belonging to religious orders to assist him in their own churches or elsewhere in preaching and hearing confessions; and to the extent that he does this he associates them with his own ministry to his people. In celebrating Mass, however, the priest, whether diocesan or regular, is not the delegate of the bishop. This is his own function in the Church which he exercises by right of ordination. Canon law may restrict the number of places in which a person can fulfill his obligation to attend Mass on Sundays and holy days; but this does not affect the nature of the priesthood. Wherever Mass is celebrated it associates those who take part in it with the whole Church. But while this is so, the unit of the Church formed by the parish and by the diocese should demonstrate its unity, at least on important occasions, by celebration of the Sacrifice in which as many as possible of the families in the parish or of parishes in the diocese are represented.

PREACHING OFFICE

In his other priestly activity and especially in preaching the priest retains his function of bringing the body of Christ to the faithful. He lends his words to Christ so that as long as his

---

2. The Second Vatican Council in the first chapter of the constitution on liturgy states that the diocese and the parish are the natural centers of liturgical life (Ch. 1, arts. 41, 42).

teaching is in harmony with that of the episcopate, whose delegate he is, it is Christ who speaks through him. His preaching
of the word forms a natural extension of his celebration of the
liturgy (cf. Vat. II Const., ch. 2, art. 52). When he preaches he
still symbolizes the physical presence of Christ in the Church
though he no longer serves as the instrument directly causing
the grace which flows from the heavenly body. But while the
Spirit is not given directly through his words as is the case when
he administers the sacraments, he is the occasion for the gift
of the Spirit sent from heaven by Christ into the hearts of the
hearers. "Labour with the gospel," St. Paul instructs Timothy,
"according to the power of God" (*JJ Tim.*, 1:8). "Take heed
to thyself, and to doctrine; be earnest in them. For in doing
this thou shalt both save thyself and them that hear thee" (*J
Tim.*, 4:16; cf. *Phil.*, 2:16; *JJ Cor.*, 3:18).

* * * * *

St. John gives us an arresting piece of information about
Christ: "Jesus himself did not baptize, but his disciples" (*Jn.*,
4:2). By his own physical presence he could produce the effects
of the sacraments for his body is the basic sacrament; it was in
this fashion that he ordained the apostles (*Lk.*, 22:19). The
only sacrament which he celebrated was the Eucharist. Here he
brings salvation not merely by touch or by word; his living body
is sacrificed and eaten; and this can only be if it is made present
sacramentally. The other sacraments become indispensable only
when his body has ascended to the Father. "It is expedient to
you that I go," he told his disciples, "for if I go not, the Paraclete
will not come to you; but if I go, I will send him to you" (*Jn.*,
16:7). The body must go; and yet it must be present and active
in the Church to achieve its fullness through the Spirit. The
body is made present and active by the priest of Christ; at his
word the Word made flesh dwells amongst us.

5 Baptism: Resurrection with Christ

It is a rare thing for the Roman liturgy to lose its urbanity. The excitement of the first Pentecost, when the risen Christ sent down his Spirit on the infant Church, has been modulated, weighed out in measured phrases, sobered by an abstract chant. The official prayer of the Church reflects the civilizing influence of what was in its origins considered an anarchic movement. The Easter Vigil liturgy is all the more remarkable in that it throws off this cloistered restraint and breaks out in a display of enthusiasm which is almost disconcertingly out of character with the rest of the Roman rite. For this one ceremony the Church reverts to the astonishment and the hardly controlled joy of the early Christians who had seen the risen Lord. Centred on the paschal candle, the Easter liturgy is a triumphant celebration of the body of Christ.

THE EASTER MYSTERY

Planted with the five grains of incense, the candle represents the wounded body of Christ; lit with the paschal fire, it stands for the risen, glorified body. From this symbolic flame the candles of the congregation are lighted while the deacon goes on to sing in praise of the Easter light: "This fire, though divided into parts, suffers no loss from the communication of its light." To bless the baptismal font the symbol of the risen body is three times submerged, contact with it symbolically rendering the waters fruitful in Christian life. Finally, each member of the congregation, holding in his hand the light of Christ, renews the promises made when that light was first given him, at baptism.

The simple, dramatic ceremonies of Easter, almost primitive in their intensity of feeling when compared with other rites of the Church, go to the heart of Christianity. The Church contemplates the mystery of herself; in the multitude of lighted candles she sees the glory of the risen Christ communicated to Christians by baptism. In celebrating the resurrection of Christ, she celebrates the fact that all her members have risen with him. "Rise thou that sleepest, and arise from the dead; and Christ shall enlighten thee" (*Eph.*, 5:14); this is the Easter hymn of the Church. Now that Christ has passed from death to everlasting life before the face of the Father, mankind has passed with him. There has been a definitive break in the history of the world; the movement away from God has been arrested; creation has found its way back to God after sin. All sin, even what still lies in the future, has been overcome; it remains for individuals to receive from Christ a share in his God-centred life, as the congregation receives light from the paschal candle.

This implies renunciation, not of anything that is authentically human, but of Satan "with all his works and pomps"; but the struggle of the individual to follow Christ, while losing nothing of its merit, is less of a personal achievement than a development of the implications of Christ's deliberate acceptance of his Father's will and his consequent glorification. The individual must be associated with the return of Christ to the Father; he must become one with Christ so that his own actions for which he is personally responsible, may be reflections, transpositions into another key, of Christ's all-embracing action. At the level of conscious choice this undoubtedly means imitating Christ in the way any person of good life might be imitated: "Learn of me . . ."; but at a deeper and more real level the initiative lies with

Christ as the one entrusted by God with the carrying out of the mystery of salvation. "No man can come to me, except the Father, who hath sent me, draw him; and I will raise him up on the last day" (*Jn.*, 6:44). God draws the individual into the Pasch of Christ, into his passing from the world of sin to the Father. It is at baptism, as the Church recalls at Easter, that this mystical identification with Christ begins to affect the individual.

The mystery of Christian baptism associates the believer with two mysteries of Christ's life, both of them baptisms.

THE BAPTISMS OF CHRIST

The New Testament speaks of two baptisms undergone by Christ: the first in the Jordan at the hands of John, the second at the end of his life, the passion, "the baptism with which I must be baptized" (*Mk.*, 10:38; *Lk.*, 12:49). The Jordan scene, as described by the evangelists, is a dramatic commentary on the effects of Christian baptism. The passion is the source of the sacrament's power.

THE JORDAN

It is in obedience to the command of his Father that Jesus approaches John and, though the Baptist demurs, asks to be baptized: "Suffer it to be so now; for so it becometh to fulfill all justice" (*Matt.*, 3:15). Jesus is plunged in the Jordan and then, coming up from the water in prayer, he sees the heavens opened to him and the Spirit of God descending as a dove and settling on him; he hears a voice from heaven: "Thou art my beloved son; in thee I am well pleased" (*Matt.*, 3:16-17 and parallel passages). The scene is an epitome of Christ's life and mission. He becomes one with sinners, accepting their purification, though he is without sin. It is in this act of obedience that is revealed his relation to the Father; the swift descent of the dove is the image of the bond of mutual love uniting Father and Son. The Spirit, the divine impulse of love for the divine nature mirrored in the Word and for creatures as they exist in the Word, the master-idea of all creation, rests on the humanity of Christ. Christ is revealed as the chosen instrument of the Spirit of love for the redemption of mankind. No new divine gift was given Christ at his baptism; he was God from the first moment of his human existence and as man was filled with grace. The Father and the Spirit simply gave audible and visible testimony of his mission at the time when his public ministry was to begin. But when one who believes in Christ is baptized the word of the Father and the coming of the Spirit bring something new into his life. He becomes like Christ, a son bound to his heavenly Father by love. He is not the Son by nature who with the Father breathes forth the Holy Spirit; that would mean that he had become God. He becomes an adopted son of God in the sense that, while retaining all of his creaturehood, he is given by grace a participation in the divine nature, from which springs a knowledge of God, destined to be perfected in face-to-face vision, and a love of God, destined to be satisfied by the possession of God achieved through vision.

CALVARY

The greater baptism is the passion. Step by step it echoes in a new key the baptism of the Jordan. "I am come to cast fire on the earth; and what will I but that it be kindled? And I have a baptism, wherewith I am to be baptized; and how am I straitened until it be accomplished" (*Lk.*, 12:49-50). Once again it is in obedience to the Father's precept that Jesus plunges himself in the suffering of Calvary, submerging himself, as in the Jordan, in the purification required of sinful humanity. This time the baptism is not a simple manifestation of his mission; it is its achievement, its predestined consummation. When Christ rises out of this purifying bath of pain the whole human race has been changed in his flesh. The Spirit descends, sent by Christ in the Pentecostal fire, upon the Church. Now the means are given men by which they may have fellowship with Christ in the baptism of Calvary and share in the divine sonship revealed at the·Jordan.

Only to the Son, God and man, does the Father say: Thou art my son. Only between these two does the Spirit pass. If men are to be adopted as sons of God it must be through association with the body of Christ rising from his great baptism.

THE BAPTISM OF CHRISTIANS

BAPTIZED INTO ONE BODY

The sacrament of baptism administered by the Church, the Spirit-bearing fullness of the physical body of Christ, achieves the union with Christ just spoken of: "In one Spirit we were all baptized into one body" (*I Cor.*, 12:12)—into the "body" of the Church, doubtless, but this means, as St. Paul's later epistles will suggest more clearly, into the physical body of Christ, rising from the baptism of his suffering. The actions of Christ in his body, which of themselves had a significance for the whole human race comparable to that of the sinful act of Adam, take actual effect when an individual submits to baptism. It is, says St. Thomas, commenting on *Romans*, 6:3-4, as though the sinner himself had suffered and died (*Summa theol.*, III, q. 69, a. 2). It is as though the body hanging on the cross were the body of the sinner, accepting with love the purification necessary for sin. There is a divinely-designed parallel between human generation, transmitting original sin, and baptism, communicating the spiritual attitude of Christ the Priest, rising from the grave to return to his Father (cf. *Rom.*, 5). All men are involved in the action of one man. Human flesh transmitted by Adam is such that the soul breathed into it by God is deprived of grace. When the body is marked in baptism with the symbol of Christ's passion, grace is restored. The sin of Adam, disrupting the spiritual harmony of man, spreads through the human race, multiplying like a cancer, setting man against man, and all men against God. The grace of Christ heals the wounds and restores unity.

The appeal of the humanist or the humanitarian to the brotherhood of man is based on a tragically misconceived idealization of a stock that is corrupt. Only Christ is our peace, drawing humanity "into one new man, making peace" and reconciling all men to God in his one body by the cross (cf. *Eph.*, 2). Political or social peace which is founded on force is at best a temporary cease-fire, honoured only as long as opposing forces are counterbalanced. We are not entitled to ask politicians to heal the sickness of the world; the most they can do is to treat symptoms, to make human society a rehabilitation centre. The remedy lies with baptism and with what the baptized make of their divine sonship.

SACRAMENT OF CHARITY

Baptism is only imperfectly described as the sacrament of faith; it is as much a sacrament of charity; certainly the New-Testament writers constantly saw it so. It is essentially a sacrament of union among men and with God. The Spirit who descends on the newly-adopted son of God at baptism (cf. *Gal.,* 4:4 f.) imparts to him the impulse of His flight. The Christian is caught up in the current of love which surges as the Father looks upon the Word and sees in Him all that is divine and all that is created. The faith of the Christian reveals to him something of what the Father sees in the Word; by baptism he binds himself to love what God loves.

It is perhaps more comfortable to say that by baptism we are bound to profess the faith. No Christian is unduly perturbed at confessing that there are three Persons in God. How much does that belief affect his conscious life, his behaviour in society? Most Catholics are prepared to acknowledge that by baptism they are under some obligation to propagate the faith, even if only by dropping an occasional coin in a collecting-box. But this is only part of the story; and not the hardest part.

We are baptized into the baptism of Christ on Calvary; this is the measure of our lives. We rise with him. Certainly we must recite the Creed, and sing it too if that is the way the Church wants it done; certainly we must preach the Gospel in whatever manner our condition of life permits; but the principal gift of baptism and the source of its most stringent demands is the union which it establishes among men as the condition of union with God. One new man rises from the waters of baptism, sharing in the sonship of Christ, possessing the Spirit of charity. "There is neither gentile nor Jew, circumcision nor uncircumcision, barbarian nor Scythian, bond nor free. But Christ is all and in all" (*Col.,* 3:11). "You are all one in Christ Jesus" (*Gal.,* 3:28). We are all meant to write into these texts our own national or social prejudices. If we feel that international affairs are too big for us or involve complications which no individual can be expected to solve, there still remain our domestic or local barriers which we can set about removing. No limit can be set to the holiness of life to which the Christian is called in virtue of his baptism, nor, which is the same thing, to his concern for his fellowmen. The baptized Christian has a contribution to make to modern society; history and personal experience prove that truth is not enough. The complete dedication of charity is indispensable.

THE CHARACTER OF BAPTISM

The grace of baptism makes the Christian a member of Christ the Priest so that every genuinely Christian action bears a priestly quality in so far as it goes to swell the hymn of praise offered to God by the whole Christ. We have already described this as the result of Christ's hidden activity in the Church, his offering of his sacrifice through the personal actions of his members. This spiritual priesthood of grace must, however, be seen in its full context as an aspect of the life of the Church. And when we consider the Church we must always look for two elements, one interior, the other exterior, visible. Spiritual union with Christ the Priest is achieved and maintained and exercised within the visible structure of the Church. The problem of lay spirituality or, as we should prefer to say, of the Christian life of the baptized, must find the foundation for its solution in the relation which exists between interior union with Christ and the function of the visible Church. The fact that Christ himself is brought within the actions of the society which is his sacrament on earth shows that spiritual union with him must be coordinated with these official activities of the Church. In the Mass Christ brings his sacrifice into the ritual of the Church; it is brought there in order that those who already offer that sacrifice spiritually may offer it also in bodily fashion. In the sacraments Christ brings his sanctifying action into the ceremonial of the Church; it is brought there in order to intensify spiritual union with Christ, and to do this in the bodily manner suited to human beings.

In the last chapter we saw how the minister of the sacraments acts in the person of Christ the Head in the liturgy. Except for marriage and emergency baptism the minister acts in virtue of his priestly character so that his external actions are those of the Church and fulfill the conditions necessary if they are to serve as the sacrament of Christ active in the ceremony. We also noted in passing that, apart from the Eucharist, the recipient has a determining role to play in the effective bringing of Christ into the liturgical action, so much so that if the recipient has no intention of receiving a sacrament then the action is simply not a sacrament. This indicates that the recipient is able to act effectively at the level of visible Church functions. It is the baptismal character which gives him the power to do this, just as it is the priestly character which gives the priest the power to bring Christ into the Church. The baptismal character might be thought of as the key which opens the door giving onto the sacramental or visible life of the Church; or it could be considered as something like the plug of an electrical appliance; it makes the connection between the sanctifying activity of Christ in the visible structure of the Church and the spiritual life of the faithful. It is of course a spiritual reality and much more intimately grafted onto the soul than either of these examples suggests. In addition, the activity flowing from the character contributes to the visible structure of the Church. Bridging the apparent gap between the hidden spiritual life of the individuals who form the Church of the faithful and the external structure of the Church, the character repays study more fully than any other element of the mystical body. The questions it raises for the theologian, involving as they do problems concerning the nature, at once spiritual and corporeal, of the Church, point the way to a comprehensive appreciation of the mystery. This is particularly true of questions about liturgical participation of the laity. All too often participation is discussed in terms of additional ceremonies attached to the sacraments by the Church in the course of her history—the making of responses at Mass, or the singing of the acclamations. These activities certainly form part of the laity's liturgical participation; they cannot be the whole of it, or even the essential part of it; for the laity were given a part in the liturgy by Christ before there were any responses to be made at Mass or any hymns to sing. If we want to get to the root of lay participation and in this way discover the absolute measure for the layman's external activity in the liturgy we have to define what exactly the baptismal character is for.

The teaching of St. Thomas on the baptismal character is approved in general terms in Pius XII's *Mediator Dei.* "By reason of their baptism," the encyclical reads, "Christians are in the mystical body and become by a common title members of Christ the Priest; by the 'character' that is graven upon their souls they are appointed to the worship of God, and therefore, according to their condition, they share in the priesthood of Christ himself" (CTSE ed. § 92). It will be recognized from what has been said in the preceding chapter that this represents an application to the baptismal character of what St. Thomas says about characters in general. Developing this summary, we may describe the share in the priesthood of Christ enjoyed by the baptized in virtue of the character as a power to take part in the visible actions of the Church in which Christ the Priest is the principal agent. Specifically, the part of the baptized is described by St. Thomas as that of one who receives divine gifts; and in this sense the baptismal character is a "passive" power.

We are standing now at a fork on the road of theological explanation of the liturgy. We have to choose between two ways of development; and the choice we make will determine the whole character of subsequent explanation of the part played by the faithful in the liturgy. We can interpret St. Thomas's phrase "passive power" as referring to a disposition in the soul for receiving the effects of the sacraments; or we can look for some other explanation. If, with many interpreters of St. Thomas, we select the first alternative then our whole attitude to lay participation will be coloured by the notion that the recipient of sacraments is basically passive, that something is done to him by the minister, that his whole function is restricted to preparing himself well to receive the sacraments; our pastoral efforts will be directed towards seeing that the recipient is "well disposed." There is no denying that this represents a well-established tradition in sacramental thought and training; nor would we be prepared to assert that it cannot achieve excellent practical results. But it will be apparent from what was said about the sacramental · character in general in the preceding chapter that this line of development is not that suggested by St. Thomas. If we want to be faithful to his mentality then we must look for an alternative explanation. For St. Thomas, as has already been shown, does

not explain the activity of any character in terms of grace, either
as something to be given or as something to be received. All
three characters for him are powers or faculties; and this means
that they are directed towards activity, never passivity. Why,
then, does he call the baptismal character passive? The explanation of this will reveal the principles of an authentically thomistic
theology of lay participation.

6 Baptism: Liturgical Activity in Reception of the Sacraments

It is our intention in this chapter to develop St. Thomas's teaching on the baptismal character so as to show the fundamental role played in the liturgical activity of the faithful by this participation in the priesthood of Christ. We shall confine the present enquiry to reception of sacraments, reserving to a later chapter the discussion of the faithful's part in the Mass.

The person primarily envisaged in all that follows is the conscious adult recipient, the term "adult" being understood of anyone who has reached the age of moral responsibility and who is, therefore, no longer an infant. Our purpose will be to show how worthy reception of the sacraments by such a person is an act of sacramental worship, made possible—apart from reception of baptism itself—by possession of the baptismal character. In accordance with this line of thought, we shall suggest that to describe the worthy recipient as "properly disposed" for grace is to adopt a terminology which does not do justice to the reality of adult and responsible sacramental participation. For practical purposes, as has already been admitted, it is adequate to instruct the recipient that he must be properly "disposed" to receive grace, having sorrow for his sins or being in a state of grace. But, the sense of our argument will be, this is like giving someone the minimum instructions necessary for driving a car with automatic gear-change; the machine will work but the driver will have no inkling of what he is setting in motion and may fail to get as much out of his machine as one who is able to control consciously its running. In what follows, when we are discussing the part played by conscious adults in the sacraments, we shall be concerned with bringing to light the basic, sometimes hidden, activity of the recipient. Our intention is comparable to that of the driving instructor who gives his pupil lessons on the internal combustion engine. By realizing more clearly what is involved in worthly reception we will become more aware of how deeply the recipient is engaged in the sacramental action. The ideal is that we should realize fully what we are doing and that our reception of a sacrament should be a deliberate act of commitment to Christ.

A further reason compels us to analyze the concept of worthy reception. It is important that Catholic teaching should be presented in such a way that non-Catholics may understand that Catholics do not have magical belief in the efficacy of the sacraments. Sincere reception of a sacrament must be shown to involve a positive act which is only very approximately described as a disposition or as the state of grace. It is an external action which signifies that the recipient in the depths of his person is actively translating into responsible human action the impetus towards God which is given by God Himself.

We have seen that there are two phases in the administration of a sacrament. The Church performs an action symbolizing the mystery of salvation; and Christ enters this ceremony to bring the fruits of his passion to the recipient. The activity made possible by possession of the baptismal character belongs to the first phase, the action of the Church; as a result of this comes the activity involved in reception of grace. For reasons of clarity we shall consider first the second phase, the gift of grace.

THE GIFT OF GRACE

EX OPERE OPERATO

It may be stated as a principle that when a sacrament is received worthily it infallibly gives grace. The Council of Trent defines that the sacraments of the New Law "contain" the grace which they signify and confer this grace on "those who place no obstacle to it" (sess. 7, can. 6 on the sacraments; Denz.-S. 1606). Theologians have not been so rash as to attempt to assess in absolute terms the measure of this gift. They term it the *ex-opere-operato* effect and are agreed in affirming that it is given in virtue of the merits of Christ so that it exceeds what the recipient could merit for himself outside the sacraments.

The meaning of the technical term is clear if it is recalled that the *opus operatum*—the "action performed"—is the sacramental action of the Church in so far as it serves as the efficacious sign of Christ's activity in the Church. The same visible action in so far as it is an external act for which the Church is responsible would be termed by St. Thomas the *opus operans* of the Church community. In other words, one and the same visible action is *opus operans*, an act of human worship, in so far as it proceeds from the Church, and is *opus operatum*, a reality independent of human worship, in so far as it serves as the sign established by Christ to signify and put into effect the divine mystery of salvation. The Church's visible act of sacramental worship is, taken over by Christ and given value of sanctification quite beyond what it possesses as an act of Church worship. The benefits granted the recipient, since they derive primarily from Christ's intervention in the ritual, are then rightly said to be "from the *opus operatum*," *ex opere operato*.

One of the most illuminating contributions which have been made to sacramental theology in recent years, due to Fr. H. Schillebeeckx, O.P., is concerned with the relationship between the personal commitment of the recipient and the effect produced by the sacrament, that is, between the individual's *opus operans* and the *ex-opere-operato* effect.[1] The outstanding merit of this

1. Cf. H. Schillebeeckx, O.P., **De sacramentele heilseconomie**, Antwerp, 't Groeit, 1952, pp. 557-663; also, C. O'Neill, O.P., **The role of the**

contribution is that it coordinates the teaching of the Church on sacramental efficacy with St. Thomas's explanation of justification of the sinner and of the increase of charity. What is important about this is that it turns the light of St. Thomas's searching analysis of the personal involvement of the faithful in the divine gift of grace onto the sacramental event, thereby revealing how the *ex-opere-operato* effect is integrated into the moral life of the recipient.

This work of synthesis achieved by Fr. Schillebeeckx involves some of the most difficult ideas in theology; but it is so essential for an adequate understanding of the sacraments that we must make some attempt to present, as simply as possible, its principal conclusions. Before doing so, we repeat our warning that we are concerned with what happens in the sacraments, not with what the recipient feels is happening. What we have to say about normal adult reception will take the form of an analysis of the activity of the recipient. Psychologically the individual may be unaware of this activity or at least of its extent; but this does not make it any less real. If he approaches the sacrament with sincerity, with such devotion as he can reasonably summon up, he will in fact be acting in the way that we shall describe. We shall deal first with sacraments of the dead—those which bring justification to the sinner—then with sacraments of the living, which bring increase of grace.

SACRAMENTS OF THE DEAD

To approach worthily a sacrament of the dead—baptism or penance—a responsible person must have at least attrition, that is, sorrow for his sins which springs from fear of divine punishment. The effect of the sacrament is then infallible; first of all, sanctifying grace is given or restored; but in addition to this the normal recipient is moved to make an act of perfect contrition, that is, sorrow for sin which springs from love of God. It is in his analysis of the recipient's acts of attrition and contrition that Fr. Schillebeeckx makes his contribution to this part of theology.

---

recipient and sacramental signification, "The Thomist," 21 (1958), pp. 257-301, 508-540.

It must be understood firstly that worthy approach to baptism or penance involves a positive act or series of acts on the part of the conscious adult recipient. Normally, this is something that the individual is aware of; he makes up his mind to receive baptism or go to confession and he has the intention of doing whatever the Church requires of him. This activity is what St. Thomas, in his discussion of justification of the sinner, calls "remote preparation" for grace. It takes place under the loving influence of God who draws the sinner back to Himself; and, since it includes, whether the sinner is always conscious of the fact or not, a desire of receiving the appropriate sacrament, it represents already an anticipated effect of baptism or penance.

The security and peace of mind given by the sacraments arise from the truth of faith that it is certain that when a penitent approaches baptism or penance with the preparation just described he will receive justifying grace. St. Thomas's theology of justification, however, makes it clear that a responsible person cannot be justified in the manner befitting his state unless he makes an act of perfect contrition. This St. Thomas calls "immediate preparation" for grace; but he makes it clear that it is a form of preparation which is achieved by the gift of grace itself (*Summa theol.*, I-II, q. 113, aa. 3, 4, 5). Grace is given by God; but it is inserted so intimately into man's person that it consolidates its influence on his responsible activity by moving him to make an act of charity and of perfect contrition. Because man is endowed with freedom he must make, under God's sanctifying influence, a free and loving response to the gift of grace. This idea may cause some difficulty because people are not always conscious, particularly at confession, of making a perfect act of contrition.

Let us take the simplest case first, that of a sinner who is actively aware of the gravity of his sin and is making his confession with all the sincerity and attention he can muster. The effect of the priest's absolution, granted that all the requirements of the sacrament have been met, is that God's justifying action moves the penitent to make an act of perfect contrition here and now. In similar circumstances baptism does the same. Psychologically, the penitent may not realize this; but it is not a question of what he feels; what is important is the work which God is bringing about within him and by him.

For our second case let us assume that the penitent has sincerely confessed his sins with the imperfect sorrow—attrition —which is adequate for worthy reception of the sacrament, and that when the priest gives absolution the penitent is distracted either deliberately or simply because his mind has wandered away from what he is doing. If the distraction is deliberate, that is, recognized for what it is and still entertained, the penitent is committing a venial sin at the moment of reception of grace, these two being quite compatible because they engage the person at two different levels of his personality. Whatever be the source of the distraction, it excludes the possibility of an act of charity at the moment of justification. That is to say, grace is truly given, but it does not achieve that fullness of insertion into the recipient's personal, responsible activity that can be brought about only by an act of charity. What has happened is that the penitent has been justified in a manner suitable to an infant; the habit of sanctifying grace has been infused but there has as yet been no personal response. The gift of grace will become a source of personal, responsible activity only when the penitent, under its influence, makes an act of perfect contrition. This may happen when the penance imposed by the priest is being recited or at any other time; once again it is by no means necessary that the penitent advert to the fact that he is making an act of charity.

All this is of the greatest significance for forming our attitude to the two sacraments we are discussing. The act of perfect contrition brought about under the influence of the gift of justifying grace is the free and personal side of the *ex-opere-operato* effect. All that St. Thomas says of justification in general is applicable to the case of sacramental justification. Consequently, all the personal activity and effort that is required for justification outside the sacraments (by an act of perfect contrition which includes an intention of the appropriate sacrament) is involved also when the sacraments are actually received. This does not at all take away from the efficacy of the sacraments. On the contrary, the precise effect of the sacrament is to move the penitent to make that moral response which is always necessary when a person responsible for his own actions is reconciled to God. The sacraments do not dispense with love of God; they make it possible.

It will be seen how positively Fr. Schillebeeckx interprets, in the case of conscious adults, the formula of Trent according to which the sacraments give grace to those who place no obstacle to it. This negative formula was selected by the Council as one which embraces all kinds of recipients, including infants who are incapable of any personal effort. It is by referring to St. Thomas's discussion of justification that we discover that if an adult is to place no obstacle to grace he must cooperate with it. If we find something strange in the idea that the event of justification has the same characteristics whether the sacraments are actually received or not, it is because we subscribe unwittingly to the Pelagian heresy, thinking that God is involved less in a sinner's return to Him by an act of perfect contrition than He is in the sacraments of baptism or penance.

The same principles clarify the case of an unconscious adult to whom baptism—or anointing—is administered; (there is some question about the efficacy of penance here, as will be explained in the chapter concerned with this sacrament). He is incapable of any act, either of attrition or contrition; but if he is a worthy recipient, if he places no obstacle, he will receive grace, not as a person here and now responsible for his acts, but in the manner of an infant. He differs, however, from an infant in that he was formerly responsible; as a consequence, his reception of the sacrament is worthy only if, before losing consciousness, he had attrition for his sins. If he recovers consciousness the grace given him in the sacrament affects his personal activity when he makes an act of contrition or charity.

SACRAMENTS OF THE LIVING

Fr. Schillebeeckx interprets reception of the sacraments of the living—those which presuppose the life of grace in the recipient—in the light of St. Thomas's teaching on the increase of charity. In accordance with the laws there laid down as governing spiritual growth, though each act of charity disposes a person for increase of the virtue, there is no increase until a person makes a more fervent act of charity (II-II, q. 24, a. 6). The process is something like that of a thermometer which has a device for registering maximum temperature in a given period; unless the column of mercury expands, the indicator cannot rise; or, to take a closer example involving the notion of life, a child does not grow with each mouthful of food, yet what he eats does promote growth.

As for justification, accordingly, St. Thomas distinguishes remote and proximate preparation for increase of charity. Each less fervent, or remiss, act of charity constitutes remote preparation; only under the influence of a new gift of grace does a person produce a more fervent act which is precisely his personal response to the divine initiative.

The application of this teaching to the sacraments is governed by the principle already invoked for sacraments of the dead. If the recipient approaches the sacrament worthily he will infallibly receive an increase of grace. Worthy reception in this case means at least a remiss act of charity. Again it must be stressed that the individual may not be aware of this act or may not realize what it is; but it is in fact implicit in the very action of going to the sacrament. In his decree on frequent communion, St. Pius X indicated that what is required of the recipient is that he have a "right intention and devotion" (*recta piaque mens*), and the decree goes on to explain that this means that the sacrament is received, not out of mere routine or through human respect, but with a desire to be more closely united with God and His will and to receive help for human weakness. A person who approaches a sacrament in this frame of mind is making an act of charity, or at least his action is governed by an act of charity made shortly before. This constitutes worthy reception of the sacrament; it is remote preparation for an increase of charity; and it brings infallibly an increase of grace.

It is much more difficult to determine the measure of this gift of grace than in the case of the sacraments of the dead where there is the clearly positive effect of justification. But it is clear that the gift is personalized only when, under its influence, the conscious adult makes a more fervent act of charity, this being proximate preparation for the increase of the virtue. The efforts of the faithful should be directed towards making this possible at the moment of reception or during the time of thanksgiving; but more important than frenzied attempts to feel closer to God is a calm and sincere readiness to serve Him.

If, for one reason or another, a worthy recipient is unable to make an act of charity at the moment of reception, then he receives grace, since this is infallibly linked with worthy reception. He does not, however, receive it as a responsible person, but, as before, in the manner of an infant. His personal response to the gift of grace will be delayed until he makes a more fervent act.

Some theologians—Cardinal Cajetan foremost among them —adopt a pessimistic attitude to the likelihood of increased grace when the recipient is deliberately distracted; but Fr. Schillebeeckx prefers to insist on the principle that a person who is worthy to receive a sacrament places no obstacle to the infusion of grace and consequently receives the increase, making his personal response when the opportunity presents itself. It must be remembered that most of the sacraments of the living are intended to give assistance to the recipient over a prolonged period of time so that the status they give in the Church constitutes a certain permanent claim to divine help; and consequently the efficacy of these sacraments is not determined exclusively by the person's response at the moment of reception. Holy communion, however, as will be seen in the appropriate chapter, is directed in a special way to procuring a more fervent act of charity when the sacrament is received. Deliberate distraction or any other form of venial sin at this moment makes such an act impossible. This means that the Eucharist is to some extent prevented from achieving its effect; and it was this that Cajetan had in mind when he expressed his opinion. Nevertheless, granted that it has been received worthily, the sacrament retains its efficacy as regards the whole orientation of the Christian life. Though it is quite impossible to express this in quantitative terms of grace increased by so many "degrees," it represents a positive influence in the life of an individual, granted that he has approached the sacrament worthily.

OPUS OPERANS

It will now be apparent that the opposition sometimes set up between the *ex-opere-operato* gift of grace in the sacraments and the *opus operans* of the recipient is artificial, at least when it is question of conscious adults. Man's *opus operans* is always dependent on God. This is true of worthy approach to the sacraments. It is also true of the new richness given to the recipient's Christian life as an effect of the sacraments. All is from God; man's *opus operans*, his personal dedication of himself to God, is the effect of God's loving action within him. What is important for practice, however, is that man is not consciously aware of God's action; he is conscious only of his own efforts, though he may perhaps at times feel intimations of God's intervention. The *opus operans* is the only reliable guide to the whole Christian life and especially to adult liturgical participation. The love of God is certainly not limited to saving only those who can respond to it, as the justification of infants and those who are unconscious shows. But God does not save the adult without his own human and free cooperation. If God dealt otherwise with men He would be denying the nature which He has given them.

It would be wrong to exclude the possibility of God's effecting a revolutionary change in a person's life through a sacrament; nevertheless, according to His ordinary Providence, He grants grace in proportion to the recipient's fervour in approaching them. What are called the dispositions of the recipient are in fact the positive acts of worship—attrition and contrition, remiss acts of charity and more fervent acts—which he offers, expressing them externally in the liturgical ceremony. The obligation lies on the recipient to exercise his liturgical function with full deliberation and whole-heartedly; this applies not only to the period of preparation for the sacrament and the actual moment of reception but also to the time afterwards. Though the sacraments, worthily received, give or increase grace, they are seen in a false light if they are thought of as sudden inputs of spiritual energy having no relation to what goes before or afterwards. They form an integral part of the whole Christian life-process which is characterized throughout by a continuous moral effort from the time when responsibility begins—it is all an *opus operans*. The fact that we submit to sacraments, receiving them from the hand of Christ, acting through the Church, serves to illumine the mystery of moral effort so that we see vividly that the *opus operans* is simply the human side of the divine mystery of salvation, that it is something which God works in us.

The scandal for non-Catholics in Catholic teaching on the sacraments does not lie in this emphasis on the divine initiative in our lives; it is in the attribution to the Church of a mediatorial function which appears to them to compromise the transcendence of God. The truth may well be that this censure is just as far as a large body of popular Catholic opinion is concerned. The firm teaching of the Church that grace is a created perfection of man, brought about in him by God's love for him, and that the sacraments are sources of grace can undergo strange transformations when translated into terms of the individual Catholic's attitude to the sacraments. Imagination plays a large part here; and it is easy to slip into the habit of thinking of the Church as a kind of supernatural supermarket with all the goods required for Christian life within easy reach of the customer. People do talk about "getting back into the state of grace" in much the same way as they speak of getting in a new supply of sugar. This does not necessarily prejudice the sincerity or the seriousness of their conduct of their own lives; but we are concerned here with popular theological thinking and not with the mysterious ways in which God can make good in our lives the inadequacies of our concepts of Him.

By thinking of grace as a commodity which God pours into the soul we can be led to interpret the Council of Trent's statement that the sacraments "contain" grace in a thoroughly materialistic fashion as though the Church had grace on tap. No Catholic would acknowledge in so many words so obvious a caricature of the Church's teaching; but unconsciously a Catholic might very well be adopting an attitude to the sacraments which amounts to something not very different. The danger of sacramental practice lies in formalism under its many guises; perhaps most damaging of all is the temptation to look on grace as a thing, a quantitative reality which can be increased merely by presence at liturgical functions. Grace is not a thing which can be passed from hand to hand. It is certainly a reality; but it is of the same order of reality as life itself. It is a development of the roots of a person's being brought about when God intervenes personally in his life. So intimately is it grafted onto human nature that it becomes a single principle with nature of responsible human action. While its presence means that God Himself is taking over control of man's human activity, this is done in so gentle and so complete a manner that man remains wholly the master of his own action.

Here once more is the paradox of grace. We are not entitled to reject the possibility of both God and man being each wholly responsible for man's good actions simply because we have no experience of such a combination of authorship in the created world. We must rather see in this unique example a revelation of the transcendent power of God. And, as far as Christian practice goes, while attributing all good to God, we must be thoroughly convinced that His directive presence in our lives heightens our own responsibility for our actions. The possession of grace by a responsible adult is inconceivable except in terms of ordination towards deliberate choice of God. To win an increase of grace is to commit oneself with ever greater personal deliberation to God. It is true, as we have seen, that the gift can sometimes precede the response; but this is not a normal occurrence in the existence of a free person; it is precisely abnormal, something which deviates from the rule determined by man's nature. The fact that it can happen serves to emphasise the gratuitousness of God's love; it is not to be taken as establishing a guide to the Christian life. The distinction made by Scholastic theology between grace and the virtues, the first an enrichment of being, the second directed towards action, if badly taught or imperfectly understood, may possibly be responsible for a static concept of grace, thought of as a perfection of the person and divorced from involvement in action. The distinction itself is invaluable for theological purposes; though obviously something should be done about bad teachers and poor students. We are not meant to carry over the dichotomy into life; and this applies with particular force to sacramental practice.

To talk about receiving grace *ex opere operato* from the sacraments and not to realize firstly that all grace is a free gift of God and secondly that it is always translated into an *opus operans* in a fully-developed human person is to betray the fact that one has lost one's bearings in the terminology of theology and, far more important, to expose oneself to all sorts of illusions about one's own Christian life. The system of the sacraments and, more generally, the whole mediatorial office of the Church do not prejudice in the slightest the transcendence of God or diminish in any way the entirely personal response which the individual must make to divine intervention in his life. In His approach to man God clothes Himself in the visible symbols of the Church which spell out the meaning of His coming and which provide the individual with the means of associating himself with the master-coming of God to man in the Incarnation which prepared the whole human race for the gift of grace. United to Christ spiritually and corporeally, by faith and by the sacraments, the Christian is open to God. It is through the Church that he finds the two-fold union with Christ that his nature demands.

We have now seen the inter-personal relationship between God and man set up when the sacraments, through the mediation of Christ and the Church, bring grace to the faithful. The emphasis here has been on the function which the sacraments have as causes of grace in the hands of Christ. In order to define precisely the manner in which the faithful take part in the sacramental activity of the Church we must now turn our attention to the first phase of the sacramental action, to the ceremony performed by the Church, which must be validly carried out if Christ is to intervene through it in the lives of the faithful. It is here that we come to the central point of our enquiry into the purpose of the baptismal character. Once again our concern will be primarily with responsible adult recipients. As the theory which we shall propose could be countered by certain objections arising from the practice of administering sacraments to those who are not conscious and to infants, we shall consider these cases after we have developed our main argument.

ECCLESIAL ACTIVITY OF THE ADULT RECIPIENT

THE SACRAMENTAL SIGN-ACTION

To understand properly the function of the baptismal character in reception of the sacraments and to grasp in consequence
the nature of the activity of conscious adults in the sacramental
order, it is essential to recall what has been said about the structure of sacraments. They are signs made by the Church and as
such form part of the visible aspect of the Church. They signify
the divine mystery of redemption in its application to individuals.
This means that they signify the gift of grace; but they do more
than this. As is specially clear when a responsible adult presents
himself to the minister of the Church to receive a sacrament, the
ceremony signifies not only the divine initiative in sanctification
but also the response that the faithful make. The ceremony, that
is, transposes to the realm of visible symbolic action the two
typical interventions of God in the Christian life, at the moment
of justification of the sinner and at the moment of increase of
grace. The ceremony reflects in stylized, symbolic form the
immensely subtle encounter between God and the human person
which takes place at these moments, and which we have described
above.

We must not fall into the trap of thinking of sacraments as
things which are given to recipients. There might be some justification for this in the case of the Blessed Eucharist where the
sacrament is completed when the priest pronounces the words of
consecration. But all the other sacraments are very clearly of the
kind that is completed only when the material used or the words
pronounced are applied to the recipient; and indeed Holy Communion also requires a recipient if the signification of nourishment is to be perfect. The sacraments are not administered in
the void; they are anchored on the individual recipient. For
St. Thomas "the sacrament is achieved where sanctification is
achieved," that is, in the recipient; and he goes on at once to
apply this principle to baptism, saying that the visible sacrament
here is not water but washing of the recipient (III, q. 66, a. 1).

Reduced to the simplest terms, the encounter between God
and man involves two elements: a giving and a receiving. God

gives; the recipient receives; this establishes the basic symbolism of the liturgical ceremony. In most sacraments of the living the gift of grace accompanies the entry of the recipient into a new phase of life in the Church and when this is so an ecclesial dimension will be added to, and will modify, the encounter between man and God. But essentially, the Church, acting for Christ, makes a positive advance through her minister in response to the recipient's request, performing an action on his body or giving some material object into his hands or pronouncing words over him; the recipient submits to this action. What is important for a theology of the laity is the nature of this act of submission.

This brings us to the heart of the matter. A sacrament is not merely a symbol of giving; it incorporates as well a symbol of receiving. It is a complex sign-action in the construction of which minister and recipient cooperate. It will be necessary to determine the extent of the recipient's cooperation, taking into account the varying states of consciousness which are admissible for him; but this central idea must be grasped first. Ignore the fact that a sacrament is a symbolic action performed by the Church, define or think about it simply as a cause of grace and at once it appears to follow that the recipient is wholly passive, like a child playing a game of Shut-your-eyes-and-open-your-mouth-and-see-what-God-sends-you.

We have noted that worthy reception of a sacrament constitutes "remote preparation" either for justification or for increase of charity. The act of receiving a sacrament is a perfectly adapted external expression of this state of mind, at once intensely active and yet open to the action of God who alone can give grace or increase of grace. The recipient acts in concert with the minister, completing the signification of the sacramental action. If, with the common theology, we denominate the sacramental action the "action performed," the *opus operatum*, then we must say that, excepting always the consecration of the Eucharist, minister and recipient have each a part to play in making or performing it. For, once again it must be stressed, what is done, the *opus operatum*, is an action, a symbolic action. If the Church attends to the making of this sign-action, Christ will fulfill his promise to give grace through the material elements of the completed sign. And the sign-action is complete only when a minister performs a symbolic action of giving and a recipient performs the corresponding action of receiving.

So much is this true that there is simply no sacrament, the whole action is invalid, if the adult recipient has not an intention of receiving what the Church offers him in the liturgical ceremony. It is this intention which makes the external action of the recipient something more than a meaningless mime. Even when the recipient is unconscious, as will be explained more fully below, he must possess some kind of intention; otherwise the sacramental action is invalid. Except for an infant, for whom the Church supplies an intention (III, q. 68, a. 9, ad 1), the recipient must be able and willing to complete the sign-action of the Church in a manner corresponding to his own condition of consciousness.

THE INTENTION OF THE RECIPIENT AND THE BAPTISMAL CHARACTER

When the sacrament being administered is baptism the adult recipient participates in the construction of the visible Church-action simply by presenting himself in bodily fashion to the ministrations of the priest or other minister and having a genuine intention of receiving the sacrament. It is clear that there is no need for the baptismal character for this act of reception. In the first place the character is given only when the visible action or sacrament is complete; and secondly the symbolism of the sacrament does not call for a character in the recipient who plays the part, not of one who already belongs to the visible Church, but of one who wishes to enter the Church visibly or sacramentally.

In all the other sacraments, however, the baptismal character is necessary. If the intention to receive these sacraments is to be effective it must spring from a mind marked by the character. This is so because the external act of reception is essentially an action of one who is inserted into the visible structure of the Church in which Christ the Priest is active; and it is the character alone which gives power to act in this sphere. The baptismal character consequently makes it possible for the recipient to complete validly the sign-action of giving and receiving which makes a sacrament.

It is now apparent that there is a similarity between the characters of orders and baptism and at the same time a radical difference. Both of them are directed towards giving visible reality to the Church, for the Church, as has been said, is visible in her official acts. In performing these acts, the Church is seen as the sacrament of Christ; and when it is question of the major sacramental actions which involve a recipient, both minister and recipient are together responsible for making this sacrament. The difference between the two is clear; the priest is responsible for the symbolism of giving, the recipient for the symbolism of receiving. Both are active in making the symbol; the distinction lies in the aspect of the symbol for which each is responsible.

INTENTION AND PARTICIPATION IN THE PRIESTHOOD OF CHRIST

By acting in this way the recipient himself forges the final link in the sacramental chain which connects him with the action of Christ in the visible Church. The recipient's action is part of the visible Church in which Christ's action is signified and through which Christ acts. Until all the elements of the visible action of the Church are, so to say, assembled, there is no possibility of Christ's priestly action being effectively signified; and until Christ's action is signified there is no possibility of Christ's intervening actively through the minister and through the material realities of the sacrament to produce the sacrament's effect in the recipient. In this fashion the recipient exercises his part in the sacramental activity of Christ the Priest; and in this sense his baptismal character gives him a share in the priesthood of Christ.

It is for the individual to ensure that his cooperation with the minister at the sacramental level is harmonized with his own interior participation. That is to say, besides having an intention to receive a sacrament, he must have those interior "dispositions" required for worthy reception. But in the light of all that has been said about sacramental participation it will now be clear why we have insisted that the link between the interior participation of the recipient and the sacramental action is much more

positive and vital than the word "dispositions" suggests. Cooperation in the sacramental action, of itself confined to external,
bodily activity expressive of an intention to receive the sacrament
and sufficient to ensure validity, demands as its natural accompaniment interior worship. It is clearly insufficient for the recipient to play his part as a member of the visible Church merely
by completing validly the sacramental sign-action. His integral
share in the life of the Church must find in this visible action
its connatural expression. His essential external participation
must be commanded by his interior fellowship with Christ. In
the technical language of Scholastic theology, his exterior actions
must be acts of the virtue of religion, the virtue of worship. If
this is so, his contribution to the visible sacrament will be an
authentic act of external worship in which he asks for divine
help; and the result will be that he will share fully in the gifts
which Christ brings when he enters the Church action.

If, on the contrary, the recipient does not make his external
act of reception an act of worship but is content to participate
purely in the sacramental sign (in virtue of a genuine intention
to receive the sacrament) then the sacrament will be valid but
unfruitful. It will not, that is, give grace. It will still be effective
in placing the recipient in whatever new phase of visible Church
life it is instituted to confer; it will give the character or matrimonial status; but these are effects which pertain to the external
or sacramental aspect of the Church; the sacrament will not have
conferred that fullness of Church life, both interior and exterior,
that it is intended to give.

It will be seen that the recipient's share in the priesthood of
Christ is a wholly personal one, directed immediately to his own
sanctification or to his own acceptance of further office in the
visible Church. It will be seen too how deeply involved in the
sacrament the recipient is, how much more there is to liturgical
participation than praying the text of the ritual. Inserted into
the structure of the visible Church by his baptism, and holding
the power of the character, the Christian is active at this external,
sacramental level as well as at the spiritual level of grace. This is
necessarily so, given the two-fold nature of the Church, corporeal
or sacramental as well as spiritual.

"PASSIVITY" OF THE BAPTISMAL CHARACTER

We are now in a position to decide why St. Thomas calls the baptismal character a "passive" power and to understand that this implies no contradiction with his attribution of activity to all characters. The baptismal character, like the other two, is directed towards action, towards contributing to the visible activity which constitutes the Church the sacrament of Christ in the world. It is at this external level that the note of passivity is attached to the recipient's participation. The recipient contributes the passive element of the sacramental sign-action performed by himself and the minister. The passivity refers to the function of the recipient in the symbol; but obviously considerable activity is required of the recipient if he is to play his part in constructing the symbol. At the deepest level also the recipient is passive, namely, in relation to God the giver of grace; but again this does not diminish his activity in preparing the sign-action through which God acts on him sacramentally. It is, accordingly, in respect of what it achieves in the external symbol and in respect of the final effect of the complete sacrament that the baptismal character is described as passive. As character it is a source of liturgical action.

OTHER RECIPIENTS

THE PROBLEM

The fact that infants and unconscious adults can validly receive certain of the sacraments indicates an obvious difficulty to the explanation just proposed of lay participation. It is clear that in their case the activity ascribed to conscious adult recipients cannot be realized; and this might suggest that their more passive role provides the norm for sacramental participation.

It is no exaggeration to say that the majority of text-book discussions of this question appear to make the unconscious person the central individual on whose situation the entire solution turns. On the face of it this looks like a shifting of emphasis from what is normal to what is extraordinary. With the exception of baptism all the sacraments are primarily intended for conscious adult recipients. It hardly seems adequate to formulate rules for liturgical participation in terms of the marginal case of an unconscious recipient. Nevertheless, on the basis of this case, it has become an axiom of sacramental theology that the recipient need not be as personally involved as the minister in the sacramental act.

This attitude is revealed when the intention required for a valid sacrament is being discussed. For the minister is prescribed at least a virtual intention, that is, an intention to do what the Church does which is here and now controlling his activity, even though he may not consciously advert at present to the terms of the intention. Such an intention presupposes that at some time in the past the minister consciously proposed to carry out his sacramental functions in accordance with the requirements of the Church. On the contrary, we find that for the recipient most authors are content to prescribe "at least an habitual intention," that is, an intention to receive the sacrament, which here and now is not controlling his activity. As in the case of a virtual intention, an habitual intention presupposes that at some time in the past the person made up his mind to receive the sacrament in question when the time for its administration should arrive. The person the authors have in mind is someone who is unconscious when the sacrament is administered; usually they are thinking of the sacrament of anointing given at death. The ambiguity of their statement is evident. It is of course quite legitimate for any author to formulate his definition of the requirements for valid reception in the widest possible terms so as to have it embrace all possible cases; but the practice can give the unwary reader the impression that what is admissible in the case of an unconscious person is sufficient for one who is conscious and responsible for his actions. The conclusion might be drawn that for any person an habitual intention is sufficient for reception of a sacrament and that consequently—since such an intention does not here and now control activity—the recipient has no part in constructing the visible sign-action. This is very far from true. For responsible reception of a sacrament at least a virtual intention is required.

In practice, the virtual intention at least is assured in anyone who approaches the sacraments with awareness of what he is doing and with a genuine desire to receive. We must stress once again that we are concerned with uncovering the activity which is implicit in receiving the sacraments with the right intention. The normal Catholic who enters the confessional or who goes up to the altar-rail has at least a virtual intention of receiving the sacrament and consequently is involved in the sign-action of the Church in the fashion described above. It is also true that a person who, for one reason or another—because he is unconscious or deliberately distracted or because he is acting out of pure habit—has only an habitual intention does validly receive the sacrament. What we want to get away from is the idea that the habitual intention is quite acceptable under any circumstances. If this were admitted the active participation of the faithful in the liturgy would be drastically reduced. They would have no active part in the visible sacramental action of the Church. In order to escape from this theology of minimum conditions we have considered first the case of conscious adult recipients. Now that the nature of their participation has been described and has been established as participation in the full sense, the task of showing how more marginal cases fit into the general scheme of sacramentalism may be undertaken.

LESS ACTIVE PARTICIPATION

It is necessary to return to a general principle. The sacraments are primarily acts of external worship offered by the whole Church. As such they signify the faith of the Church in the divine mystery of salvation; and, in the case of sacraments other than the Mass, what is expressed is faith in the application of this mystery to the individual recipient. If the recipient is a conscious adult he must make his personal contribution to this act of community worship, firstly by an intention of receiving the sacrament, and secondly by an authentic act of worship; lacking the first, the sacrament will be invalid; lacking the second, it will be unfruitful as far as grace is concerned. If, on the contrary, the individual is incapable of personal participation in the ritual he is carried on the faith and charity of the Church. He is presented to the sacramental action in the exact condition in which he is by the Christian community to which he belongs.

Infant baptism is the clearest example. The Church, in submitting an infant to the sacrament, accepts responsibility, normally shared by the parents and the sponsors, for his Christian education, for placing him in conditions which will permit the due development of grace within him. Obviously, nothing is required on the part of the child himself; not merely is the sacrament valid, it is infallibly fruitful. The recipient is justified by the grace of Christ and is incorporated sacramentally into Christ precisely as a member of a community which cares for its young. The important thing to grasp is that the symbolism of infant baptism is satisfied by the Church's presentation of a person incapable of any action of his own.

With baptism or anointing of an unconscious person the case is somewhat different. Once again the charity of the Church presents one who is incapable of personal action; but now the recipient has behind him a history of personal decisions and attitudes of mind. The Church's act of worship signifies this situation; it is an act of submitting to the mercy of Christ an unconscious individual who is presumed to be adequately prepared. Investigation of the person's past might give grounds for supposing that, when conscious, he had some genuine intention of being baptized or receiving the sacrament of anointing; positive law requires at least a summary investigation of this kind where possible, as well as a similar enquiry into the person's worthiness to receive the sacrament. But whatever judgment is made on these two questions by the person responsible will be conjectural. Whether the sacrament is valid or not will depend on whether or not the objective state of the recipient's mind corresponds to what is signified by the rite. Once again the deciding factor is the precise symbolism of the sacramental action in this particular situation; and the symbolism varies according to the state of the recipient.

Our conclusion is that it is the concrete symbolism of the individual sacramental action that determines the measure of active participation required of the recipient. Consequently, none of the various marginal cases which occur affect what has been said concerning the participation of the conscious adult. For in his case the signification of the Church's act of sacramental worship is that of supplication made by the Christian community in favour of one who is responsible for his own present actions.

Here the recipient who has the "right intention" cooperates to the full in the sign-action; and indeliberate distraction does not prejudice his involvement.

If, instead of this, the conscious adult deliberately entertains distractions so that he has not even a virtual intention of receiving the sacrament, if, in other words, in spite of his decision to receive the sacrament, he is committing venial sin at the moment of reception, then as far as the sacrament is concerned he is not acting as a conscious adult at all. He contributes to the visible sign-action nothing more than his bodily presence and his habitual intention of receiving the sacrament. As has been said about such a person's gift of grace, the sacrament is received by him as though he were an infant, carried by the worship of the Church. The validity of the sacrament is saved; but the recipient has failed to respond to the demands which the action makes upon him. Because the sacrament is valid the recipient acquires whatever new status and powers in the Church are given by the sacraments. To what extent he may benefit spiritually has been discussed above.

THE LESSON OF LITURGICAL ACTIVITY

The act of receiving a sacrament reveals the Christian in his situation as one of the baptized, a member of Christ, and an integral part of the Church. The spiritual and ecclesial context in which, often unaware, he constantly moves is here laid bare. The sacraments are designed to make him conscious of the structure and life of the organism into which he is incorporated, much as if he were to become conscious of the process of breathing and the circulation of the blood which maintain his bodily life.

The fact that there are sacraments teaches him that to fulfill the obligations of his baptism he needs the constant support of God, the unfailing mediation of Christ. The intervention of the Church shows her hierarchy in its typical role at the service of divine love and gives concrete expression to the charity of all her members solicitous for one. The spiritual co-operation of the recipient himself, varying according to his condition from infancy to death, reveals the mystery of the Christian life, a gift from God at every moment, yet a free giving of oneself to Him. The external part that the recipient must play in the liturgical ceremony is designed to make him conscious that he belongs to the visible Church and has responsibilities towards it and consequently towards his fellowmen. The implications of this last are more wide-reaching when the Christian has received confirmation; this is the next subject for consideration.

7 Confirmation: Witness to Christ

Confirmation remains a mystery sacrament; there is no general agreement as to what exactly it does. This ought to make the preparation of children or adults for its reception an extremely difficult task. It is all very well to say that it makes "perfect Christians and soldiers of Jesus Chirst"; but this is nothing like as clear-cut as what we can say about any of the other sacraments; and, while the efficacy of the sacrament does not depend entirely on the recipient's, or even the Church's, grasp of its implications, it does seem to be an unsatisfactory state of affairs if the only clear notion that people retain of confirmation is that the bishop gave them a blow on the cheek. If memory serves, this blow—which, after all, is only a very ritual tap—figures prominently in the confirmation class. To tell the children that this signifies the duty they now have to stand up to the difficulties of living as Christians in an unsympathetic, if not a hostile, world does no great harm, however distressed an historian might be at this free interpretation of the ceremony; but it does seem to reflect the defensive attitude of an unpopular minority group. Is this all that can be said about one of the three structural sacraments of the Church? And what will happen to this catechesis when the bishop's blow is removed from the ceremonial?

No blame attaches to catechists if they have recourse to expedients of this sort to compensate for the lack of more solid preparation for a sacrament which, since it gives a character, marks a decisive stage in the life of a Christian and has significance for the whole visible Church in its function as sacrament of Christ in the world. Theologians have been making public confession during the last few years of their failure to provide an adequate understanding of confirmation. As in so many other areas of theology, the Protestant Reformation has had a determining influence on the course taken, from the sixteenth to the nineteenth century, by studies of confirmation. The early Protestants rejected confirmation, denying it the status of a sacrament. "A useless piece of ceremonial" Melanchthon called it, and it was generally agreed among those of like mind that it was an invention of the Church. After the Council of Trent had reaffirmed the sacramental nature of confirmation, St. Robert Bellarmin led the way to a scholarly defence of this teaching, so establishing the subsequent orientation of this department of theology. A great deal of research has been done recently on the original form and the early explanations of the sacrament in an attempt to break out of this artificially limited field of study. Certain general conclusions have been formulated; but still no specific definitions of the nature and purpose of confirmation have yet won acceptance.

THEOLOGICAL APPROACH

THE RELEVANCE OF ST. THOMAS

By way of general comment on theological method it may be observed that historical research of the kind just mentioned into origins and patristic writings forms an indispensable part of the theologian's task. By bringing to light the practice of the Church and the teaching of tradition over the centuries, it shows the Church in her handling of the revealed truth of which she is guardian and interpreter, and this provides an invaluable guide to the work of theology. But while there can be no substitute for return to the sources of theology with their incomparable freshness of pastoral zeal and their immediacy to the Scriptures, it must not be forgotten that the patristic period, according to the more general reckoning, ended in the West with St. Isidore of Seville (d. 636) and in the East with St. John Damascene (d. 749). The life of the Church continued and it shared in the great revivals of learning of the ninth, twelfth and thirteenth centuries.

The theologians of the middle ages brought the reflection of the Church on revelation a stage further than the Fathers had done. Peter Lombard, Alexander of Hales, St. Bonaventure, St. Albert the Great, and above all, St. Thomas, among a host of others, laid the foundations of a systematic organization of revealed truth. Their aim was a synthesis which would present in human terms the divine truth revealed in the course of history. In this they were developing the inherent logic of revelation itself, for God has spoken to man through the human words of the prophets and of His Son, thereby guaranteeing the validity of human concepts for expressing accurately, however imperfectly, His divine truth. The thirteenth-century theologians brought to the study of revelation the methods of Greek philosophy, foremost among them the searching analysis of terms and concepts. Though they were at work in Europe and at a particular epoch of history, what they produced had and has a significance which escapes all local and temporal limitations. They had discovered in Aristotle and, to a lesser extent, in Plato the natural heritage of the human mind, the true *philosophia perennis*, a metaphysics which does not change, though it may have to confront new problems, with the advance of other branches of human learning. In doing this the medieval theologians learned how to control the use of the human intellect which is the image of God's own intellect.

St. Thomas's burning conviction and guiding principle was that reason and faith cannot contradict each other, that it must be possible to integrate one with the other, because both are from God and both are participations in His all-perfect knowledge. The truly stupendous task which these medieval theologians undertook was the coordination of these two intellectual lights given to man by his Creator and Redeemer. They were not so presumptuous as to think that they were capable of carrying their task to fulfillment; but what they began represents one of the major functions of the Church's mission, the bringing of divine truth to man. The essential task of the Church is to preach, to proclaim the message of Christian redemption to every individual, and to administer the sacraments. But the salvation of the individual does not take place in a social and cultural vacuum. It is something which is accomplished within the context of human society; it demands the renewal of the whole of human culture; above all, it requires that man as such, in his supreme natural dignity as a rational being, receive divine truth as an enrichment of his intellect. Only if the Church fulfills her mission to human society and civilization will she be in a position to reach the individual.

The name of St. Thomas appears again and again in these pages because it was he who made the definitive advance in the accomplishment of this mission to man as rational. We have chosen this place to outline the meaning of what he did because his teaching on confirmation provides a model example of his method and demonstrates how much modern theologians need to return to him if they are to pick up the threads of the Church's meditation on revelation, which had to be cast aside in the years following on the Reformation crisis. St. Thomas may not have enjoyed the advantages of twentieth-century methods of historical research, but he was well aware of the theologian's obligation to consult the teaching of tradition, and, like all his contemporaries, he was steeped in the Scriptures. An analysis of any question of his *Summa theologiae* reveals his constant preoccupation with the sources of theology and shows him as a master workman, picking out unerringly the major themes of scriptural and patristic thought. It is to him that we shall go to discover the key to the Church's teaching on confirmation.

THE PROBLEM OF CONFIRMATION

The difficulty about finding out exactly what confirmation does derives largely from the fact that the usual sources of sacramental theology—teaching of the Church, the New Testament, early rituals and the instructions given by bishops of the

early centuries—offer very little material for systematic organization. Confirmation as a general rule was administered in the
early Church immediately after baptism. It was natural that one
instruction was given for both; the result usually was that the
catechist made no clear distinction between the two sacraments,
treating the whole ceremony as the rite of initiation into the
Church.

Anglican scholars, who were among the first to raise the
problem of confirmation in recent years, have not all escaped
the confusion latent in this unreflective approach to the relationship between the two sacraments. Some of them have suggested
that baptism was originally nothing more than an introductory
ceremony to the "sealing" of the Christian in confirmation and
have gone on to propose that baptism has a purely negative
effect, the remission of sin, while confirmation brings the gift
of the Spirit; others have insisted, as Catholics must, that the
Spirit is given in baptism because, as Catholic teaching would
specify, grace is given; but then the problem remains: what does
confirmation do? The easy answer to this is that it increases
grace and gives strength "for the battle"; but it is just this answer that theologians find unsatisfactory for it appears to make
baptism sufficient for Christian initiation and to assign to confirmation a simple accessory function. The new insistence of the
Church, expressed in the decree of the Congregation of the Sacraments of 14 September, 1946, that all those in danger of death
should be confirmed, even by a priest, if the sacrament has not
already been received indicates how inadequate the "battle"
theory is. Confirmation has some positive contribution to make
to the status of the Christian.

TRADITIONAL TEACHING

Medieval theologians had at their disposal two principal
texts summing up for them the meditations of their predecessors
on confirmation. One of these texts is the ancestor of the tradition of commentaries developed in military terms. Considerable
respect was paid this document in the middle ages because it
was attributed to a fourth-century pope, Melchiades (Miltiades).
Theologians have known for some time that the text is of rather

later date and of less eminent authority, having been inserted in the False Decretals, a group of forged documents compiled in the ninth century with the object of enhancing the authority of diocesan bishops; but it was not until Dom Gregory Dix, the Anglican liturgical scholar, wittily described the process by which a very unimportant sermon of a minor sixth-century bishop was transformed into early papal teaching that doubts began seriously to be felt about the legitimacy of describing confirmation as an arming of the Christian for the combat. Not a few Catholic writers were drawn into rejecting the description outright.[1]

More recent studies have shown that, forgery or not, the pseudo-Melchiades faithfully represents one element of the Church's traditional teaching on the sacrament.[2] But to be told this is only to have the pieces of the jigsaw puzzle put back on the table after someone has knocked them off. We must accept the military description; but it is clearly metaphorical; the problem is, what is the reality behind it? That it implies a development or a further stage of the Christian initiation commenced in baptism is deducible from the early catechesis; but the existence of a second, distinct sacrament is indication of some specifically distinct effect. What this is the military metaphor does not adequately express. Even a simply baptized Christian is obliged to profess his faith in the face of opposition; he is called to the standard of Christ; he is Christ's soldier, as is recognized in the whole tradition based on St. Augustine's interpretation of the baptismal character. Justice is not being done to the autonomy of confirmation as long as this sacrament is thought of as though it were an eccentric addition made by Christ to the ritual of his Church, which could quite easily have been done without. Insistence on its autonomy does not exclude seeing in confirmation a relation to baptism. The two sacraments form the complete initiation of a person into the Church, but each has its own function which it is adequate of itself to fulfill.

The other text which influenced the medieval theologians dates from the ninth-century Carolingian renaissance. It is a pass-

---

1. E.g., L. Bouyer in "La vie spirituelle," Suppl., May, 1949.
2. Cf. P. T. Camelot, O.P., in "Rev. des sciences phil. et théol.," 1954, pp. 637 f.

age from Raban Maur, Archbishop of Mainz, and is one of the most informative commentaries on confirmation that we possess. The Holy Spirit, it notes, is given in both baptism and confirmation. Baptism procures the indwelling of the Blessed Trinity; in confirmation the Spirit comes "with all the fullness of holiness and knowledge and power." And, more significantly: "By the laying on of the bishop's hand the Paraclete is given to the baptized Christian that he. may be strengthened by the Holy Spirit for preaching." This text gives rise to several questions, in particular in its reference to preaching; but its genuine sense within the context of Christian tradition is revaled only when it is read in the interpretation of St. Thomas who incorporated it into the foundations of his theology of confirmation and used it to clarify the theme of military commitment.

SCRIPTURAL INDICATIONS

DIRECT REFERENCES

St. Thomas's genius as a theologian lay in his ability to organize coherently the scattered elements of Christian truth revealed piecemeal fashion in the course of history and preserved in the Church. The scriptural documentation in this case is slight. There are two accounts in *Acts* of the administration of confirmation, by Peter and John in Samaria, and by Paul at Ephesus (*Acts*, 8:4-25; 19:1-7); and two rather vague references which, at most, give evidence of the existence of the sacrament in apostolic times (*Heb.*, 6:1-6; *II Cor.*, 1:20-22). These passages, however, do little more than pose the problem of the theologian. The account of the evangelization of Samaria gives a vivid picture of the infant Church in action. Philip, a deacon, goes to the city "preaching Christ unto them" and healing his hearers in soul and body (*Acts*, 8:5-8). "But when they had believed Philip preaching of the kingdom of God, in the name of Jesus Christ, they were baptized both men and women" (ibid., v.12). When the success of the mission was reported to Jerusalem two of the apostles, Peter and John, visit the new church. "And when they had come, they prayed for (the converts) that they might receive the Holy Ghost. For he was not as yet come upon any of them; but they were only baptized in the name of the Lord Jesus. Then they laid their hands upon them and they received the Holy Ghost" (ibid., vv.14-17). That this invisible gift was manifested externally by charismatic gifts is indicated by the attempt of Simon to buy from the apostles the power of laying on hands and is mentioned explicitly in the case of Paul at Ephesus where the confirmed speak in tongues and prophesy (*Acts,* 8:18 f.; 19:6). It is clear from these accounts that the laying on of hands was reserved to the apostles and took place only after baptism. But the precise difficulty about confirmation is raised in terms of its effect. It is said to give the Holy Spirit whereas elsewhere *Acts* itself shows that He is already given in baptism (2:38; cf. 10:47). The visible charisms appear to indicate a new kind of gift; but they do not specify very clearly what form it took. The apostolic ceremony is seen to form a complement to baptism, something which is required if converts are to be fully accepted by the body of bishops.

Faced with this lack of direct scriptural evidence, theologians, and St. Thomas among them, turn to two other manifestations of the Spirit reported in the New Testament. It should be made clear at once that these can offer only a generic likeness to confirmation; it would be a mistake to think of them as exact parallels. In the life of Christ and in the history of the Church, as told in the New Testament, there occur in each case two related events which correspond to the two sacraments of Christian initiation.

CHRIST AND THE SPIRIT: FULLNESS OF AGE

The prophets had foretold the messianic age as a time of fullness of the spirit; the apostles, when their eyes were opened to the meaning of the Scriptures, were quick to understand that these prophetic texts were fulfilled in the coming of the Holy Spirit in Christ. "I will hide my face no more from them, for I have poured out my spirit upon all the house of Israel, saith the Lord God" (*Ezech.,* 39:29). "I will pour out upon the house of David, and upon the inhabitants of Jerusalem, the spirit of grace and of prayers" (*Zach.,* 12:10; cf. *Joel,* 3:1-2). The Spirit intervenes in the personal mystery of Christ first at the Incarnation

(*Lk.*, 1:35) and again at the baptism in the Jordan (*Lk.*, 3:22 and parallel passages). On the first occasion Christ is constituted the Messiah; on the second he makes public acceptance of his mission as Messiah and as the Suffering Servant. In him is the supreme fulfillment of the prophecies; from him will be derived their fulfillment in his members. At baptism the individual receives the fruits of Christ's messianic mission; he becomes a son of God, united to Him by the Spirit of love. Confirmation, says St. Thomas, conforms the Christian to Christ in the mystery of his baptism. We have already suggested that sacramental baptism conforms the Christian to Christ at the Jordan; but this is in respect of divine sonship and the giving of the Spirit. St. Thomas sees in confirmation a further assimilation to Christ as he was revealed in his baptism. It was a time of fullness of grace; so too is confirmation. But, whereas the descent of the dove simply manifested the fullness possessed by Christ from the moment of his conception, confirmation actually confers a fullness (*Summa theol.*, III, q. 72, a. 1, ad 3). By this is not meant that the person who receives confirmation attains perfection of virtue, for this is patently not the case, though without doubt sanctifying grace is increased if the recipient participates devoutly in the sacramental action. The fullness that St. Thomas has in mind is less interior than this. The Spirit descended visibly on Christ "at the time when Jesus began to teach and preach; for this function full age is required, that is, thirty years" (III, q. 39, a. 3).

Now—and this is where the parellel between Christ's entry on his public ministry and our confirmation breaks down and must break down—Jesus derived his mission as preacher and teacher from his personal identity with the Word of God and from his fullness of habitual grace which was the natural accompaniment of the hypostatic union. The person who is confirmed is conformed to Christ as he was at the beginning of his public ministry in the sense that he attains to full age *in the Church*. Since the Church is not purely an assembly of the faithful or of the justified but is also a visible society with an external organization and public activities which serve as the sacrament of Christ in the world, to attain fullness of age in it is not something to be measured only in terms of sanctifying grace; it involves also, and indeed primarily, acquiring adult status in the visible organization. As always when we compare the Church with Christ and derive the characteristics of the body from those of the Head, we find that the functions exercised by Christ in virtue of his personal union with God and his personal holiness are reproduced in the Church on the two inter-related levels of grace and visible structure. For Christ is active in the Church not only as the Head who is actually united to his members by the bond of grace but also as the Head who works through the Church's official acts in order to bring sanctity to the members of the Church and to the world. Union with Christ and conformity to him is achieved not only on the plane of personal moral commitment but also on the plane of official status in a visible society. This makes the fact of being a Christian much more complex than the simple notion of following Christ would at first suggest; but it reveals too the mystery of Christ on earth in his sacrament the Church. From what has been said about orders and baptism it should be clear that it is the external ceremony of confirmation which achieves for the Christian his new position of adulthood in the structural organization of the Church and that the character supplies him with the power necessary for fulfilling the new functions which thereby devolve upon him; but before developing this point St. Thomas completes his examination of the scriptural parallels to confirmation.

There emerges from the comparison of confirmation with the baptism of Christ the key-stone of St. Thomas's theology of the sacrament: its effect is to confer fullness of age in the spiritual life as this is lived in the Church. The temptation when discovering this idea of his for the first time is to abandon strict theological reasoning and to indulge in rhetorical considerations on the sense of Christian maturity and responsibility which the confirmed person should cultivate; that, in fact, is the line taken in the confirmation class and, if textbooks are any indication, in most theology classes. It is all true and it is admirable that candidates for confirmation should be instructed in it; but it is telescoped theology. The catechist and the theologian know already that the Church expects the confirmed Christian to take some kind of active part in her apostolate and they discover in the notion of responsibility an adequate explanation for this; the result is frequently an immediate union of the two ideas.

This is an exact parallel to the tendency to denominate the minister of a sacrament a giver of grace without any qualification. All St. Thomas's carefully constructed theology of sign is swept aside in eagerness to stress the result of the minister's action. Likewise with confirmation, its practical consequences are emphasised at once without any thought for how they are to be achieved in the context of the Church. What part does the character given by the sacrament play in a sense of responsibility? Clearly none at all. The merit of St. Thomas's treatment of the matter is that by "fullness of age in the spiritual life" he does not mean just an adult attitude to religious obligations; he has in mind the more complex thing which is the status of adult in the Church. There is some kind of advancement in the official category to which the Christian belongs in the organization of the Church, some new role that he has to play in forming the sacrament of Christ in the world. The second scriptural parallel to confirmation fills in some of the details.

THE CHURCH AND THE SPIRIT

As with Christ himself and the Christian, there are two divine interventions in the establishment of the Church. The visible mission of the Word—the earthly mysteries of Christ, culminating in the passion and resurrection—forms one element in its foundation; the visible mission of the Holy Spirit at Pentecost completes it. The coming of the Spirit marks the opening of the public ministry of the Church, exercised under apostolic authority in preaching and administration of the sacraments. The apostles are transformed from a group of disciples gathered in prayerful memory of their heavenly master into a band of active missionaries, propagandists of the faith.

Considerable care must be taken when this decisive turn in the history of the Church is used to interpret confirmation; and indeed St. Thomas, while indicating the traditional parallel between the two events, is at some pains to point out also how different they are. It would be far too facile, not to say theologically dangerous, to apply directly to the confirmed Christian the transformation that was brought about in the first pope and his collaborators by the descent of the Spirit. The point of comparison which St. Thomas selects is a very general one, doing no violence to the distinction between clergy and lay people. Whereas before Pentecost the apostles were concerned only with their personal relations with Christ, afterwards their attention was also turned outwards to their fellowmen. And is not this, asks St. Thomas, just what we understand by attaining adult age? The child lives for himself; his whole activity is directed towards his own development. The adult, on the contrary, is involved in the give and take of social relations; he contributes something to the life of others; he "communicates his actions to others" (III, q. 72, a. 2).

The Church's coming of age at Pentecost was marked by the first public move of the hierarchy; but evidently the individual Christian, when he has received confirmation, is not expected or empowered to take up the kind of activity that is assigned the clergy. Interpreting the symbolism of the chrism used in confirmation (which was, at any rate in the middle ages, the matter of the sacrament, a development of the apostolic laying on of hands) St. Thomas says that its recipient is meant to be the "good odour of Christ" (cf. *II Cor.*, 2:15), "acting in such a way as to build up the faithful" (III, q. 72, a. 2, ad 1). This may appear a very non-committal description of the confirmed Christian's duties towards others; but this is because a precise definition cannot be given of what those duties are. No single activity can be said to be distinctive of the confirmed; circumstances determine in each case the particular way in which the individual will "build up" the faithful.

Once again, what is essential to grasp is that the character of confirmation plays a determining role in the Christian's public activity. He is the "good odour of Christ," not exclusively because of any developed degree of virtue he may possess, but also because of the new position he has acquired in the organization of the Church in so far as this is the sacrament of Christ. It is just this that distinguishes him from the simply baptized, all of whom, when they reach the age of responsibility, are as much obliged as he is by the demands of charity and good example towards others. Once again, then, it becomes clear that the secret of confirmation lies in the character. It is from this that the gift of the Spirit, proper to this sacrament, takes on its distinctive characteristics. If it can be discovered what is the function of the character the mystery of confirmation, if not solved, is at least on the way to a solution. To explain the connection between the character of confirmation and the gift of the Spirit a word must be said about the missions of the divine Persons.

THE CHARACTER OF CONFIRMATION

THE DIVINE MISSIONS

The mystery of the involvement of Christians in the life of the Blessed Trinity is expressed by theologians, following the indications of the Scriptures, in terms of missions of the Son and the Holy Spirit and the "coming" of the Father into the world.

What is called the invisible mission of the Holy Spirit is quite simply the life of sanctifying grace; this way of describing it is an attempt to account for the new vital relation with the Blessed Trinity into which the person in the state of grace enters. The three divine Persons are present everywhere in the universe, holding it in being; but only the creature raised to the supernatural order by grace can become aware of this presence in such fashion that he knows and loves the three Persons and in a mysterious way almost perceives them for what they are. (True perception is reserved for face-to-face vision in heaven.) It is this supernatural awareness of the three Persons active in the soul, which we think of as a new kind of presence of the Blessed Trinity, that constitutes the divine indwelling. To call it a mission of the Holy Spirit is to concentrate attention on the divine love which makes it possible; but it involves also an invisible mission of the Son and a coming into the soul of the Father; for the three Persons are never separated in their action on creatures. Now, since all the sacraments, if received properly, give grace, it is clear that in all of them there is an invisible mission of the Spirit. Confirmation does not differ essentially from baptism from this point of view; it simply procures a new gift of the Spirit, a new gift of grace, adapted to the special functions conferred by confirmation.

There is another kind of mission, the visible mission of the Son and that of the Spirit. These are visible manifestations of the two divine Persons in the world: the Son in the Incarnation, the Spirit at the baptism of Christ, at the transfiguration and at Pentecost. Clearly, there are substantial differences between the visible mission of the Son and those of the Holy Spirit. The Son drew a human nature into personal union with himself; the Spirit, on the contrary, was manifested in the world simply by a symbol: a dove, a cloud, tongues of fire. But the two kinds of visible mission have this in common that they reveal to some degree the inner life of the Trinity and the special mode in which the Son and the Spirit intervene in the life of the Church. The primary function of the Church is to bring about with all the means at her disposal the invisible mission of the Spirit, the indwelling of the Blessed Trinity in man, for this is the meaning of "the mystery of godliness" (*II Tim.*, 3:16). The visible missions illustrate the part played in this work of sanctification by the Son and the Spirit, and consequently by the Father from whom they proceed.

The whole Trinity is the Author of salvation; but the incarnate Son alone intervenes in the world by human action as the Priest of mankind, responding in the name of all men to the gift of divine love. After his ascension the High Priest, in his humanity, shares with men his own holiness; that is, he makes the divine love effective within them so that the Blessed Trinity may dwell in them by grace. The inception of this work of sanctification, supremely a work of divine love, is revealed to men in the visible mission of the Spirit at Pentecost. The Spirit does not become incarnate; there is no task reserved to Him as redemption is reserved to the Son. The Spirit's mission is accomplished by a symbol, by something which does no more than direct man's attention to the mystery of the Blessed Trinity and provides him with a way of thinking about the impenetrable mystery of grace. At Pentecost too, and by reason of the same symbolic descent of heavenly fire, it is revealed that the Church is involved in the mystery of trinitarian love and has been instituted to convey the sanctifying action of the heavenly Priest to mankind.

The significance of the visible missions of the Spirit lies in the designation of Christ and of the Church, in subordination to Christ, as the means established in the world by the Blessed

Trinity to procure the invisible mission of the Spirit, the divine indwelling. It is in terms of the visible mission of the Spirit to the Church—which presupposes the visible mission of the Son— that the three characters are to be understood. This has special relevance to confirmation, the sacrament of the Spirit.

THE CHARACTER

The sacrament of orders inserts the clergy into the Church of Pentecost as official ministers of the heavenly Priest in preaching the word and administering the sacraments. The corresponding character gives them the power to exercise their sacramental function. The sacrament of baptism inserts Christians, both laity and clergy, into the Church as individuals who can draw life from the heavenly Priest through the sacraments; the character gives the necessary power. It is certain that the sacrament and character of confirmation are to be explained in similar fashion. As one of the three structural sacraments it inserts the Christian into the visible Church as it is the earthly sacrament and organ of the heavenly Priest, and its character supplies the requisite power to fulfill the consequent functions. The question is, in what manner confirmation does this.

The general orientation of St. Thomas's reply to this question is already clear enough. The sacrament of confirmation places its recipient in a new official position in the society which forms the sacrament of Christ. It is a position which implies adult participation in the visible Church's mission of bringing to men the fruit of Christ's priestly action. The fact that the participation is adult means that, unlike the simply baptized, the confirmed person co-operates in applying the fruits of Christ's priesthood to others and not to himself alone. Once again, for the sake of clarity, it must be stressed that it is question all the time of function in the visible Church. By the very fact of possessing grace even the baptized person is involved in the community life of the mystical body and shares in all its benefits as well as its obligations. But as far as position in the visible society goes, the baptized person's co-operation with the sacramental priesthood of Christ is confined to making the final application of its sanctifying activity to himself. It may well be that this will ultimately benefit others; but this will be by reason of the holiness of the individual, not by reason of a function in the visible Church. The confirmed Christian, on the contrary, while retaining all the advantages and obligations of the baptized arising from grace, has in addition a sacramental mission to the world arising from his official position in the structure of the Church. Corresponding to the external sacrament which confers this new status is the character of confirmation which, as with orders and baptism, gives the power needed for fulfilling the duties involved.

PARTICIPATION IN THE PRIESTHOOD OF CHRIST

The position conferred by confirmation and the power given by the character have a priestly quality, but not at all in any sense which would imply an over-lapping of the functions of clergy and laity. The activity of the confirmed person, whatever form it may take, is priestly because it is exercised 'in virtue of the character which gives its bearer an official function in the Church, the sacrament of Christ. All the official activity of this Church is priestly because it depends on Christ the Priest, because it is a development of the fruits of his sacrifice and the channel through which he is active in the world. Consequently, any action performed by the Church is a "sacred" action; and this is why St. Thomas, whose whole treatment of the mystery of the Incarnation is placed in terms of Christ's priesthood, can maintain that the confirmation character, like all characters, is directed towards sacred actions (III, q. 72, a. 5), and at the same time declare that it is a "power of publicly professing the faith of Christ in words, in an official capacity" (ibid., ad 2). Certain modern writers have adopted the second statement while rejecting the first, suggesting that confirmation assimilates the Christian to Christ the Prophet. One would hesitate to denounce this as a rejection of thomism; but it does appear to represent a failure to enter fully into St. Thomas's profound understanding of the priesthood of Christ and of the Church. His source, as an examination of *Summa theologiae*, III, q. 22 will show, is the *Epistle to the Hebrews* so that he sees in the priesthood of Christ the unifying principle of his whole mission. If Christ teaches it is because he is a priest, fulfilling in his person all that was foreshadowed in the office of Moses and of the Levitical priesthood. As a priest he is mediator of the New Alliance, bringing the things of God to man, bringing, that is, the New Law of grace: "For the lips of the priest shall keep knowledge, and they shall seek the law at his mouth" (*Malach.*, 2:7; cf. III, q. 22, a. 1). While, then, it is legitimate to speak of the prophetic office of the Church and to distinquish it, at least in part, from her priestly office, it seems clear that for St. Thomas such a distinction is not profitably applied to Christ since his teaching was an exercise of his priestly office. He prefers too to see all the activity of the Church in the light of Christ as the development of his priestly sacrifice.

ACTIVITY OF THE CONFIRMED CHRISTIAN

The breadth of St. Thomas's view of the activities of the confirmed may now be grasped. There is no specific task assigned them; every Christian thing they do, from reception of the sacraments to preaching at the street corner (if their bishops permit them to do this), takes on the quality of witness to Christ, active in the Church as priestly sanctifier of the world. This is not just good example, which derives from charity; nor, consequently, does it depend solely on personal holiness or conscious intention. By reason of their objective status in the Church the confirmed truly act in the power of Christ and co-operate in the invisible mission of the Spirit to the world. Their confirmation character, like all characters, is directed towards making official signs of faith; it functions whenever confirmed Christians act out of the conviction of their faith. In a fashion similar to the characters of orders and baptism, it makes their external professions of faith different from those of a person who has not received the sacrament. It makes these actions objectively part of the fabric of the visible Church. This is the Church in action in the world, whenever the confirmed act as Christians; this is the sacrament of Christ. And Christ uses the actions of the confirmed, as he uses the sacraments, but in a different way, for bringing grace into the world. There is no need for confusion about this; it is simply an application to the confirmed of what has already been said in general terms about the whole visible Church in so far as it constitutes the sacrament of Christ. It goes without saying that only the seven principal sacramental actions of the Church directly procure the invisible mission of the Spirit in grace. But the other activities of the Church, including those of the confirmed, are privileged occasions of grace. For there is considerably more to bringing the fruit of Christ's priesthood into the world than simply administering the sacraments. It is necessary that bishops and priests instruct men in the faith and that they obtain the assistance of certain laymen in this; and there still remains the task of impregnating society at every level with the Christian message, of preparing men for the sacraments through the infinitely varied personal contacts of human social intercourse.

This last task is entrusted to the confirmed; they are the people who must bring Christ into factories, not priests whose work lies elsewhere. The idealism of the priest-workers would not have led to such unhappy results if there had been confirmed Christians in sufficient numbers willing to do what they said they would do when they received the sacrament. While the hierarchy may entrust specifically apostolic tasks, such as catechesis, to adequately prepared laymen, the laity do not necessarily have to teach by word of mouth. Before anything else they must simply live as Christian members of society, making their contribution to the common material good, but doing this in such a way that they give a practical demonstration to their fellows of what it means to follow Christ. One of the most striking passages in Pope John XXIII's address at the opening of the Second Vatican Council (11 October, 1962), and one which aroused most interest in the secular European press, was his reading of *Matthew*, 6:33. "Seek first the kingdom of God and his justice"; this lays down the guiding principle of all Christian thought and effort. "But we must not pass over the rest of our Lord's charge: 'and all these things will be added unto you'." The religious orders and congregations of the Church bear witness to this programme of seeking Christian perfection while at the same time serving human society. But this teaching, went on the Pope, must "penetrate to all levels of man's activity, to the life of the individual, the family, society." If this is to be achieved "the Church's first obligation is to hold fast to the sacred heritage of truth received from the past; but she must at the same time look to the present, to the novel modes and conditions of life of the modern world, to the new forms of Catholic apostolate which they demand." The Church acknowledges the "extraordinary progress achieved in the field of science and does not fail to recognize its authentic value"; her duty is to remind men that while God gave them the task of "subduing the earth and ruling over it" (cf. *Gen.*, 1:28), He also commanded them to "adore the Lord God and to serve Him alone" (*Matt.*, 4:10); for true progress is impeded if men pursue only technological perfection. This recognition of the inherent goodness of material progress and consequently of the basis of modern social reform and technical discovery offers the confirmed Christian the charter of his status in the Church. Periodicals published by Catholic laymen now and again put forward unusual suggestions about ways in which the laity could cooperate in the life of the Church. There are proposals that laymen should control parochial finances or select their parish priest or have a hand in any of the other things at present controlled by the clergy. Without pronouncing on the merits of such suggestions, and without wishing to be judged guilty of the new clerical crime of wanting to keep the laity in their place, we may be permitted to observe how marginal this sort of discussion is. There are evidently many spheres where competent laymen can give the benefit of their experience to their parish clergy; but no matter what organizational changes might be made in the Church the number of laymen involved would be slight. Exotic proposals, besides being diverting, can be diversionary. They can only too easily distract attention from the principal function of the confirmed Christian which is to bear witness to Christ as a qualified member of the Church in the day-to-day life of society. A laity, convinced of its faith and grasping its application to every human activity, is an essential constituent of the Church on which the Spirit descended at Pentecost and which is a sign, raised up among the nations, of the mystery of salvation. Confirmation lays an obligation on the Christian to contribute to this sign; but as well—and laymen should be convinced of this—the character of confirmation lends to such activity an efficacy deriving not simply from the individual's personal merits or ability but above all from Christ. For Christ has chosen to bring salvation to the world through the visible Church; and this Church is formed not only of clergy but of laymen too.

These ideas on confirmation, and in particular on the character, are put forward in the belief that they represent St. Thomas's interpretation of the traditional metaphors and explanations of the sacrament. In the middle ages a "soldier of Jesus Christ" was called to the crusades. At the present time he may enrol in Catholic Action, becoming what is unattractively called in Europe a "militant" Catholic. But these are just two of the activities suited to the confirmed. The Church indicates the more profound significance of the sacrament when she requires that it be received before marriage and before religious profession.

8 The Blessed Eucharist: Union with Christ

"Take and eat; this is my body. Drink ye all of this. For this is my blood of the new alliance which shall be shed for many unto remission of sins" (*Matt.*, 26:26, 28). The physical realism, the earthiness, of the thing our Lord did at the supper-table can be easily overlooked. It is the most obvious aspect of the unprescribed ritual which he introduced into the ceremonial paschal meal that he was eating with his followers; yet we can become so busy explaining the meaning of what he did that the fact itself loses for us its plain significance. It was a piece of bread provided for the meal that he took into his hand; he said that it was his body. He took up the cup of wine being used at the meal; he said that it contained his blood. The Church assures us that he meant what he said; so perhaps we could pause for a moment and give ourselves the too obvious answer to the question: what is the Blessed Eucharist? It is what the priest says it is: lying on the altar is the body of Christ; in the chalice is the blood of Christ; and one looks like bread, the other looks like wine.

THE BODY OF CHRIST

Children being prepared for first communion are told that they are to receive our Lord, present under the appearances of bread; the hymns and prayers they learn speak of a friend coming to visit them; the catechism class is orientated towards making vivid for them the fact that the person of Christ is contained in the sacrament. This is not quite the same thing as saying, as our Lord said, that what he held in his hands was his body and that the cup contained his blood. There are very good reasons for developing for children in the way described the implications of our Lord's words. The Christian mind grasps almost without reflection that the meaning behind the Eucharist is that it unites us to the person of Christ. Catechetical experts have canonized this Christian common sense into a principle according to which it is essential for the teacher to establish a person-to-person relationship between the child and our Lord in the sacrament. All this is perfectly valid; and it is equally valid to exploit further the sense of the Eucharist and to state, as the catechism does, that under both species are contained the body, blood, soul and divinity of Christ. It still remains that all that Christ himself said was: "This is my body. This is my blood." And he instructed his disciples to eat and drink what looked like bread and wine.

THIS IS MY BODY

What upset the Jews when they heard Christ speaking of the Eucharist was that they understood very clearly a good deal of what he was suggesting; more clearly in one way than the child in the first-communion class. They knew that he was talking about his body; and they knew that he was saying that they must eat it (*John*, 6:54, 61 f.). They were repelled by what they took to be cannibalism proposed by an unbalanced preacher. It was to correct this crude impression that our Lord added: "It is the spirit that gives life; the flesh profiteth nothing" (ibid., v.64). He was taking back nothing of what he had already said; he was simply appealing to the principle of incarnation, the mystery of God coming to men through human flesh.

ᐧ Christ gave his body and his blood to the Church in the Blessed Eucharist before his bodily presence was removed from earth to the heavenly sanctuary. It was his physical body in its integrity that he was giving. He gave it under the appearances of bread and wine, one containing the flesh, the other the blood, because he was leaving his body with the Church as something which could be used in a community meal commemorating his death. It had to be given under the form of nourishment, food and drink, and it had to be given in a fashion symbolic of death, shed blood signified by one species and bloodless flesh by the other. Christ had in mind, in other words, liturgical considerations, arising from the use he intended the Church to make of the sacrament in her worship, when he gave the two-fold form to the Eucharist. But the central idea to grasp is that Christ's primary intention was to leave his body with the Church.

The part played by Christ's glorious body in the sacraments and in the life of the Church has been stressed several times in the preceding chapters. His body is the foundational sacrament of the mystery of redemption. Crucified and glorified, it is the supreme visible manifestation of the love of the Blessed Trinity for men: "God so loved the world as to give his only-begotten son" (*John*, 3:16). At the same time the most sublime act of creation, the act of charity with which man responds to the love of the Trinity, and the act of worship which is the creature's first duty to God, are bound up inextricably with what happened to the body of Christ. ᐧ All the human love of Christ for his Father and for men and all the intensity of his perfect worship were concentrated on the hour of Calvary; they found their divinely-ordained proof and symbol in that act of sacrifice made visible in the broken body and the shed blood.

ᐧ The divine love of the Blessed Trinity and the human love of the heart of Jesus now reach out to individual men to awaken in them an echo of the love of Christ for the Father; and the body and blood, now restored and glorified, are still the instrument of this redemptive love. From this body flows the Holy Spirit sent by the Father and the Son into Christians, drawing them into the life of the Blessed Trinity by grace. From this body

the Spirit is sent too into the visible functions of the Church, the
sacrament of the body, making them life-giving.

At the centre of Christianity is the body of Christ. It is the
vehicle of expression for Christ's and God's redemptive love; and
it is the visible instrument united to God through which all
graces are given.

Corresponding to these two functions of the body in the
work of redemption are two relations of Christians to the body.
Firstly they depend on it for all their supernatural gifts since
God uses the humanity of Christ as His instrument for sanctifying the world. Secondly they have in the sacrificed body of
Christ the master-expression of their charity and their worship.
It is the capital sign of man's response to the gifts of God. By
it humanity in the person of Christ, the sinless Head of mankind,
first purged itself of sin and proved itself worthy of receiving
the divine gifts. When God gives grace to men, using Christ's
humanity as His instrument, men are associated with the reparation and worthiness of the Head which are accepted by faith
and communicated by the physical contact established with his
body. After grace has been received and men are in a position
to make their own response of reparation, love and worship to
God, the sacrificed body and blood remain as the great unifying
symbol which gathers together in a single outward expression
all that mankind offers to God. United with Christ inwardly,
loving the Father with him, Christians share with him one visible
sign of their common love.

THE BODY IN THE CHURCH

It is this physical body of Christ which is present in the
Church in the Eucharist. Christians eat the body, impregnated
with the Spirit who gives life. Christians eat it; the sacrament
is absorbed by the nutritive organs of their bodies, though the
presence of Christ's body remains only as long as the species of
bread retain their natural qualities. The words used by Christ
fix our attention on these corporeal details. That the sacrament
has a spiritual effect, personal, affective union with Christ, goes
without saying; and that this is the most important truth about
the sacrament is beyond question. Christian common sense—

that is, living faith, guided by the Holy Spirit—picks out unerringly this central truth about the Eucharist. But Christian common sense could miss the genius of sacramentalism which consists not so much in the effect produced by the sacraments as in the human fashion in which it is produced. Faith and charity and all the other virtues are the substance of the Christian life; but since the Son of God became man, assuming a complete human nature, men can become sons of God only by full exercise of their humanity, using their bodies as well as their souls. Eden is lost to us, the inner Eden of purely spiritual communion with God as well as the garden. The materiality of the Blessed Eucharist reminds us that we are not disembodied spirits and no longer children of innocence, that we can find union with God only in the physical conditions of our earthly life. The sublimity of loving God is anchored in bodily contact with the humanity of Christ and in eating what appears to be bread. Nor does the gift of grace when once received through the bread liberate us from our bodily condition. The altar and the tabernacle remain as constant reminders that the one acceptable sign of union with God is the broken body of Calvary. We are called to the Christian life, not to a spiritual life. Our worship derives from a God enfleshed; we serve God with our bodies as well as with our minds. Wherever the human body and the material goods which serve it are despised or distrusted there is failure to understand in its integrity the Christian message. If the great Christian mystics give another impression we are misreading them. God does not mean us to deny the nature which He has given us. If we attempt to do so we fail in our Christian responsibilities to the world and, in addition, as likely as not, we are on the way to the psychiatric ward.

UNDER THE APPEARANCES OF BREAD

The humanistic and social implications of a Christian life centred on the Eucharist extend to the whole of our earthly existence. It was not by chance of personal piety that St. Thomas Aquinas drew his inspiration from the Blessed Sacrament, nor was it simply because his theological acumen revealed to him its splendours. His life-work, the achievement of the Church's basic co-ordination of faith and reason, of the divine and the human in man's mind, is implied in the fact that the body of Christ is contained in a host made by man's hands. Christ transforming man's daily bread, this is the symbol of the Church. The Christian message must be permitted to illuminate every human activity; all the resources of human nature must be put to the service of the message. Not only must the word be preached from the pulpit, it must be made part of human life, it must become the vital, guiding influence in the professions and trades of the earthly city.

It was not simply because their conduct was disrespectful to the sacrament that St. Paul reproved the Corinthians for drinking too much and sharing too little at the meal which preceded their celebration of the Eucharist. The sacramentalism of the bread, the bodily contact which is necessary for the Christian to enter into union with Christ, teaches us the inescapable lesson that Christianity is real only when it is a way of earthly life, when an attitude of mind is expressed in common social intercourse. The people who surround us, some of them agreeable to us, some of them not, whom we have to meet and work with and live with, these, together with ourselves and our personal quirks of character, provide the material for the Spirit who dwells within us. All this must be transformed, transubstantiated as it were, into Christianity because Christianity is the mystical body of Christ and it draws its nature from the Eucharist. This —the common object picked up from the ordinary table—is my body. There is no better way to reach an understanding of the Church than by meditating on the Eucharist, and no better way to grasp the sense of fraternal charity. The bread used for the sacrament may be rough or smooth, the wine sweet or bitter; within there is Christ. There is nothing superficial about Christian charity; it is too human, too divine for that. It springs from deliberate acceptance of people and things as they are and from the knowledge that the Spirit who moved over the waters at the creation is sent by Christ to renew the face of the earth.

This way of looking at the Christian life is sometimes called "incarnational" because it sees the day-to-day history of the Church as a process by which the revealed word of God, accepted by faith, is made flesh through charity in human activity.

Yet in fact the logic of the union of the divine Word with humanity was not fully developed at Nazareth in the womb of Mary. There was a further implication to be revealed at the last supper when the Incarnate Word took into his hands a piece of bread, the fruit of human labour, and said: This is my body. Christianity is not simply incarnational; it is eucharistic. It is Christ in the world that was created by God and that is being reshaped, humanized, Christianized, divinized by men. The members of the Church form the active, dynamic sacrament of Christ in the world. At the centre of the Church the Eucharist, the permanent sacrament of Christ, symbolizes and nourishes all Christian activity.

To speak of the social implications of the Eucharist is only to give a new turn to an idea that runs through the tradition of the Church. The materials from which are made the sacrament of Christ in the Church have always provided theologians with grounds for developing its significance. The dominant theme of all such interpretations derives from St. Augustine: "Our Lord gave us his body and blood in materials which form a unit made up of many parts; a single piece of bread is made from many grains of wheat; wine has been pressed from many grapes" (*In Joann.*, tr. 26, n. 17). The Eucharist is a symbol of Christian unity in charity: many members form one body with one another and with Christ in the charity given by the sacrament. "Sign of love, symbol of union, bond of charity" (ibid., n. 13). In this traditional theme is expressed the true source of the humanistic and social implications of the Eucharist. The activity of the apostle, cleric or lay, involved in the Christianization of society must be like the bread of the Eucharist; it is meaningless unless it is inspired by love of God and men in Christ.

LIFE-GIVING FLESH

The meditation of the Fathers and of theologians on the symbolism of the species of bread and wine has a curious origin. It seems clear that its inspiration was a faulty translation of a passage in *I Corinthians* (10:7; the inexact version is reproduced in the Douai text). This takes away nothing from the suggestiveness or validity of these commentaries; they form part of the contemplative treasure of the Church and represent a legtimate exploitation of the symbolism of the sacrament. But even more suggestive is the idea contained in the translation of the verse proposed by modern exegetes: "Because the bread is one, we, many though we are, are one body because we all share in the one bread." According to this version St. Paul bases the unity of the mystical body, not on the symbolism of bread and wine gathered together from many ingredients, but on the presence in the sacrament of the one body of Christ which makes all the bread of the Eucharist one bread. Because all Christians eat this one body they form one body. It will be seen at once how this interpretation harmonizes with the idea that the mystical body is the fullness of the physical body. Through contact with Christ's body Christians are built up in charity to form its fullness in grace.

THE REAL PRESENCE

ST. THOMAS'S CENTRAL CONCEPT

St. Thomas, who was absorbed by the idea of the function played by the body of Christ in the life of the Church, does not fail to recognize that the mystery of the Eucharist centres on the Real Presence. At first sight this may appear to be a very obvious point of view; but in fact many liturgists have been embarrassed in recent years by St. Thomas's apparent lack of appreciation of the sacrificial aspect of the Eucharist. By way of apology for his insistence on the Real Presence they explain that he was involved in the aftermath of the controversy with Berengar who falsified the teaching of the Church on this point. While it is very probable that if St. Thomas were writing his *Summa* at the present time he would develop considerably his treatment of the Mass as a sacrifice, there still does not appear to be any reason to suppose that he would modify appreciably the emphasis of his discussion of the Eucharist. It is very clear from reading his pages attentively that for him the essential characteristic of this sacrament is that it contains the body of Christ. He has a great deal to say too about the sacrifice, though much of this may be missed by those who think of the *Summa* as an encyclopedia which may be consulted piecemeal. But in his scheme of eucharistic thought this is a secondary theme, none the less important for that.

The reason for his choice of this point of view is, it may be suggested, to be found in the Prologue to the Third Part of the *Summa*. This is the Part in which he treats of Christ and the sacraments and, according to his original plan which he was unable to complete before his death, immortal life. The theme of the whole Part he states in these words: "We must finally consider the Saviour of all and the gifts which he has brought to the human race. This involves discussion first of the Saviour himself, second of his sacraments through which we attain salvation . . ." The principal significance of the sacraments, in other words, lies in their being the means through which Christ applies to us as individuals what he has won for us by his life and passion. The mystery of redemption is here very clearly before St. Thomas's mind. It is a gift of grace to man. Within this framework of thought the primary function of the Eucharist is to bring the body of Christ into contact with men so that they may be sanctified by it.

When liturgy is considered from another point of view as an exercise of the virtue of religion to which man is bound by his creaturehood St. Thomas will say that sacrifice is the principal external act of this virtue. Since, then, among the sacraments of the Church there is a sacrifice the problem arises as to which kind of sacrament is more important, or specifically in relation to the Eucharist: which aspect of it is central, the sacrifice or communion?

As will appear more clearly in the following chapter, the problem is to be solved in terms of the use that the faithful make of the Eucharist. The fact that the Mass is, according to Thomists, actually offered by Christ is not the decisive point. This may, perhaps, already be clear when it is recalled that sacraments are basically acts of the Church.

St. Thomas would reply to the problem with a distinction. From the point of view of liturgy, the exercise of the moral virtue of religion, sacrifice is the central external act. But from the point of view of sacramentalism, when the whole sacramental system is seen as the means through which salvation is brought to men, communion is primary. Comparing the two branches of the distinction, which holds the absolute primacy? Without any doubt, the second. The gift of God must precede any virtuous response on man's part. Man cannot have active fellowship in Christ's sacrifice until he has received grace from Christ. For the Church, accordingly, which is instituted to apply to men the fruits of Calvary, the central aspect of the Eucharist is that it contains the body of Christ, the created source of all grace. From this sacrament, received actually or in desire, derives the possibility of man's response to God. It should be noticed, however, that this solution is proposed to a theological problem of method. It is not intended to solve the practical problem of a person who has to choose between assisting at Mass and receiving communion when for any reason it is not possible to do both. Particular circumstances will play a determining role here.

THE EFFECT OF THE EUCHARIST

St. Thomas's insistence on the Real Presence is in harmony with his theology of grace. The principal indication of the efficacy of this sacrament, he says, is the fact that it contains Christ "who, when he came visibly into the world, brought to it the life of grace (*John*, 1:17); and who, in similar fashion, when he comes to a person sacramentally, works in him the life of grace: 'he that eateth me, the same also shall live by me' (*John*, 6:58)." He goes on to quote a passage from St. Cyril which interprets this presence of Christ specifically in terms of his flesh: "The life-giving Word of God by uniting to Himself His own flesh made it also life-giving. It is a fitting consequence of this that through the instrumentality of His sacred body and precious blood which we receive in the bread and wine as a life-giving blessing He should be in some sense united to our bodies." (*Summa theol.*, III, q. 79, a. 1). This is perhaps one of St. Thomas's most illuminating comments on the concept of the Incarnation held by the Greek Fathers. For them the human race was redeemed by the very fact that the Word united to Himself a human nature; all men were affected by the entry of God into their midst. The Western Church insisted more particularly on the specifically redemptive role of the passion and death. This view is without doubt more precise than that of the

Eastern Fathers for it takes into account the divinely-ordained culmination of Christ's earthly mission; yet St. Thomas recognizes the authentic insight into the economy of the Incarnation suggested by the Greek idea. He skilfully combines the two traditions by means of the notion of the instrumental function of Christ's humanity. By the very fact of the Incarnation God enters into every man in the sense that the humanity of Christ is definitively united to the Word as the instrument through which all men will be sanctified if they are brought into contact with it. The passion purifies the human race and prepares it to receive the grace of God; but the purity and worthiness of the Head of the race must still be communicated to individuals. In the Eucharist above all this contact and this communication are achieved. Because this sacrament contains the body that suffered for men and that has risen to glory to be the source of all graces the Eucharist is the supreme sacrament. The others derive their power from the body of Christ active through them; this one contains the body; "of itself," concludes St. Thomas, "it has power to give grace" (ibid., ad 1).

Since communion is at the centre of St. Thomas's thought he finds that the primary effect for which the sacrament was instituted is indicated in the way the Church uses it. The body is eaten as food to nourish us, as our Lord suggested to the Jews, spiritually. It does for man as Christian what ordinary food and drink do for his bodily life. St. Thomas is not "spiritualizing" Christianity here; he is simply distinguishing nourishment for the Christian life from material food and recognizing the primacy of the spirit in man. As food, then, not just for the soul but for the whole Christian, the Eucharist sustains, gives growth, restores energy, brings pleasure (ibid., corp.). This means, continues St. Thomas in a bold metaphor inspired by the wine and justified by a text from the *Canticle* (5:1), that the restorative power of the Eucharist derives from the pleasure it gives man's spirit which is made drunk with the goodness of God, experienced in the act of charity produced by the sacrament (ibid., ad 2). There are few passages of the *Summa* in which the contemplative character of St. Thomas's theology, always present as an under-current, appears more clearly; here a saint speaks of his own experience of communion. The Eucharist, he says, recalling a theme of Eastern theology, is like the live coal taken by a seraph from the altar with tongs and touched to the mouth of Isaias; it is aflame with God. "Behold this hath touched thy lips, and thy iniquities have been taken away, and thy sins have been cleansed" (*Is.*, 6:6-7).

EUCHARISTIC BODY AND MYSTICAL BODY

THE UNIVERSALITY OF THE EUCHARIST

There can be little doubt that it was St. Thomas's own devotion to the Eucharist which enlightened his mind to plumb the depths of its mystery. He is not content to explore the sacrament in isolation as one of the seven. He sees it as dominating the whole sacramental system, as the central reality of the Church. On it converge all the other sacraments, all ecclesiastical functions, all grace; from it these derive their significance in the mystical body on earth. The words of Christ: "Except you eat my flesh and drink my blood you shall not have life in you" (*John*, 6:54) are literally true for St. Thomas as they were for St. Augustine. "Nobody," we find in the *Summa*, "possesses grace before he receives this sacrament at least in desire, his own in the case of an adult, that of the Church in the case of infants" (III, q. 79, a. 1, ad 1). It is as though St. Thomas saw that in the apostolic preaching, centred on the risen Christ and calling men to repent and enter the Church by baptism, was implicitly contained the revelation that the only way in which union with Christ can be achieved is through the Eucharist. All that the Scriptures say of the glorified Christ as the source of grace may be applied to the eucharistic Christ. It is not that St. Thomas shifts the centre of Christianity from the heavenly sanctuary to the Church's liturgy; rather he sees within the earthly ceremonial and its sacraments the liturgy of Christ before the face of the Father described in the *Epistle to the Hebrews*. Christianity is eucharistic in the absolute sense so that St. Thomas can finally say that the words of Christ just quoted are equivalent to the theological axiom: Outside the Church there is no salvation. If we were to express this in the form: Apart from contact with the physical body of Christ there is no salvation, its validity, at least within the thomistic scheme of thought, would at once be apparent. But St. Thomas goes a most significant step further. Contact with the physical body of Christ from which the mystical body derives is possible only through the Eucharist.

Anyone with a feeling for theology will sense the background to St. Thomas's thought on this point; but something more positive than that is needed if an uneasy suspicion that a rabbit has been pulled out of the hat is to be allayed. What is easily recognizable in St. Thomas's view is the relation between the physical body and the mystical body. Theologians have a short-hand way of putting this. The physical body, they say is signified and contained by the sacramental food; technically put, Christ's body is the signified reality (*res et sacramentum*) which serves as symbol and cause of the final effect. The unity of the mystical body in charity is the ultimate reality (*res tantum*) signified and effected by the physical body of Christ contained in the Eucharist. The Eucharist, in short, causes the unity of the mystical body because it causes charity. This is a commonplace of sacramental theology. What is distinctive about St. Thomas is that he interprets the Eucharist's efficacy as being universal. There is no charity and nothing belonging to the Church which escapes the influence of the sacrament. This is clearly very different from simply saying that the Eucharist intensifies the union of the mystical body, which is the common teaching.

As always, St. Thomas considers the Eucharist as communion when he delineates his concept of its universal influence, though, as will appear later, his framework of thought is adapted to explaining the sacrifice. As communion, the eucharistic body is the cause of the *res*; it unites the men and women who live in the Church to Christ by charity. This is clear in the case of those who actually receive communion with the right intention, who make their act of reception a profession of faith in Christ their Redeemer and who desire to be one with him by charity. But this is not enough to establish that the physical body in the sacrament is the universal source of the mystical body. Grace comes to the members of the Church from the risen Christ through other channels than the Eucharist; that is to say, there are other efficient causes of grace. There are the other sacraments in which Christ is active. Most important, there is baptism the specific function of which is to initiate individuals into the mystical body. As well there are the graces given in prayer and in other virtuous activities. St. Thomas is well aware of all this; he shows his deep understanding of the Eucharist by his explanation of how it is involved always in the other sacraments and in acts of virtue.

DESIRE FOR THE EUCHARIST AND INCORPORATION INTO CHRIST

The key to his thought is his concept of desire for the Eucharist. This is something which he sees implanted in the Church in two ways, corresponding to the two elements of the Church, structure and interior union with Christ. Grace and charity imply always in the faithful on earth a desire for the Eucharist. The sacramental structure of the Church is centred on the Eucharist; it has a tendency towards, or ontological desire for, this sacrament which is at its centre.

First, as regards grace St. Thomas writes:

> The effect symbolized and produced by this sacrament (that is, the *res tantum*) is union with the mystical body, which is essential for salvation; for the way to heaven is closed to those who do not belong to the Church; in the same way, during the Flood no one was saved who did not enter the ark of Noe, the symbol of the church (*J Pet.*, 3:20-21). But . . . the effect of a particular sacrament may be obtained before actual reception of the sacrament by means of a desire of receiving (the sacrament). From this it follows that a person can be saved even before actually receiving the Eucharist if he desires to receive it; as is the case with baptism where desire (of the sacrament) is sufficient for salvation (*Summa theol.*, III, q. 73, a. 3).

In another place St. Thomas identifies spiritual communion, desire of eating the sacrament, with incorporation into Christ by charity; it is obvious, he comments, that without this no one can be saved (III, q. 80, a. 11; etc.). It will be seen that St.

Thomas identifies every act of charity with desire for the Eucharist. Since only a conscious adult is capable of such an act infants are directed sacramentally towards the Eucharist by the sacrament of baptism. Just as this ceremony expresses the faith of the whole Church and communicates it to the infant, so too baptism expresses the desire of the Church, springing from charity, for the Eucharist, and the infant benefits by the gift of grace (III, q. 73, a. 3). St. Thomas sees the Christian as beginning the Christian life by baptism and grace and by that very fact being directed towards the Eucharist which provides the consummation of the Christian life on earth because it gives union with Christ by charity. A person would not begin if he did not desire the goal; and this remains true of every new gift of grace received, whether through the other sacraments or otherwise. Even the grace of marriage, the most earthbound of the sacraments, finds its logical outcome when husband and wife are united with one another and with Christ at the altar-rail. Men are baptized for this moment. Their baptism and their confirmation involve them in a thousand different activities but none of them is Christian activity if it does not spring from union with Christ in communion and if it does not draw the Christian back to the Eucharist. Here is the necessary corrective for an excessively human approach to the Christian task of humanizing society. It is not mere humanism the Church promotes; the primacy remains with union with God through Christ. The Eucharist, Christ in bread, is the inspiration; from it come the balance and the judgment so necessary for the difficult task of living a Christian life as a contributing member of human society.

In the visible structure of the Church also the Eucharist is supreme. Whatever contributes to the general sacrament of Christ in the world finds its justification and its transcendent exemplar in the prime sacrament. St. Thomas explains this in two ways: First in terms of Christ's activity in the different sacraments; secondly in terms of office or visible function in the Church. The Eucharist, he says, developing the first point, contains Christ substantially, whereas the other sacraments contain only an instrumental power derived from Christ. Those familiar with the Fourth Way for proving the existence of God will recognize here an application of its principle: in any given class the primacy is held by that being which by essence possesses the quality characteristic of the class; others in the class participate in the perfection of this first. As to office or function in the visible Church, all are directed towards the Eucharist. Priestly orders are for its consecration. Baptism and confirmation in different ways are for receiving the Eucharist. The distinction between these two sacraments of initiation is not clearly made by St. Thomas here. The connection between confirmation and the Eucharist has to be developed in terms of the apostolic function of the confirmed, along the lines already suggested. Penance and anointing of the sick prepare the Christian for communion, both interiorly and in the eyes of the Church. The union of man and wife symbolizes the coming together of Christ and the Church, while the unity between these two is symbolized and achieved by the Eucharist. Marriage, accordingly, as an element in the visible structure of the Church, serves to represent in the most human of terms the divine mystery of the Eucharist (III, q. 65, a. 3).

Accordingly, in terms both of grace and of ecclesiastical function the Eucharist, as the theologian puts it, acts as the final cause of all that is in the Church; it is the magnet, attracting everything to itself. It is Christ in the Church, drawing all things to himself. If we are thinking in images we should not imagine two parallel lines drawn through grace and through the visible structure of the Church to the Eucharist. The lines are converging. The line of structure is throughout its length the sign of the interior reality of grace, though, while the Church retains her earthly, imperfect state, it remains possible that the reality does not correspond to the sign. Those who hold office in the Church or who in any fashion contribute to the visible sacrament of the Church's life may not fulfill interiorly what they profess externally. The sacraments of grace may be impeded from achieving their intended effect. But when the lines converge in the Eucharist the Church is seen in her ideal state. Within the visible appearances there is nothing but Christ; all that is signified is realized in the sacrament. When the Church uses the sacrament human frailty may reassert itself so that the final effect of charity may not be achieved. But the sacrament itself, in its permanent reality, represents the Church as immaculate, the ideal towards which the Church of imperfect individuals is striving.

THE UNIVERSAL SACRIFICE

So far we have attempted to follow St. Thomas in his explanation of the universal causality of the Eucharist as communion. But as well as being given to the Church as the food of Christians the sacrament is a sacrifice. The Mass is a memorial meal as was the Jewish paschal supper. An event of redemption, central to the history of God's people, is recalled and renewed in a community repast. The nature of the Mass will be studied more closely in the following chapter; here we want to try to see it in its wide context as a function of the mystical body.

The eucharistic body and blood as communion symbolize and cause—by efficient and final causality—the union of the mystical body in charity. This is because bread and wine or what have the appearance of bread and wine signify nourishment; but the two-fold form of the Eucharist, the designation of the things on the altar as the body *and* blood of Christ, has another dimension of signification. The Church possesses the body of Christ as sacramentally separate from the blood and consequently in the state of a sacrificial victim. This is the unique acceptable sign of Calvary, transposed into a new realm of reality. In other words the Eucharist brings into the Church the body of Christ in a form in which it fulfills within the liturgy the two functions assigned to the physical body of Christ in the mystery of redemption. Christ's body is the instrument through which God sanctifies man; it is present in the Church as communion. His body on Calvary was nailed to the cross by the soldiers and Christ was left to die. He accepted his passion and death, willed them in obedience to his Father's decree, and consequently made them, as far he personally was concerned, an authentic external act of worship, a sacrifice. As with any external act of worship the visible event was a sign of his interior act of dedication to God. What happened on Calvary has established his mutilated body as the supreme expression of the charity and worship of the Christian community; it is present sacramentally in the Church as the eucharistic sacrifice.

As sacrifice, the eucharistic body and blood have a relation of signification to the same reality as that which they signify as communion; they signify the *res,* the charity of the mystical body. The difference is that as communion they signify this charity as something which they cause, but as sacrifice they signify it as possessed by the faithful and actively inspiring them to pay their debt of worship and reparation to God who has created and redeemed them and against whom they have sinned. The Church stands justified before God because she has this visible sacrificial sign constantly on her altars. Her members bring to it all that they have received from Christ, all that they do in Christ's name. From eternity God has seen the Church so, rising out of the charity of the Sacred Heart of Jesus, offering the body and the blood. The Mass gathers the prayers, works, sufferings and joys of men into the unique sacrifice of Christ. Towards it are directed all the secret stirrings of men's hearts when they seek sincerely to serve God. If all supernatural life in the world has implanted within it a desire for union with Christ in communion, it also finds in the Mass the centre of its worship.

SACRAMENT OF CHRISTIAN UNITY

We are now in a position to enter into the heart of St. Thomas's thought on the Eucharist and attempt to share in his grandiose vision. For him the sacrament's influence extends to the same limits as does that of the risen Christ, active within the world. In terms of human psychology this implies at least a desire, however obscurely formulated, on the part of all those who come under the saving influence of Christ to receive the Eucharist and to worship in the Mass. This constitutes on the part of the sacrament an exercise of final causality; it is a goal to be reached, a means of union with God to be used.

It should be noticed that final causality is a reality; it is true causality. Nevertheless, the primary form of causality exercised by the sacraments is not final but efficient; they were instituted, that is, as direct channels through which Christ could act upon the faithful who actually receive them. The Eucharist, if it is to fulfill integrally its function in the mystery of salvation, is meant to be received actually in communion and to clothe actually the worship of Christians at Mass. It does not serve this integral function for those who have never actually used it in communion and at Mass; for these it is no more than an object of desire, an unacknowledged centre of their lives. To the degree that it is not actually used by adult believers in the conditions in which Christ intended it to be used—that is, in the Roman Catholic Church—there is imperfection in the unity of Christians. But, conversely, to the degree that it does influence all Christians, whether as a sacrament received or as an object of desire, there is unity; not the perfect unity that Christ desired for his Church, which is realized only by those in open communion with Rome, but an initial and imperfect form of that unity.

This is a matter so close to the hearts of Christians today that it is vitally important that St. Thomas's thought be meditated upon searchingly and prayerfully. The remainder of this chapter is an attempt to indicate the significance of his views. What is outstanding in his theology is that, according to the principles which he proposes, the unity of Christians is primarily to be discovered, not in their common submission to Christ in heaven, but in their relation to the Blessed Eucharist, the sacrament of Christ possessed rightfully only by the Roman Catholic Church. This means that there exists at the centre of the Church on earth a visible reality which symbolizes and causes the union of all believers in Christ.

VISIBLE UNION WITH THE CHURCH

The Roman Catholic Church maintains uncompromisingly that she is identified with the mystical body of Christ and that consequently outside her fold there is no salvation. She does not admit the possibility of exceptions to this rule; but the apparent rigour of her attitude found its most authoritative commentary in the warmth of personality of Pope John XXIII who called all Christians his children. It has never been part of Church teaching that those who are not publicly known as Roman Catholics cannot be saved; what the Church teaches is that no one can be saved who does not in some fashion enter within the one ark of salvation. That this implies that all who are saved must have at least the desire of baptism is the common teaching of theologians in accordance with the Council of Trent (sess. 6, ch. 4; Denz. - S. 1524, 1618). Baptism is the established ceremonial profession of faith in Christ and the required rite of entry into the visible society of the Church. Wherever baptism is validly administered it is the baptism of the one Church.

Wherever there is only faith in Christ and its obligations are accepted by charity there must be desire of baptism because faith implies acceptance of the whole divine revelation even when individual elements of it are as yet unknown. But when baptism has been received only in desire the believer in Christ has made no sacramental profession of his faith; he is not inserted into the visible structure of the Church by reason of the rite of initiation. There is here a considerable difficulty for theologians who attempt to discover the relation of such believers to the Church. It is vital to maintain that Christ has so ordered the means of applying the power of his passion to men that interior union with him by grace is always reflected or expressed in visible union with the Church on earth. When the problem is placed in terms of baptism or of acceptance of the guidance of the pope and bishops the only solution that can be offered is the non-baptized believers with charity are mentally incorporated in Christ and desire sacramental incorporation; and that their submission to the hierarchy is implicit and non-juridical. But this solution brings nightmares to theologians when they reflect on it and fear to see in it the hidden spectre of an invisible Church. For it has been made clear by the teaching authority that the Church is not invisible and that solutions to the problem of membership must not imply that it is. Without baptism is it possible to be visibly united to the Church?

Though the distinction between mental and sacramental incorporation is St. Thomas's (III, q. 68, a. 2; cf. ibid., q. 69, a. 5, ad 1; II-II, q. 1, a. 9, ad 3), introduced in his discussion of baptism, his final word on incorporation into Christ is found in his pages on the Eucharist. It is this sacrament which provides the one, visible, sacramental bond of all who belong to Christ. It must be emphasised how tenuous this bond is in the case of the non-baptized. They do not possess the character of baptism and are consequently not of the number of those who can validly receive the Eucharist or offer the Mass. The Eucharist is not for their use in the way that Christ intended it to be used. Nevertheless because it is the symbol of the mystical body and its cause, and further because it acts as a final as well as an efficient cause, it provides within the Church a sacramental expression of the interior union with Christ enjoyed by whoever is not baptized yet possesses the gift of grace.

Basic to this development of St. Thomas's teaching is his concept of sacraments as signs of faith. The external sacrament of baptism is the last and most perfect of a variety of rites of initiation into the people of God. It succeeds to circumcision as the prescribed sign of adherence to the mystery of Christ and to the society within which faith in him must be professed (III, q. 70, aa. 1, 2). It is because baptism is prescribed as a sign professing faith that the Eucharist can supply in some degree for lack of association with the visible Church through the sacrament of initiation. The Eucharist is the one existing and real sacramental sign symbolizing here and now the charity of those who are drawn towards it by Christ.

This is very far from giving jurdically verifiable membership of Christ; but we should not for that reason dismiss it as insufficient to give even a measure of visible union with the Church. Clearly, the individual men and women concerned cannot be known by their fellows as members of Christ and of the Church. But the Eucharist is truly their profession of faith in Christ and in the Roman Church. It is the symbol and cause of their salvation, though they do not recognize it; and it belongs to the one apostolic Church. Some of those who are thus drawn to the Eucharist will later receive baptism; but at present their baptism is not a reality. The Eucharist is already real for them, manifesting their union with Christ. The union with the Church which it grants them would be utterly inadequate for membership in any other society; but the Roman Church is the mystical body of Christ and it cannot be thought of in the same categories as those which are appropriate for merely human organizations.

There is no question of saying that one religion is as good as another if all men of good will can be saved. The tragedy of disunion is that so many of those with a longing for the Blessed Eucharist in their hearts do not recognize it for what it is, that they are deprived of so many of the earthly helps entrusted to the one Church by Christ to prepare men for receiving the Eucharist. But the firmest hope for reunion lies in the fact that, in spite of humanly contrived disunion, one strong bond remains uniting objectively all who call upon the name of Christ, and uniting them, unconscious of the fact though they may be, under the care of Christ's vicar on earth.

Theologians of the Orthodox churches of the East recognize in the Eucharist the sacrament of unity, but reject the authority of the bishop of Rome. But unity in worship is not sufficient for the perfect unity of the Church. There must as well be unity of belief and practice; and this is implied in worship which is fully aware of the obligations of Christianity. Baptized non-Catholics have withdrawn themselves even further, renouncing the Eucharist; but they still retain a form of worship that derives from the Mass and, more important still, they possess the baptismal character which permits them to offer the Mass. As they take part in their own services they are drawn into the one great sacrifice, celebrated on the altars of the Church. Catholics, as they gather in their parish church for Sunday Mass, should be aware of their fellowship with other Christians, worshipping in other places, reaching out unknowingly for the true sacrifice.

The unbaptized are excluded from worshipping with the Church, yet her worship affects them. As she offers the body and the blood, she intercedes for all men, and in her ritual Christ himself worships his Father, asserting his claim as universal Redeemer. The Eucharist, symbol of all who belong to Christ, is offered for all, even for those who have not yet accepted his mediation.

Disunion may well have its place in divine Providence as an occasion for increasing our love of the Church to which God's mercy has brought us. Above all it should teach us to enter into the mystery of the Eucharist. So many of those who have at their disposal this sacrament which is Christ raised aloft in the world, drawing all things to himself, do not realize that the white host fulfills on earth all the longing of the human heart. How much responsibility for continuing disunion must be borne by those who profess belief in the sacrament of unity?

THE BREAD OF ANGELS

The focal point of all that belongs to Christ in the world, the Eucharist opens onto heaven. The substance of the bread is withdrawn from this world and changed into the substance of the glorified body of Christ; those who eat the transubstantiated bread are themselves drawn into the sphere of eternal happiness. The first Christians celebrated the eucharistic meal not only as a memorial of Christ's death but also as an anticipation of the banquet to be enjoyed with him in heaven. "I will no more drink of the fruit of the vine with you," he said, referring to his death, "until that day when I shall drink it new in the kingdom of God" (*Mark*, 14:25; cf. *1 Cor.*, 11:26). By eating at the sacramental table of the Church, Christians share already, in the manner suited to their state, in the community life of heaven.

It is related of Bl. Imelda Lambertini that she died after receiving communion for the first time. Though there are theological obscurities about the nature of the host which, according to the traditional account, miraculously appeared before her, the chronicler's concluding words are worthy of meditation. When the child had received the host, "she went to make her thanksgiving in heaven." This sacrament, writes St. Thomas, bringing with it, as it does, the saving efficacy of Christ's passion, is sufficient of itself to place us in glory; but first, he adds, we must suffer with Christ that we may be glorified with him (III, q. 79, a. 1, ad 1; cf. *Rom.*, 8:17). There is in the eating of Christ something which is common to both heaven and earth. This eating, spoken of by Christ himself (*John*, 6), means, says St. Thomas in another place, to be united to Christ by charity and in knowledge of God. Christ is, accordingly, the bread of both men and angels; both are united to him by knowledge and love; their union differs only according to the mode of knowledge of each. "Both belong to the society of the mystical body though in different ways, men on the basis of faith, the angels by reason of their clear vision of God." When men enter heaven they too will "eat Christ" in the manner of the angels, being united to him by vision and by charity (III, q. 80, a. 2).

It is at this point, having expressed the life of the whole mystical body in terms of "eating Christ," that St. Thomas gives the ultimate theological reason why all Christian life on earth is directed towards the Eucharist and why, consequently, the Roman Catholic Church is identified with the mystical body on earth. The sacrament of the body, he says, is "proportioned to the state of those who remain in the obscurity of faith." To be saved men must "eat" Christ; to eat him by faith—which is the only way to approach him on earth—the sacramental bread must be consumed, either actually or in desire. While man's knowledge of God is based on faith he has no choice but to use symbols, corporeal things which express his interior union with Christ. Only when there is vision of God is direct spiritual contact possible, for then God reveals Himself in a manner which surpasses all human concept and which renders symbols irrelevant. In the present state the supreme symbol is the Eucharist, resting on the altars of the Church.

Eating the Eucharist with faith, membership of the visible Church on earth, is a temporary expedient, a preliminary to full enjoyment of Christ in heaven. "For this reason," concludes St. Thomas, "man is said to eat the bread of angels" for the sacrament gives him some part in their happiness which in heaven will be his (III, q. 80, a. 2; cf. *Ps.*, 77:25; *Deut.*, 8:5; *J Cor.*, 10:3). Heaven and earth, the whole mystical body, are united through the Eucharist.

9 The Blessed Eucharist: Offering with Christ

The body of Christ is life-giving only because it bears the imprint of the passion and death in a humanity united with the divine Word. It is with a sacrificed body and bearing his own blood that our Saviour enters into the Holy of Holies and stands before the Father interceding for us. When he gave his body to the Church in the Eucharist, he gave it under these two modalities, as a source of grace and as a victim of sacrifice. The sacrament is given to us as food under two species; this implies that the Mass is not merely a meal but a sacrificial meal. For the use of both bread and wine is not absolutely necessary for the signification of nourishment. The symbolism is more perfect when the two are used; but the present practice in the Western Church of giving communion to the laity under one species indicates clearly that nothing essential is at stake here. Each of the species contains Christ as he now exists in heaven, though there is a difference between the two in what might be called sacramental focus. The compelling reason for Christ's giving his body and his blood under distinct symbols was that the consecration of the Eucharist was to be a sacrifice.

THE NEW PASCHAL SACRIFICE

The sacrificial character of the Mass was something that was very clear to the early Christians and, in a particularly vivid way, to the Jewish converts. The New-Testament accounts of the last supper bring us back to the teaching of the apostles on the nature of the Mass. In spite of the difficulties encountered by exegetes in establishing the precise date of the supper, the fact that it was the solemn paschal meal emerges as evident from the texts. For those who were present this circumstance at once placed it in a framework of redemptive sacrifice. The paschal meal was a commemoration of God's bringing His people out of slavery and of the subsequent Alliance which He formed with them in the desert. At the same time it reminded the Jews each year that the Alliance was maintained and renewed through the sacrifice of the paschal lamb. The lamb itself was placed in the centre of the table and the meal was conducted according to a strict ceremonial, with symbolic dishes. There was a tradition-hallowed explanation given by the head of the family of the significance of the celebration.

This was the paschal meal of which Christ said: "I will eat of it no more" (*Lk.*, 22:16) for the time had come for the shadows of the Old Alliance to give way to the reality of the New. Their sense of the Jewish tradition would have already made it clear to the apostles that when Christ gave them his body and blood he was performing a sacrificial action of which the victim was no longer the lamb but himself. "Christ our pasch is sacrificed," St. Paul would later say (*J Cor.*, 5:7), summarising what must have been one of the early commentaries on the Mass.

The words too which Christ used made it more explicit still that the New Alliance between God and man was being sealed by the sacrificial blood of Christ. "Take and eat; this is my body for you" (cf. *Matt.*, 26:26; *Mk.*, 14:22; *Lk.*, 22:19; *J Cor.*, 11:24). "Do this in remembrance of me" (*Lk.*; *J Cor.*). "This is my blood of the New Alliance which is being shed for many unto the forgiveness of sins" (*Matt.*, 26:28). "Do this as often as you drink it, in remembrance of me" (*J Cor.*, 11:25). Nowadays it is only by an effort of imagination that we can recreate for ourselves the atmosphere of that last paschal meal and hear the resonances of Jewish history behind our Lord's words. There is no reason to suppose that the apostles could have given a reasoned account of the mystery that was being realized in their midst; but they could not have failed to be aware of the utter transformation that the supper had undergone. The paschal lamb was superseded; a new Victim was set out on the table. A new celebration of a new alliance was committed to them so that they could themselves repeat what Christ had done. The paschal meal of the new Lamb would henceforward bring the body and blood of Christ in sacrifice into their midst as a memorial of God's new act of redemption and as a pledge of His continuing love for His people. The first groups of Christians are to be found carrying out Christ's command and *the* breaking of the bread becomes one of the characteristic marks of the new community (cf. *Acts*, 2:42; 20:7-11). "As often as you shall eat of this bread and drink the chalice," comments St. Paul, "you shall show the death of the Lord until he come" (*J. Cor.*, 11:26). This is the mystery of the Mass which the Church accepts unquestioningly from Christ and which she continues until the time for visible sacrifice is past.

THEOLOGICAL BACKGROUND TO THE MASS

MERIT AND ATONEMENT IN HEAD AND MEMBERS

The mystery of divine redemption is first revealed and consummated in Christ; through him it is communicated to his members in whom is repeated in moral terms the Pattern of the mysteries established in the Head. For both Head and members the essential Pattern has two motifs: there is the gift of God and there is the human response to God. The whole Pattern is the work of God in both Christ and his members. The response to God is the human side of the divine gift. Union with God must be given by God; but at the same time it must be achieved by free, meritorious action on man's part. The absolute priority of the divine gift is clearly seen in Christ whose human nature was united to the divine Word gratuitously, without any possibility of merit on the part of Christ; for he did not exist in human fashion and capable of meriting before the Incarnation. Christ's human response to God's gift is itself, utterly free though it is, a gift of God through grace. Supremely expressed in the sacrifice on Calvary, Christ's response to God is the condition for the full development of the divine gift in the rest of mankind. When grace is given to Christ's members, to those who by grace itself are associated with Christ's sacrifice, they too must respond to God's love; they must, that is, in their turn translate the gift of grace into free, meritorious action by which they advance towards final union with God.

We shall think that the Church's teaching on man's obligation to reparation and his possibility of merit is derogatory to the universal merit of Christ and to the all-sufficiency of his atonement only if we have the crudely commercial notion of merit and satisfaction that has already been shown to be inaccurate. We must not forget that the ideas taken from human labour contracts which are used to express our relations with God are analogies only, spring-boards for theology. When applied to the Christian life these notions must be purified of anything that suggests our placing the Author of all goodness under obligation to us. The life of union with God is such that of its very nature it implies merit and, when man belongs to a sinful race, reparation. For this life is precisely a life; it implies organic growth; not physical growth, but growth in knowledge and love of God, deriving from a likeness to God given by grace. It is God who gives this growth; but His action is utterly within us so that it is by our own actions that we grow. This is merit; under God's action we dispose ourselves for greater intimacy with Him; and there is no other way for free creatures to advance towards final union with God. If we speak of merit in terms of a right that we have to increased grace or to heaven we are thinking of this growth in terms of God's intention when He gives us grace. Our right to heaven derives from God's free decision to set us on the way to perfect union with Himself. He gives us the grace which begins within us the life of heaven but which must develop in us, preparing us for perfect union. So long as we possess grace, accordingly, God is bringing us to heaven; this is our right. It does not oblige God to us; the only "obligation"

is within God Himself, binding Him to the design of His own
wisdom (cf. *Summa theol.*, I-II, q. 114, a. 1, ad 3). Similarly,
our right to increased grace means that God is acting in us so
that we may dispose ourselves for more intimate union with
Him on earth. Atonement or reparation is likewise implied in
the life of union with God when man is a sinner. A person is
unadapted for perfect union with God as long as he has not
re-established within himself the order of justice which requires
that excessive indulgence of one's own will contrary to the intrinsic laws of the universe be off-set by corresponding restrictions (I-II, q. 87, a. 6). Merit and reparation, in short, are events
in the life of man, reflecting God's working within him; they
cannot affect God; rather they reveal His design for man.

Very far, then, from taking anything away from Christ's
prerogatives, the Church's teaching on merit and reparation mag-
nifies his mediation. Other men can merit and atone only because
God draws them into union with Himself; and God makes them
worthy of this union by associating them with Christ's merits
and atonement, that is, with Christ's worthiness. Concretely, this
means that when a man is justified by God he is given the grace
to believe that God is justifying him through the mystery of
Christ (cf. I-II, q. 114, a. 5, ad 1; q. 113, a. 4, ad 3). It is this
act of faith in Christ's role in salvation which provides the basis
of man's worthiness before God; for, since it is an intellectual
acknowledgment of Christ's headship, it establishes that *personal* relationship of submission to Christ which constitutes
fundamental union with him. From this flows trust in Christ's
mediation; and the gift of charity provides that fullness of personal union with Christ which unites our will to God as his will
is united. Were it not for Christ man would not receive grace,
for in Christ the fundamental worthiness of humanity lies; when
man is given grace and begins to grow in union with God it is
always on the foundation of his association by faith with Christ
who has once and for all merited—proved himself worthy of—
all the grace that is given to men. Far from Christ's mediation
making our merit and reparation superfluous, it makes them possible.

These ideas form the background to the theology of the
Mass. It is essential to understand that the Mass takes its place

within the context of the repetition of the Pattern of Christ's
personal mystery in his members. It is a mystery of the Church
and therefore belongs to that sphere of the mystery of redemption in which Christ's merits and reparation are communicated
to other men. This is indeed evident from the fact that it is a
sacramental mystery, a eucharistic mystery. Christ instituted the
Eucharist in order to draw men into fellowship with his own
unique mystery. If it is grasped clearly that the Mass is one of
the means given the Church by which men may enter into fellowship with Christ, then it will be at once apparent that difficulties
based on alleged injury done to the unique and all-sufficient
sacrifice of Calvary are beside the point. This is not to say that
there will be no more difficulties about the Mass. In particular,
the central problem of how it can be a true sacrifice remains.
But to argue that the Church's teaching on the Mass takes away
from the universal efficacy of Calvary is to betray that one has
failed to understand what the Church teaches.

TEACHING OF THE CHURCH

The Council of Trent in its chapter on the Mass affirms in
the first place that "through the merciful Providence of God the
Father a new priest was to be raised up according to the order
of Melchisedech in the person of our Lord Jesus Christ, who
would be able to lead into perfection and fullness whoever was
to be sanctified (cf. *Heb.*, 10:14)"; and the Council goes on to
profess its belief in the uniqueness of Christ's sacrifice (cf. *Heb.*,
7:27) and in its efficacy to procure eternal redemption for men.
Christ's institution of the Mass is then affirmed; but it is placed
at once in the context of the application of the power of Calvary
to members of the Church. At the last supper "Christ offered
to God his Father his body and blood under the appearances
of bread and wine. It was his purpose to leave to his beloved
spouse, the Church, a sacrifice which was (in accordance with
the requirements of human nature) a visible one, and by which
the unique blood-spilling sacrifice later to be offered on the
cross should be represented, its memory preserved until the end
of time, and its saving power applied to the remission of the
sins which we daily commit" (sess. 22, cap. 1; Denz. - S. 1739,

1740). The whole mystery of the Mass, in other words, is part of the communication to the Church of the efficacy of Calvary. Just as Christ's merit makes our merit possible, so Christ's sacrifice makes that of the Church possible. Neither our merit nor the Church's sacrifice detracts from the power of Christ's mediation; on the contrary, they demonstrate its supreme efficacy.

MORAL CONTEXT OF THE MASS

What we must fix our attention on, accordingly, in connection with the Mass is first of all the interior activity of Christ and of his passion in the members of the Church. The grace that the heavenly Christ communicates to his members draws them into union with God. The very nature of this union, with its destined perfection in heaven and its possibility of growth on earth, carries with it the possibility of merit, the process of attaining full growth. Likewise, it carries with it the possibility of reparation for sins committed. The response that Christ made to his Father's love finds an echo in the hearts of his members. The gift of grace, when assimilated by the human person and made the inner source of action, becomes his response to God's love. The Pattern, as it is repeated in Christ's members, has undergone a modification. It incorporates now the added themes of faith in Christ's mediation and of repentance for personal sins. The Church realizes by faith that her merits and her reparation depend on her association with Christ's merits and reparation. She understands by faith that the sacrifice of Calvary covers over all her good actions for it is the condition of their realization and the necessary complement of their inadequacy. With this mind the Church celebrates Mass.

A SIGN OF FAITH

THE REASON FOR THE MASS

In the practical exercise of her mission the Church does not reason about her liturgy. She simply acts in obedience to Christ's command. So with the Mass; she holds by faith that it is a true sacrifice and that by celebrating it "with a true heart, with orthodox faith, with fear and reverence, going to God in sorrow and repentance," her members will "obtain mercy and find grace in seasonable aid" (Trent, sess. 22, cap. 2; Denz. - S. 1743; cf. *Heb.*, 4:16).

Because the Church has on her altar the Victim of Calvary she has at her disposal to express her interior submission to God in union with Christ the very same sign, adapted to her sacramental system, that expressed visibly on Calvary the redemptive submission of Christ to his Father. There are two elements here. Firstly, the life of grace, deriving from Christ, makes it possible for the Church to share in the union with God which he enjoys and consequently to arouse in her heart an echo of the loving obedience to God which he possesses supremely. Secondly, the Eucharist makes available to her in the form of a victim the body and blood of Christ, which on Calvary formed the material of his sacrifice and which now form the material of a sacrifice common to her and to Christ.

Leaving to theologians the task of seeking an explanation, the Church acts on the conviction that by reason of the Real Presence she has a true sacrifice in the Mass. She insists that in no way is there question of repeating Calvary, which, as the first Protestants justly asserted, would be blasphemy. The sacramental immolation of Christ on the altar of the Church is something which corresponds to the grace of the Church. Christ is principally responsible both for the grace and for the visible sacrifice; but just as he gives grace to his members so that it is their own, so he makes available to them in the Mass the immolated body and blood of his own sacrifice. The Victim supplies the visible sacrificial expression for the grace of the Church, active through the virtues. This relation to the grace of Christians indicates that the Mass belongs to the sphere in which Christ's merits and reparation are applied to his members. It is the mystery of the Mass that the external sacrificial sign of Calvary is in this fashion made available to the Church and that Christ actually offers it. There is no mystery as to why it is made available. The sacrificed body and blood constitute the supreme visible expression of mankind's response to the divine gift of grace; all mankind's surrender to God is summed up in the immolation of this Victim. The Victim itself is given to the Church in the Eucharist so that Christians may have before them and use in bodily fashion—as their nature requires—the unique sacrificial sign of their fellowship with Christ.

FAITH IN CALVARY

✚The Mass is, accordingly, basically a sign of faith. Because it is a sacrifice it is an act of religion and an expression of the love of Christ and his members for God. But faith supplies the link with Christ which associates at all times the Christian's interior self-offering with the obedience of Calvary. By faith the Church acknowledges that the death of Christ was the divinely-instituted means of redemption. By faith the Church obeys Christ's command to repeat his action at the last supper. By faith the Church believes that on her altar she has the unique Victim offered by Christ, made present to clothe her own self-offering.

The faith of the Church is centred on the consecration of the Mass, the moment when the body and the blood are made present on the altar. This is her moment of sacrifice, her moment of offering. In order to make more vivid for her children the meaning of this moment, she has surrounded it with readings and prayers; these draw their meaning from the consecration. It is to be noted in particular that the offering of the bread and wine before the canon of the Mass has no significance in itself. It would be to misinterpret gravely the Christian mystery to think of this ceremony as some kind of supplementary sacrifice or oblation, something wholly belonging to the Church. There is only one sacrificial expression of Christian submission to God, and that is the body and blood of Christ. The offertory of the Mass is overshadowed by the consecration; it simply makes explicit for the faithful the attitude which should be theirs when the unique Victim is made present. "This is my body. This is my blood." When the priest pronounces the words, the faith of the Church bursts out of the confines of purely spiritual union with Calvary. It has before it the Victim itself.

THE UNIQUE VICTIM

The Mass is the sacrifice of the Church. This is not contrary to saying that it is the sacrifice of Christ. Indeed it could not be the sacrifice of the Church were it not the sacrifice of Christ, for his is the only true sacrifice. But there is no other reason for bringing the body onto the altar in the state of victim except that the faithful should be able to enter Christ's sacrifice. That the self-offering of the faithful is immeasurably enhanced by visible, bodily association with the sign of Christ's loving obedience is certain. For the Mass is a sacrament and as such is one of the means instituted by Christ to bring the fruits of Calvary to men. But as far as Christ himself is concerned there is no novelty in the Mass. It does not add anything to what he did on Calvary. He still offers the sacrifice, but he no longer merits or makes reparation. The sole addition to the Christian mystery procured by the Mass, which could not be procured by any other means, is the insertion of the Church's worship into the unique sacrifice. "Insertion" is a metaphorical way of saying that the immolation of Christ—what was seen by the onlookers at Calvary—which was Christ's own external act of worship, becomes in the Mass the Church's external act of worship. This goes completely beyond anything that faith alone can do. When we say that the Christian offers the sacrifice of Calvary by faith we do not mean that the sacrifice is his own act of worship in the fashion, for example, that a genuflection is. All we mean is that the Christian acknowledges the divine mystery revealed on the cross and accepts Christ's mediation. Calvary was Christ's act of worship; and, as we shall see later, Mary's also; it was not the Church's; rather it was the meritorious cause, the condition for the coming into existence, of the Church. The Mass, on the contrary, permits Christians to offer the sacramental Victim as their own community sacrifice. The Real Presence, with its twofold form, gives the Church sacramentally the unique sacrifice of Christianity as her own.

St. Paul describes the sufferings of his captivity as filling up in his own flesh what is lacking in the sufferings of Christ for the Church, his body (cf. *Col.*, 1:24). He is speaking of the reparation which Christians are called to make by reason of their interior union with Christ, a reparation which, as has been said, does not imply any inadequacy in Christ's own mediation but is rather the result of Christ's sufferings which must in some measure be repeated in those who through him are united to

God. The full measure of sufferings must be made up in St. Paul and in other Christians, not in Christ, except in so far as he lives in his members. The Mass complements this logic of Christian grace, developing the union of faith. It permits the Christian to lay hold in bodily fashion on the Victim of Calvary, made present sacramentally, and to offer the body and the blood of Christ as the symbol of his interior unity with Christ. All that is involved in this interior union, not only reparation but as well love, adoration, merit, the whole life of the Christian, is expressed in the visible sacrifice of the Victim common to Christ and to his members. Interior union with Christ implies that the Christian by grace repeats in his own life the Pattern of Christ's life of loving obedience. It is a form of union which necessarily implies distinction from Christ because it involves the personal translation of grace into free, responsible activity. In the Mass the personal lives of Christ and the Christian are reunited by the Eucharist in the common act of external worship. As in all the sacraments, the faith of the Church transcends itself; the Christian is brought into immediate contact with the body of Christ, in this case not as the channel of grace but as the sign of humanity's love for God. The Victim, which on Calvary expressed the worship of the Church only in so far as this was contained in the worship of Christ the Head, now actually expresses the worship of the community of Christ's members.

This situation of the Mass as the sacrifice of the Church through which the fruits of Calvary are applied cannot be too much emphasised. From this it follows that its efficacy is determined by the devotion with which the faithful offer it. Thomists in particular must insist on this point because they, unlike some other theologians, teach that the Mass is also actually offered by Christ himself and, accordingly, they attribute to the Mass infinite value. But their opinion, which we share and which will be developed in the following section, must be properly understood. The fact that Christ enters personally into the liturgical sacrifice of the Church—as Victim and as Priest—means that the Mass has an *ex-opere-operato* effect; that is, in virtue of Christ's passion, the act of Church worship brings to mankind far richer benefits from God than the merits and reparation of the faithful would of themselves warrant. But, as in all the sacraments, the devotion of the faithful determines the measure of these gifts in the sense that the gifts are given in proportion to the devotion (cf. III, q. 79, a. 5; a. 7, c. and ad 2). This point, which is central to Christian understanding of the Mass, will be developed later when the sense of Christ's entry into the ceremony has been explained.

CHRIST ENTERS THE MASS

SACRAMENTAL IMMOLATION

Up to this point it has been accepted without enquiry that the Mass is a sacrifice. This is the teaching of the Church; because it is accepted on faith by Catholics a great part of catechetical instruction can be given on the Mass without raising any question about how it is a sacrifice or what is its relation to Calvary. It is only when we attempt to define precisely the manner of Christ's intervention in the Church's ceremony that these questions demand reply.

When the Church celebrates Mass her function as sacrament of Christ is brought to its peak of intensity. The ordained priest speaks the words of consecration in the person of Christ, designating what he holds in his hands and what is in the chalice as the body and blood of Christ. Considering this action at its surface value it is a symbol of Calvary, repeating that of the supper room. Distinct realities are denominated respectively body and blood; this is a translation into symbols of the violence done to Christ by his executioners. Were it not for the Real Presence the Church would have on her altar simply a symbolic memorial of Calvary, a material representation of Christ's death, which would serve to stimulate and focus the faith of Christians in his mediation. The majority of non-Catholics recognize so far the utility of the ceremonial of the Mass; and whatever values they admit are in fact incorporated in it.

We know that there is more than this. Because the priest possesses the character of orders the sign-action which he performs at the consecration has validity as an official act of the Church in which Christ himself intervenes to realize what is signified. What the priest holds in his hands after the consecration is truly the body of Christ; what is in the chalice is truly the blood.

Now it is quite true that the Christ present in the Eucharist is the risen Christ in heaven in whom flesh and blood are united with one another and with his soul and with the divine Word. Consequently, when the body of Christ is made present in the species of bread it is not separated from the blood, the soul or the divinity; and likewise the blood of the Eucharist is not separated from the body, the soul or the divinity. Nevertheless, since a sacrament realizes formally only what it signifies, what is present in the species of bread directly as a result of the words of consecration is the body of Christ; whatever else belongs to him is present, not formally by reason of the words, but simply because in the glorified Christ it cannot be separated from the body. The like is true for the blood contained in the species of wine. In other words, as far as sacramentalism goes, the body is present as distinct from the blood. To object that this is only make-believe is to reveal that one is thinking of Christ as he exists in his natural state in heaven. The sacramental presence depends on the realization of what is signified; and since two distinct symbols are placed by the priest, two distinct sacramental presences are procured. There is no question of anything happening to Christ in his natural state; everything turns on the mode in which he is present in the sacramental species. We might say, as has already been suggested, that the species of bread focus on the body of Christ, the species of wine on the blood; whatever else is present under the two kinds is out of focus, not relevant as far as strict sacramentalism is concerned. Or possibly television provides a helpful example. The screen carries the image of the announcer, the loudspeaker carries his voice; in the studio these two are united in one person. Moreover, a lip-reader could understand what is being said without assistance from the loudspeaker; nevertheless all that the screen formally carries is vision. But the only way to reach a true grasp of the mystery is by meditation on the nature of a sacrament: it effects precisely what it signifies.

Since the visible species constitute a symbol of Christ's violent death on the cross, and since by transubstantiation the species really contain what they signify, the Church has on her altar the Victim of the New Alliance in sacramental form. The Eucharist does not contain the death of Christ; that is an event of past history. Transubstantiation is not an assault on the body of Christ; it affects only the bread and wine in conformity with the words of the priest. Accordingly, the Eucharist in the Mass refers to the death of Christ in so far as the two separate species constitute a symbol of the death and in so far as each species makes Christ present in its own way, one focusing on his flesh, the other on his blood. The hosts reserved after Mass in the tabernacle do not, properly speaking, constitute a symbol of Christ's death; for that is required the simultaneous presence of the chalice of blood.

The Mass brings about neither a purely symbolic, nor a physical immolation of Christ; it brings about a true immolation, but a sacramental one. There is nothing else like this on earth and consequently new words have to be found to apply to the mystery or old words have to be adapted to a new sense. For example, Pius XII says: "A commemorative showing forth (*memorialis demonstratio*) of his death which took place in reality on Calvary is repeated in each Mass, because by distinct representations Christ Jesus is signified and shown forth in the state of a victim" (*Mediator Dei*, §74). The Council of Trent is less explicit, describing the Mass as "representing" the sacrifice of the cross so that "its memory may remain" (sess. 22, cap. 1; Denz.-S. 1740). The Second Vatican Council speaks of the sacrifice of the Cross being "perpetuated" (Vat. II Const., ch. 2, art. 47). St. Thomas chooses the words "a certain kind of image representative of the passion of Christ, which was his true immolation" (III, q. 83, a. 1); but he is well aware that by defining the relationship between Mass and Calvary as that between "image" and "truth"—or, as we might say, between shadow and substance—he is giving only a generic definition, one which applies equally well to the figurative sacrifices of the Old Law. This is, of course, simply an application of the first principle of his sacramental theology according to which a sacrament is defined as "a sign of faith." This definition too applies to both Old- and New-Law sacraments. What is distinctive about those of the New is that they signify in a special way;

they signify Christ as actually producing through them the effect for which they were instituted. St. Thomas follows the same procedure of specifying a generic definition here when he discusses the Mass. It is not a mere symbol or image of the Calvary immolation. Christ is immolated because through the Mass we share in the fruits of the passion (ibid.). It must always be kept in mind that no theologian attempts to prove that the Mass is a sacrifice. He accepts the fact as revealed; he can try to illustrate the meaning of the truth by comparing this sacrifice with Calvary, by comparing its mode with the form of reality proper to sacraments, by indicating what role is assigned the Mass in the scheme of salvation. He approaches the mystery by all sorts of converging paths and in this fashion tries to build up a composite picture of it in which will appear its significance. The conclusion of the approach by way of the doctrine of transubstantiation is that after the consecration the Church possesses the unique Victim of the New Alliance, sacramentally immolated.

CHRIST OFFERS THE MASS

For several theologians what has been said about immolation represents an adequate account of the Mass. Principal among these are those who consider the Eucharist as exclusively the sacrifice of the Church. They add that this means that Christ offers the Mass through the Church. As has already been pointed out, Thomists and many others are of the opinion that more is contained in the mystery than this. According to their view, Christ actually offers the Mass, he is not involved merely because he instituted the sacrifice and because the Church acts in his name. The statement of doctrine at Trent is deliberately framed in such a way as to exclude neither of these opinions: "The Victim is one and the same; the same one now offers through his ministerial priests who in the past offered himself on the cross; the difference is solely in the manner of offering" (sess. 22, cap. 2; Denz.-S. 1743; repeated in Vat. II Const., ch. 1, art. 7).

To grasp the significance of the Thomist position the terms used must be clearly understood. Christ is said to have offered the sacrifice of Calvary. This means firstly that Christ by an act of his human will submitted in loving obedience to the divine will; this was and remains a constant attitude of mind in Christ. In him as in others it is termed offering of self to God or spiritual sacrifice. Accordingly, the phrase "Christ offered himself" refers to his interior obedience. This obedience was manifested externally in all the actions of his earthly life, in what he said and what he did. His inner attitude of mind, in other words, controlled his exterior action so that the movements of his body were acts of obedience and love. Other virtues too were involved, but these two always held a central place. The crucifixion was simply one of a whole series of bodily expressions of Christ's submissiveness to his Father; what was unique about it was that it was decreed by God as the one acceptable sacrifice of fallen humanity. Here "sacrifice" is being used of a specific form of external ritual. Visible sacrifice is intended to express in as complete a manner as possible man's interior offering of himself to God. A living thing is slaughtered and "offered" to God. The new sense of "offer" must be noticed carefully. It means that the priest of the sacrifice designates the victim as a symbol of man's interior self-offering. The whole ceremonial is for man's sake, to represent vividly for him in the destruction of the victim the meaning of renunciation of self-will and submission to the will of God, and to stimulate this renunciation in him (cf. II-II, q. 81, a. 7). On Calvary Christ was both priest and victim. The *value* of what he did derived from his charity and obedience, from his offering of himself interiorly. But his specifically *priestly act* was to designate the violence being done to his body as the sacrificial sign of his charity and obedience: he "offered" his body and blood; these were the sign of his self-offering. This priestly act is said to be an external act because, though hidden in Christ's mind, it made the external event of Calvary personally significant for Christ.[1]

---

1. For reference during the following discussion. We distinguish in Christ:
   1⁰ His **self-offering**: acts of love, worship, obedience; spiritual sacrifice; characterized Christ's whole life.
   2⁰ His **priestly offering**: the act by which he designated on Calvary his violated body and blood as a sacrificial victim symbolic of his self-offering, thereby making the event an external act of worship. As will be said below, this is an act of the practical intellect.

Having made this distinction between the two modes of offering, we must now observe that in Christ the two were not in parallel, as the words "interior obedience" and "exterior sign" might at first suggest. The offering of the body and blood was rather subordinated to the interior self-offering. That is to say, the specifically priestly act of Christ was, like all his other external actions, controlled by the charity and obedience of his will and immediately by the virtue of religion. It was, in other words, an external act of worship, directed by charity and obedience. Accordingly, while preserving its own specific function, is was itself an element of Christ's self-offering; it was an unfolding of the consequences of the basic attitude of will which affected Christ in his whole being as man, composed of body as well as soul.

THE PRIESTLY ACT OF CHRIST

When Thomists say that Christ actually offers the Mass, what sense do they attach to the word "offer?" The truth is that most of them concentrate on the religious unity of Christ's offering in the sense just explained; they do not analyze the significance of the two modes of offering which it implies. This approach is adequate for expressing the principal point of the Thomist position, namely, that the Mass is a visible manifestation of Christ's love and obedience so that he offers himself to his Father in the liturgical action as he did on Calvary. Fr. W. Barden, O.P., has considerably clarified this common Thomistic explanation by pointing out, in accordance with St. Thomas's teaching on the virtue of religion, the necessity for making the distinction between Christ's interior self-offering and his priestly offering of the visible Victim. Christ's intervention in the Mass is achieved formally by way of his priestly act whereby he designates the body and the blood as the visible sign of his self-offering. Fr. Barden specifies that this is an act of Christ's practical intellect, this being the function of the human mind which, under the movement of the will, directs deliberate bodily actions or, as with Christ and the violence done to him, adopts what is done to the body by others as something of which one personally approves. In the Mass, as on Calvary, it is this act of Christ's mind which is directly brought to bear on the body and blood and which designates them as the sacrificial sign of his self-offering. It is through the priestly act that Christ's interior self-offering is referred to the Mass which thus becomes an external act of Christ worshipping in heaven.[2]

The close connection established by Thomists between Mass and Calvary is now apparent. It is the same self-offering of Christ which is manifested in both sacrifices. Further, it is the same specifically priestly act which in both designates the Victim as sacrificial sign of the self-offering. And the Victim is the same, except that in the Mass its state of victimhood is purely sacramental. It is only at the surface level of sign that there is any real distinction as far as worship goes; Christ's offering is sacramentalized. Further, since the value of the sign derives from what it signifies, it is clear that Christ does not merit through the Mass nor does he make reparation for sin, for the interior self-offering signified is that of one who is in heaven and who is consequently no longer in the state to merit or atone. Christ still adores the Father in heaven, still offers Him thanks, still, as *Hebrews* teaches, makes intercession for us; and all this is expressed in the Mass.

Fr. Barden, carrying his investigation of the nature of Christ's priestly act a step further, suggests an even closer affinity between Mass and Calvary. Having identified this act as belonging to the practical intellect, he recalls that a single act of Christ's infused knowledge can be maintained unchangingly throughout the passage of earthly history. It is to this knowledge, he suggests, that Christ's priestly act belongs so that it is held, identically the same, from the supper to the end of time as long as the need for visible sacrifice remains.[3] On this supposition even the external act of Calvary and that of the Mass are identified; for what is done to Christ's body by others is not Christ's act but rather the material of his act. All of his personal activity on Calvary is preserved in the heavenly Christ and brought to bear on the sacramentally separated body and blood. Fr. Barden's proposal is no more than a hypothesis, but it is one which ac-

---

2. W. Barden, O.P., **What happens at Mass**, Alba House, S.I. N.Y., 1963.
3. Ibid. The background to this question has been discussed on pp. 76-78.

cords admirably with revelation and provides an answer to one of the most agitated questions in present-day theology of the Mass. It is perhaps the closest approach made by a traditional theologian to Dom Casel's suggestive but unacceptable insight into the presence of Christ's mysteries in the sacraments. The distinctions which Fr. Barden makes show that the visible historical event of Calvary was only one element of Christ's external act of worship and, while indispensable to the sacrifice, not the most important element. Only this is different in the Mass, being replaced by the sacramental separation of the same body and blood.

THE CELEBRANT, AN IMAGE OF CHRIST

While developing this account of the act by which Christ offers the Mass we have spoken of his priestly act as entering into the Church ceremony and as being brought to bear on the sacramental Victim. These expressions are obviously metaphorical; the reality behind them must be explained. The function assigned the act is clear; it is to designate the sacramental Victim as the sacrificial sign of Christ's heavenly worship. Without this priestly intervention the eucharistic body and blood would not be Christ's sacrifice but simply a very perfect symbol of his death. The question is: by what means is his priestly act brought into contact with the Victim on the altar?

In a very significant passage St. Thomas applies to the ordained priest of the Church in his relation to the High Priest the same term which he uses to describe the relation of the eucharistic Victim to the passion. The priest, he says, acts as the "image" of Christ when, in his person and by his power, he consecrates (III, q. 83, a. 1, ad 3). Now, it is common Thomistic teaching that the divine power of transubstantiation is brought to a particular altar through the priest who celebrates the Mass. As in the other sacraments, God uses as His instrument for producing the effect signified both the humanity of Christ and, in subordination to this, the human minister. The celebrant's independent activity is confined to the performance of the ritual. As in the other sacraments, his intention of doing what the Church does makes available to the Church his external actions so that they constitute a sign of faith in Christ, instituting the Eucharist. Here we have the response of the Church to Christ's command: Do this in memory of me. The function of the priest in this sign-action should be noted. He speaks in the person of Christ, that is, he forms the sacrament or symbol of Christ, as he was at the last supper. Consequently, at this visible level of sacrament (*sacramentum tantum*), the celebrant is the sign or image of Christ not only as transubstantiating but also as offering the Victim. The celebrant's priestly character ensures that the whole sign-action is sacramentally valid, signifying, that is, Christ's own intervention to achieve what is symbolized. The result is a two-fold presence of Christ at the altar: first in the sacramental species where he is present as Victim; second in the celebrant through whom Christ's specifically priestly act is made present and is applied to the sacramental body and blood.

Christ uses the celebrant as his instrument in two ways: to transubstantiate the bread and wine and to apply to the sacramental Victim that act by which Christ designates it as the sacrificial expression of his self-offering. If we now turn our attention from the celebrant to Christ we see that he, in his turn, is the instrument of God in the action of transubstantiation. This means that his human activity is used instrumentally by God, being applied through the celebrant to the bread and wine. Now, one element in the human activity of Christ thus applied is his priestly act. It is, therefore, by divine power that this act is brought into the Mass; but once brought in it is able to perform its own function of designating the Victim as sacrificial. The application of Christ's priestly act to a particular eucharistic Victim is achieved through the celebrant who is an instrument of God subordinated to the humanity of Christ. The whole action is thus achieved by divine power. God transubstantiates through Christ and through the celebrant. By using Christ's human activity in this way, He not only elevates it to instrumental efficacy in respect of transubstantiation, but also enables it to fulfill its own specifically priestly function of designating through the celebrant the sacramental body and blood as Christ's sacrifice.

It may perhaps be thought that this is an unnecessarily complicated account. Why should we not simply say that Christ from heaven directly designates the eucharistic body and blood as his sacrifice using the celebrant as an instrument purely for transubstantiation? The simplest reply is that, in this case, the celebrant would not offer the Mass; he would simply be the minister of transubstantiation. To offer, one must designate the Victim as sacrificial sign. This the celebrant does, in the fashion of an instrument, when he applies Christ's priestly act to the host and the chalice. A more fundamental reply to the objection is that Christ cannot eliminate the celebrant from the act of offering. The Victim is a *sacramental* one, enclosed in that world where effect is produced through signs. The Eucharist is something that belongs to the Church, to those who need corporeal signs proportioned to the state of faith. The offering must be *sacramental* also, made, that is, through an official of the Church who is a symbol of Christ offering. Certainly, at the last supper Christ could directly designate the eucharistic body and blood as his sacrifice; but there Christ was present in body, seated at the table. This satisfied the demands of sacramentalism, his words and gestures symbolizing the hidden mystery which they were bringing about. But now that Christ has ascended to heaven he must make use of ministers to embody himself on earth, to establish that complete sign-action of sacrifice in the Church which will be sacramentally effective.

This brings us back to St. Thomas's description of the celebrant at Mass as an "image" of Christ the Priest, offering his sacrifice. To use spatial imagery: at Mass the action at the altar, with all the sacramental elements which it comprises, is inserted between the priestly act of Christ's practical intellect and his body and blood. Whereas on Calvary there was a simple act of external worship, the priestly act immediately designating the death as sacrificial, in the Mass the same act of Christ's worship is exercised in and through the complex structure of the Church's liturgy where signs contain the reality signified. The Church, who by her liturgical actions forms the sacramental fullness of the body of Christ, provides the visible realities which express on earth by sacrifice Christ's heavenly worship.

THE CHURCH IN THE MASS

THE VALUE OF THE MASS

When Thomists say that the Mass has infinite value they are taking note of the fact that Christ himself actually offers the body and the blood which consequently express, as they did on Calvary, the infinite worship of Christ's heart. If this mystery is isolated from its context it might easily give rise to some confusion of ideas. Quite often one hears it said that in the Mass the Church "appropriates to herself," "makes her own," or "lays hold on," Christ's sacrifice with all its values as a perfect act of worship and that this compensates for the imperfection of the faithful's personal response to God. This is an extremely ambiguous statement and could encourage a dangerously quietistic approach to the Mass if the conclusion were drawn that the faithful's devotion is a secondary consideration. The contrary is true; the personal worship of the faithful provides the principal reason for the sacramental representation of Calvary. Evidently, in the perspectives of the whole mystery of salvation their worship is something secondary, being wholly dependent on the gift of God through Christ. But the mystery of the Eucharist, like everything else in the Church, is directed towards applying the fruit of Christ's passion to men so that they in their turn may make their personal response to God's invitation to union with Himself. In this sense the focal point of the phase of redemption constituted by the Church is the individual merit of the faithful, always, naturally, bearing a reference to God's gift and Christ's merit. It has already been stressed that the sense of the Mass must be sought in this sphere. Christ's personal offering of the sacrifice does not alter this.

The source of confusion lies in vagueness about what exactly in Christ's sacrifice the Church does appropriate. Does the Church appropriate his worship? Does she offer it? The reply is that she does; but by faith; the Mass does not introduce any new element as far as this is concerned. It must be clearly understood that Christ's worship is his own; it does not belong to the Church; rather it is the source of the Church's existence. This worship springs from the virtues in Christ's soul. Certainly, it affects the Church since Christ is the Head of the mystical body. By faith each member of the Church acknowledges that Christ's worship is mediatorial and in this way benefits from it. This permits us to say that the faithful offer his worship or offer Calvary; but this is simply a way of describing their own self-offering in terms of its meritorious cause. It is a way of expressing the fact that the faithful depend on Christ for the grace they possess; consequently their grace is an index to the measure in which they have fellowship in Christ's redemptive sacrifice. An effect of the Mass is obviously to increase this fellowship by increasing grace; but as far as the offering of Mass goes it is vital to realize that the grace and worship of the faithful represent the full measure in which they offer Christ's worship.

What, then, does the Church appropriate of Christ's in the Mass? Through the celebrant she appropriates his priestly offering of the body and blood and through this his heavenly worship. But this is a purely sacramental appropriation; that is to say, her ritual is used by Christ as a means of offering sacrifice. From this, as has been said, derives the infinite value of the Mass and its *ex-opere-operato* effect. The function of the celebrant here is purely ministerial; he offers the sacrifice as an instrument of Christ. The Church does not in any fashion appropriate morally Christ's sacrifice because of the celebrant's role. It is *Christ's* sacrifice, *his* worship, which is expressed in the Church's liturgy. This will draw down blessing on men; but this is the application of Calvary and is an *effect* of the Mass. The faithful can, of course, offer Christ's eucharistic worship by faith; but this does not differ essentially from their offering of Calvary; their personal grace and devotion determine the measure of their fellowship.

Our question must be made more specific: what does the Church appropriate as her own in the Mass? There can be only one reply: *she appropriates the Victim actually being offered by Christ, and this constitutes the essential complement provided by the Mass for the Christian life.* At Mass the faithful can offer the sacrificial body and blood because Christ has placed them at their disposal in the Eucharist; this is something that the Church possesses as her own and which she can offer personally. Undoubtedly this is a victim of infinite dignity because it is united hypostatically to the divine Word. But its value as a sacrifice derives from the devotion with which it is offered, that is, from the intensity of self-offering which it signifies. Christ himself offers it with the fullness of devotion which springs from his fullness of grace; the intrinsic value of the Victim serves to indicate the completeness of his submission to his Father. The Church, on her side, offers the same Victim with the devotion of her faithful. As a consequence the devotion of the faithful is associated with that of Christ in the offering of the single Victim. What the Church makes her own is the *visible expression* of Christ's devotion and she can use it to express simultaneously her own devotion. Because he is worshipping through her ritual she will benefit more fully than the devotion of the faithful would of itself warrant; but the determining factor, in proportion to which she benefits, is the contribution made by the faithful.

SACRIFICE OF THE FAITHFUL

What must be avoided in our thinking about the Mass is any suggestion that by some magical process our personal moral standing is represented as other than it is. That would be to consider the Mass as a sort of confidence trick worked on God. We offer the Victim of the Mass as members of Christ in the condition in which we are, with the promptitude of will in the service of God which we actually possess; and consequently we can offer it half-heartedly if, while being prepared to submit to God in essentials, we reserve to ourselves a margin of independence in things which we consider not to matter, if, that is, we have no intention of trying to remove venial sin from our lives. We can, in a certain sense, offer it without charity, not by a true offering but as a cry from the sinner for help. It is also true that one of the purposes of the Mass is to improve our moral condition; but this is an effect of the Mass and must not be confused with the offering itself.

It is because we are permitted in the Mass to use as the expression of our imperfect worship the supreme sign of perfect Christian worship that this sacrifice is a privileged moment in our lives, communicating to us a share in the gifts merited by

Christ. If this is what is meant by another phrase sometimes used, namely: our offering is "taken up" into Christ's offering —then the phrase is acceptable. It might well, however, be clarified by definition of the terms used. To repeat what has been said: our interior offering depends on Christ's redemptive sacrifice, a visible act of religion drawing its value from Christ's charity. In this sense Christ offers in us or, alternatively, we offer in Christ. Consequently, our whole Christian life is to this extent "taken up" by faith into Christ's offering. At Mass our interior offering is given sacrificial expression by the eucharistic Victim. The sign of Christ's self-offering becomes the sign of ours. In this sense our offering is "taken up" into the unique sacrificial sign of Christianity. The Eucharist, in other words, does for our offering, for our charity, what baptism does for faith. At Mass our offering in Christ is no longer based simply on faith; it is inserted in bodily fashion also into his visible sacrifice. It is "taken up" visibly as well as interiorly. What must be avoided here is once again the idea that this represents our offering as anything other than what it is. As far as offering of self to God goes the Mass simply externalizes in sacrificial fashion our personal condition.

The text of the Mass which has grown up round the central sacramental moment is wholly directed towards developing in the faithful the spirit of true worship. The *Orate Fratres* and the prayers of the Canon which ask that the sacrifice may be acceptable often prove disconcerting to those who concentrate their attention on Christ's part in the Mass. In fact these prayers touch the essential point. They raise no question about Christ's sacrifice being accepted; its acceptance has been demonstrated by the resurrection and ascension. What the Church has to concern herself about is whether her own sacrifice will be acceptable, whether her faithful will make the Victim the sign of their devotion. For on the fervour of this devotion depends the actual benefit drawn from Christ's sacrifice.

Having now sketched out with broad strokes the role that the faithful play in the Mass, we must fill in the details, enquiring how precisely the faithful enter the sacramental sacrifice. This investigation will corroborate by papal teaching the point of view already outlined.

PARTICIPATION OF THE BAPTIZED

In *Mediator Dei* Pius XII lays down very clearly—and more extensively than the *Constitution on Liturgy* of Vatican II—the general principles which govern the theology of the laity's role at Mass. The passages of the encyclical devoted to this matter are a brilliant summary of traditional teaching together with its application to a current problem. There is repeated insistence on the distinction between layman and priest; and it is specified that the latter does not act in virtue of a function delegated to him by the community. "The priest acts in the name of the people precisely and only because he represents the person of our Lord Jesus Christ, considered as Head of all the members and offering himself for them; the priest, therefore, approaches the altar as Christ's minister, lower than Christ, but higher than the people; the people, on the other hand, because it in no way represents the person of the divine Redeemer and is not mediator between itself and God, can in no way possess the priestly right. All this is certain with the certainty of faith" (*Mediator Dei*, CTSE ed. [=MD] §§ 88, 89). The sense of this passage will be clear from our exposition of St. Thomas's teaching. Only the priest transubstantiates; only he is the instrument through whom Christ offers the Victim; only he, as Christ's minister, makes the Mass a true sacrifice.

✓ The encyclical goes on immediately: "Yet it must be said that the faithful do also offer the divine Victim, though in a different way" (MD § 89). "Precisely because the priest places the divine Victim on the altar he presents it as an oblation to God the Father for the glory of the Blessed Trinity and for the benefit of the Church. Now, understood in this restricted sense, the oblation is in their own way shared by the faithful" (MD § 96). There are two grounds for saying that the faithful offer the Victim; "for not only do they offer the sacrifice *through the hands* of the priest, but also in a certain way they offer it *with* him" (MD § 96; cf. Vat. II Const., ch. 2, art. 48).

OFFERING THROUGH THE PRIEST

No difficulty arises about the first mode of offering. It depends on the fact that the Mass is the sacrifice of Christ, Head of the mystical body. His sacrifice is mediatorial, offered in the name of all his members. In this sense the members by faith offer "through" Christ and consequently "through the hands of the priest." Pius XII, abstracting from the theological question whether Christ actually offers the Mass or simply delegates the celebrant, writes: "The minister at the altar acts in the person of Christ considered as Head, and as offering in the name of all the members" (MD § 97). He uses the phrase "through the hands of the priest" to indicate that, whatever theological position one may adopt, the celebrant's function is purely ministerial, carried out in subordination to Christ, the unique mediator. It is not through the priest as an individual that the faithful offer; but through Christ and through the priest as minister of Christ. The Thomist will interpret the passage in terms of the instrumental use of the celebrant by Christ. In accordance with what has already been said, it will be clear that the offering of the Mass through the hands of the priest does not differ essentially from the faithful's offering of the sacrifice of Calvary. The sacrifice is Christ's; the members share in it by faith, accepting his mediation. Consequently, all who possess supernatural faith in Christ can share in the sacrifice of the Mass through Christ. In fact, Christian life and offering the sacrifice through Christ —or through the hands of the priest—are synonymous.

OFFERING WITH THE PRIEST

It is the offering "with" the priest which constitutes the specfically sacramental participation of the faithful. Here union with Christ's sacrifice is given visible expression in that same sacrifice as offered in the Eucharist. In the terms used earlier, the self-offering of the faithful in union with Christ is symbolized by the priestly offering of the Victim. This is to give the faithful a part in Christ's own sacrifice, making it their sacrifice. No longer do they simply offer through him; they are with him in offering it. Pius XII goes to some pains to define clearly the extent of this offering by the faithful. The reason for his concern is apparent. We are now in the realm of liturgical ceremony where the divinely-instituted hierarchy of the Church has reserved functions. The specfically priestly act of designating the

Victim as sacrificial sign of the community's self-offering can be performed only by the ordained priest. In this the Church's liturgy reflects the economy of salvation in which Christ alone is the Priest of the redemptive sacrifice. His priestly act is exercised exclusively through his liturgical embodiment or representative. Accordingly: "When the people are said to offer with the priest, this does not mean that all the members of the Church, like the priest himself, perform the visible liturgical rite; this is done only by the minister divinely appointed for the purpose" (MD § 98).

What, then, is the faithful's part in the liturgical act? "They unite their sentiments of praise, entreaty, expiation, and thanksgiving with the sentiments or intention of the priest, indeed with those of the High Priest himself. . . ." So far there is nothing specifically liturgical about this; the faithful could do as much even if there were no true sacrifice in the Mass, even if it were simply a memorial service of Calvary. But the encyclical goes on to the key-phrase: ". . . in order that in the very oblation of the Victim, those sentiments may be presented to God the Father *also by the priest's external rite*" (MD § 98; italics ours). It is made quite clear that this means that the faithful offer the Victim (cf. MD §§ 91, 103). Here is the novel element introduced into Christian worship by the sacrifice of the Mass. What the priest does at the altar makes available to the faithful a bodily, sacrificial expression for their praise, prayer, reparation and thanksgiving, offered in interior union with Christ. "The external rite of sacrifice must of its very nature be a sign of internal worship; and what is signified by the sacrifice of the New Law is that supreme homage by which Christ, the principal offerer, and with him and through him all his mystical members, pay due honour and veneration to God" (MD § 98).

Only the baptized can offer this sacramental Victim with the priest. This is because it forms part of the visible structure of the Church and only those who are baptized are inserted into this structure and possess in their sacramental characters the power necessary for acting in this sphere. In order to determine precisely the role played by the baptismal character we must delineate clearly the sign-action performed at Mass for, as has been seen, the character gives validity to a person's intention to participate in the sacramental actions of the Church.

THE SIGN-ACTION OF THE MASS

All that has been said about the celebrant's function indicates that there is an essential difference between the sign-action of the Mass and that of any other sacrament. When a person receives a sacrament his external participation determines the validity of this action of the Church. In the Mass, on the contrary, the essential sign-action is performed by, and its validity depends on, the celebrant alone. He is the symbol of Christ, unique High Priest, and he pronounces the words of consecration, thereby procuring the Real Presence. At the consecration, accordingly, the celebrant with the species of bread and wine, acting as priest, is the sign of Christ the Head offering his mediatorial sacrifice. By faith we know that the sign is efficacious and that Christ does actually offer through the celebrant. The faithful have no part in constructing this sign-action; obviously not, since the sign is that of the sacrifice of the Head. But the mediatorial sacrifice is not brought into the Church for Christ's sake; it is there precisely so that his members may have a bodily sacrifice to express their interior union with him. Consequently, the integral sign-action of the Mass, as the sacrifice of the Church, calls for the participation of the community of members of the Church. While the celebrant as visible instrument takes the place of Christ, the rest of those who are inserted into the visible structure of the Church form the sign of the body redeemed by Christ. It is the function of the baptized, at this level of ritual sign-action, to fill out the symbolism of the celebrant's action, by forming the visible gathering of those who offer the unique sacrifice with and through Christ. Only in this way is the meaning of the Mass spelled out on the level of symbolism. This does not at all imply that the priest must have a congregation if he is to celebrate Mass. The very existence of the Church in the world as a visible society suffices to develop in this symbolic fashion the meaning of the Mass; and the celebrant himself, as a priest of the Church, provides an adequate token symbol of the whole assembly even when he celebrates alone.

In both Mass and the other sacraments the baptized person contributes to the visible Church-action the symbol of dependence on Christ, thus reflecting the inner event of grace. In the Mass it is the personal, responsible activity flowing from grace received which comes to the foreground. While one person acts as priestly mediator all who belong to the Church by faith and baptism are members of Christ the Priest, forming one mystical person with him, capable of worshipping with him. Accordingly, the liturgical enactment of this mystery involves not only the intervention of the ordained priest, representing Christ, Head and mediator, but also the possibility for the individual members of the Church to offer the Victim with the priest. The liturgical act symbolizes and realizes not only the initiative taken by Christ in redemption but as well the union with Christ in his sacrifice of those who are incorporated into him.

The implications of incorporation into Christ the Priest are normative for liturgical participation. At the level of faith incorporation means that Christians acknowledge the Victim of Calvary as the supreme expression of their worship in Christ. At the level of liturgical representation the mystery is reflected and realized. Those who are sacramentally incorporated by faith and baptism, while they are powerless to designate the eucharistic Victim as sacrificial, can adopt the Victim of the sacrifice as the expression of their worship. Their spiritual union with Christ's sacrifice develops into bodily union; members of the one Priest, they offer the visible Victim with him.

FUNCTION OF THE BAPTISMAL CHARACTER

In conformity with its nature, the sacramental character has the function at Mass of giving validity to the intention of those who participate in the external sign-action. An intention, as we have seen, is required of those who take part in sacramental actions. Without it, their bodily involvement does not interpret authentically their personal attitude. Explicitly this intention need not be more, on the part of the faithful, than a desire to share in the Mass at which they are present or in all the Masses of the

Church. The very fact of going to Mass through devotion or out of obedience to Church law implies such an intention. Implicitly at least, what it involves is a desire to adopt the eucharistic Victim as the sacrificial expression of one's own worship and to offer It with Christ. It is the baptismal character which gives efficacy to such an intention. In virtue of the character the faithful participate in the priesthood of Christ as it is exercised in the liturgy of the Church. They share in the power of the specifically priestly act of Christ in the restricted sense that, presupposing his present sacrificial offering, they can offer the body and blood with him and with the celebrant.

When the baptized offer the Victim with Christ it is in one sense he who offers through them, just as he is active in them sustaining their spiritual union with God. He offers the Mass through the celebrant as Head of the mystical body, entering the Church through his sacramental representative. He offers it through the faithful because they are his members. There is no reduplication here for the two modes of offering are utterly distinct. The celebrant is the sacramental minister of Christ, applying his priestly act to the eucharistic Victim. On the contrary, Christ offers through his baptized members in the sense and to the degree that they have received grace by his mediation and are able to insert their own personal worship into the sacrifice. The immolated body and blood, which on Calvary signified the redemptive love and obedience of Christ the Head, signify in the Mass the love and obedience of the members with his. Their worship, which was included in Christ's worship on Calvary as in its universal meritorious cause, is now explicitly signified by the one Victim, sacramentally renewed.

The offering of the body and blood by the faithful through the celebrant and with him are not, it should now be clear, two disparate modes of participation. The relation between the two corresponds to that between faith and sacraments, between spiritual union with Christ and integrally human union. The mediatorial sacrifice is made present through the action of the celebrant. The baptized—in common with all believers—are united with it by faith; and by this very fact they offer the sacrifice through the celebrant just as they offer Calvary through Christ. But because they also possess the character the baptized are further united with the sacrifice sacramentally, in bodily fashion; that is, the Victim is as much their external sign of worship as is the posture of their own bodies when they make a genuflection. They are sacramental members of Christ the Priest and as such they have certain rights over his sacramental body. Within the sacramental mystery, it is their own body which is immolated on the altar for they are inserted into the sacramental fullness of Christ. The common priesthood of the baptized, active through the character, permits them to adopt the Victim directly, without the mediation of the celebrant. The celebrant, as sacramental mediator, must indeed first place the Victim on the altar; but once the body and blood are sacrificially present the baptized faithful can, in virtue of their spiritual and sacramental participation in Christ's priesthood, offer them to God themselves; and in this—but only this—they do not depend on the celebrant. This is their privilege and duty as members of Christ the Priest.

When we say the priest must "first" place the Victim on the altar, this must not be understood as though the faithful's offering followed in time the consecration. The sacramental offering of priest and people are contemporaneous; and, since Christ offers through the priest only at the consecration, the people's strictly sacramental offering is also confined to this moment. Morally and psychologically, of course, their attitude of worship may be stimulated or maintained throughout the ritual, and indeed constitutes a basic attitude of the whole Christian life; but corporeal participation in Christ's sacrifice is achieved only while Christ is active in the celebrant, using him as his instrument. An involuntary distraction at the consecration does not rob the faithful of their part in the sacrifice, nor for that matter does a deliberate, venially sinful distraction wholly exclude them. The basic pattern of their Christian life is the essential contribution they have to make to the sacrifice; but it is desirable and obviously more beneficial for themselves and for the whole of humanity if they are attentive to the significance of what they are doing.

The non-baptized, though they may be believers, cannot offer the Mass with Christ, just as they cannot receive communion. They have no power of acting in the visible sacrament of Christ constituted by the liturgical acts of the Church. Even a catechumen who believes explicitly in the Real Presence and in the sacrificial nature of the Mass is excluded from sacramental participation, though by faith he can offer the Mass through Christ. To offer with the priest a person's intention of participating in the sacramental action must be reinforced by the character of baptism, the power corresponding to sacramental incorporation into Christ and the Church. This associates the person with the sacrifice of the visible Church.

PRACTICAL CONSEQUENCES

The urgently practical conclusion to be drawn from all this discussion of the faithful's part in the Mass is one that we have already seen the Council of Trent stating as basic doctrine: Christ's sacrifice is given the Church so that it may serve as the visible sacrifice which the faithful offer with Christ and so that it may apply the fruits of Calvary to men. The necessity for the faithful to make it a true act of personal worship derives, not simply from the general principle that they ought to pray when they go to church, but from the very nature of the sacramental sacrifice. There is no need on the part of Christ for the eucharistic sacrifice; he redeemed us on Calvary and his intercessory worship continues for ever in heaven. He actually worships in the Mass primarily so as to make available to the worship of the Church the unique bodily sacrifice.

By being incorporated into this sacrifice the worship of the Church, while preserving the moral value which the faithful give it, takes on new qualities. It evidently becomes sacrificial so that the faithful, in spite of the once-for-all character of the Christian sacrifice, can constantly participate in the supreme act of worship, in the bodily fashion that their nature demands. The Victim offered imparts to the worship of the Church a reparatory character. By appropriating to themselves and offering the eucharistic image of Christ's death the faithful share in the reparation made by Christ on Calvary. We have said earlier that the union with God which they enjoy by reason of grace requires of them that they personally make reparation. But of themselves they can never atone adequately for an offence against God; they depend on Christ's atonement, made by him as their Head; and in the sacramentally immolated Victim of the Mass all the richness of that atonement is made available to them and imputed to them in proportion to their devotion.

Atonement, it should be understood, unlike interior repentance can be made over to another. Christ's sufferings are sacramentally represented in the Eucharist; they are attached to the Victim that is given to the Church as hers. Moreover, as the practice of accepting stipends indicates, the Church has a certain power to nominate the individuals whom she wishes to benefit from the imputation of Christ's atonement granted through the Mass. But it must be clearly understood that the measure of this imputation is determined proportionately by the devotion of the faithful who offer the Mass—and primarily of the person who contributes the stipend—as well as by the state of grace of the person nominated as beneficiary. Cardinal Cajetan, one of the foremost commentators of St. Thomas, does not hesitate, in his work *De celebratione Missae*, to draw the evident conclusion that the greater the number of those for whom an individual offers Mass the less each one benefits. But mathematics may not be the best guide to liturgical practice. The important factor is charity; and who is to say whether there is not greater charity in extending one's intercession to the many rather than the few? What the Christian should concern himself about is that he personally must make the Mass an authentic act of worship. It seems particularly important to insist that when a stipend is given to a priest the offerer should form an intention to participate in the Mass to be celebrated. This Mass can then be made a centre towards which are directed all the good works that the offerer performs during a certain period. The worship of the whole Church will be directed towards the benefit of the individual named; but there is something lacking if the offerer himself is not fully implicated in this worship. Above all we should get away from the idea that having a Mass celebrated is like sending flowers through a telegraphic agency, simply filling in a name and leaving the rest to the organization.

Pius XII recalls a traditional theme indicating the significance of the faithful's offering of the Victim slain for sin. They also must "become victims, as it were: cultivating a spirit of self-denial according to the precepts of the Gospel, willingly doing works of penance, detesting and expiating their sins ... dying mystically with Christ on the cross" (MD § 85). St. Augustine is quoted on this: "In the sacrament of the altar a sign is given to the Church that in the sacrifice she offers she herself is offered" (*City of God*, bk. X, ch. 6; MD § 109). This readiness to restore the order of justice by doing penance for sin finds its true perspectives in the Mass where it is associated with Christ's atonement and draws down upon the living and the dead the reparatory value of Christ's own sufferings. The union of the mystical body in charity, which identifies the ruling interests of the many individuals involved, already makes possible vicarious reparation; the further corporeal union achieved in the Mass, when the single Victim expresses the desire of Head and members to atone for sin, brings an immeasurable fullness to the offering of the Church. In similar fashion the praise, thanksgiving and prayer of the faithful, because offered in corporeal union with Christ, are filled out by the perfect worship of Christ; they are reunited with their source and take their place in the great hymn of love and obedience that goes up from the heart of Christ. The blood of Christ in the Mass is a daily pledge of the New Alliance in which all that man has is given by God through Christ, and what man gives in return is only what he has received.

To offer the eucharistic Victim is to adopt a whole programme of life. Calvary was not an isolated event in Christ's earthly existence; it was the logical outcome of his constant submission to his Father's will and summed up his whole life. The Mass has the same significance for the faithful, except that it is a beginning rather than an end. The cup of water given in Christ's name takes from the Mass the dignity of being a part of Christ's sacrifice. The Christian should consciously direct all his actions towards the Mass. From this habit will grow an appreciation of what the Mass really means for Christian life and from this, true liturgical piety. The more fully the individual participates in this virtuous or Christian fashion, the more ready will he be to discover in the prayers and ceremonial of the Mass a natural expression for his Christ-given love of God; and, even more important, the greater will be the benefits won for himself and for the world, for, let us insist again, the effectiveness of Christ's sacrifice depends on the devotion with which the Mass is offered by the Church with Christ. All the grace brought to man by the Church derives from the eucharistic sacrifice for it is the sacrifice of Christ in the daily world. The baptized are called on to redeem the world with Christ and in subordination to him through the Mass.

CEREMONIAL PARTICIPATION OF THE FAITHFUL

CONFUSION ABOUT ACTIVE PARTICIPATION

Of set purpose only passing mention has so far been made of the various prayers, responses and actions assigned the congregation by the ritual of the Roman Mass. This has not been through any lack of appreciation for such modes of assisting at Mass, but solely for the sake of establishing first the essential characteristics of the faithful's participation which is based on their baptism. For it cannot be denied that there has been, and unfortunately still is, an unhappy confusion in some minds as to the exact meaning of the term "active participation." It has come to be applied exclusively to vocal or other communitary forms of worship; and some unwary enthusiasts give the impression that it is their opinion that a congregation which does not take part in the Mass by these means is not actively participating. Such an attitude betrays, if not a superficiality of understanding, at least a failure to come to grips with the reality of the layman's place in the Church, which carries with it a profound involvement in all her actions; it cannot but do harm to true liturgical revival. On the contrary, by defining carefully the role played by the ceremonial, not only its limitations, but also its potentialities, will be brought to light and, moreover, an objective guide to its use will be to hand.

The desire of the Church that the faithful should take their proper part in the ceremonies has been made increasingly clear in recent years. The Instruction of the Congregation of Rites, September 3, 1958, leaves no doubt on this. More authoritative still is the First Chapter of the *Constitution on Liturgy* of the Second Vatican Council. Part 3 of this chapter lays down rules governing reform of the liturgy. Among these, some are derived from the hierarchic and intrinsically communitary character of the liturgy, the second of which states that whenever possible the form of ritual which is externally communitary is to be preferred to one which is more individual and private (art. 27). The third requires that the active participation of the people is to be promoted by their making the responses, by acclamations and by singing; moreover their part is to be noted in the rubrics (arts. 30, 31).

The Council and the Instruction just referred to term such activity "actuosa participatio"; but this cannot be translated simply as "active participation" because this is the English term properly applied to the function belonging to the baptized in virtue of their sacramental character. This is a function which does not depend essentially on saying prayers or making responses of ecclesiastical institution; it derives from the very nature of the Church as founded by Christ. The baptized exercised it before such prayers existed; they exercised it throughout all the centuries when they were reduced to silence in the pews; they can still exercise it, and most profitably, today if they sincerely wish to worship. It is a function which is exercised at the consecration when they worship with Christ actually offering the Victim, and which is complemented when they receive communion. All the other parts of the Mass are secondary to these two moments and derive their significance from them. Since this is the essential active participation of the baptized some other term must be found, if confusion is to be avoided, for the part they play in the subordinate ritual. "External or visible participation" will not do because this is precisely what the power of the character implies. "Ceremonial participation" might be suggested.

PURPOSE OF CEREMONIAL PARTICIPATION

The purpose of ceremonial participation is, in the words of Pius XII, "to enable the faithful to take part more easily and more profitably in the Mass" (MD § 111); "to foster the devotion of the faithful and their close union with Christ and his visible minister, and to arouse in them those sentiments and attitudes of mind in which they must become like the High Priest of the New Testament" (MD § 112). The non-essential parts of the Mass still pertain to its integrity as an act of human worship. The whole forms a sign of faith in the mediation of Christ's sacrifice and of man's response to it. Christ's entry into the liturgical assembly takes place when the sign-action reaches the point where the words used at the last supper are repeated. Psychologically there should be no break for the faithful, only an awareness of new realism. While faith in Christ's coming may well increase devotion at this particular moment, it is normal that the preceding ritual—with its silences as well as its vocal prayers—should build up, in a way adapted to human reactions, the worship of the faithful. The essential function of the cere-monial is consequently religio-psychological: it stimulates devo-tion and orientates it towards the moment of sacrifice. This is a function common to all external acts of religion so that it does not by any means imply that ceremonial participation is not genuine worship. It can be made such by the individual mem-bers of the congregation; the obligation lies on them to ensure that it is. Certainly, a pastor cannot be satisfied that he has re-stored the liturgy in his parish simply because he has succeeded in persuading his people to overcome the shyness or disinclina-tion that formerly prevented them singing out the responses. This is only a beginning which has, of course, its own practical educa-tive value if not positively resisted; but nothing can provide a substitute for patient and clear explanation of the sense of it all. Prudence and tact, together with a balanced view of the liturgy, are indispensable if the Council's instructions are to be put into fruitful effect.

ITS SIGNIFICANCE

Granted the principle that it would be better if all the faith-ful were adequately prepared and disposed to participate in the ceremonial, understanding must still be shown to the many in-dividuals who complain that they draw little profit from it. The argument so often put forward against such people, that the official text of the Mass expresses the intentions of the Church, has a certain validity; but it should not be pushed too far. The intentions of the Church are not at all complicated, and the texts, apart from the epistles and gospels, are nothing more than variations on a simple and recurring theme. There are all manner of other means of achieving essentially the same effect that they are intended to produce. No matter how convincingly a preacher tells the people that the text of the Mass helps them to pray better, some of his hearers will still maintain that they do not find it so. As far as they are concerned this is the final word. To appeal to religious experience has validity only for those who are already won over. Liturgical education, if it is to be universal in its appeal, must build on the nature of the liturgy, not on subjective reaction to it.

The only intrinsically compelling reason for ceremonial participation lies in the symbolic function of the congregation. While the celebrant acts in the person of Christ the Head, the people represent the Church of the redeemed. Corporate redemption requires corporate ceremonial participation. The sacramentalism of the Mass is brought to its logical conclusion only when the congregation as a body takes its part in the ritual in accordance with the rubrics. The sacramentalism is that of the Eucharist and accordingly has two levels of signification. The inner reality (*res tantum*) signified by ceremonial participation is charity, the bond which unites the mystical body. The intermediary reality (*res et sacramentum*) signified by the ceremonial and, together with it, signifying the inner reality is the offering of the body and blood by the faithful with the priest and with Christ; the uniqueness of the Victim and the corporate union of the priesthood of the faithful calls for complete unison in ceremonial action.

This line of argument must not·be exaggerated. The simple willing presence of a congregation at Mass is already symbolic of the union of charity and of offering; it satisfies to some extent the demands of sacramentalism. But it is a symbol which can be made more perfect. Seen in this light, community singing or dialogue with the celebrant reveals its true values. We should not, however, be too quick to paint all of these values in the rosiest of colours. Singing in a non-professional choir is not al-

ways an aesthetic experience; and for people of retiring or independent temperament the discipline of taking part in a dialogue
Mass can quite easily be distressing or irritating. It is unreal to
complain that people who do not feel any relish for community
prayer lack a sense of the Church and .to try to dragoon them
into conformity. The communitary character of the mystical
body does not suppress individual personality, as the very nature of the people's offering at Mass makes crystal clear. If an
individual finds ceremŏnial participation a trial then this will
have to be made to represent one of its values for him. It is not
just a question of putting up with something unpleasant because
of the Church's desire in this matter; though an element of
reparation is not at all out of place at Mass. It is rather that the
experience of something uncongenial reveals an authentic aspect
of life in the mystical body.

We are apt to be over-romantic about the mystical body, not
in the sense that we exaggerate its splendour, but because we do
not pay enough attention, when we are thinking about its dogmatic formulation, to the stark realities of what is involved in
the union of charity. The idea of charity is a magnificent one;
living in charity with the people we meet can be a struggle in
which the magnificence is only distantly perceived. It means a
whole series of triumphs, small and great, over selfishness, putting up with the faults of the people we live with, fitting into a
community where temperaments, education, interests differ
widely. It means, in a word, supernatural—but intelligent—compromise with circumstances. The woman in the congregation who
is always a note ahead in the Creed, the man who fancies himself as a virtuoso tenor, or just the plain din of a dialogue Mass
when we do not feel up to it, all have their sacramental function
at Mass. Some people are uncomplicated enough not to be wor-
ried by any of this. They could be people who lead good Christian lives and find the obligations of charity light; or on' the other
hand their idea of charity could be very superficial. Some people
like community singing; they do it at home and with their friends;
naturally they like to do it in church. This does not necessarily
make them better Christians than those of less out-going temperament. Perhaps those who are upset by the rest of the con-

gregation are unduly complicated or sensitive or critical; but they have to live in charity with the temperament they have and they cannot do better than offer their Mass as a symbol of what Christian living means for them. They will object that they cannot pray in such conditions. It depends on what is meant by prayer. There may be less feeling of devotion than when they kneel in silence before the altar; but feeling of devotion can be deceptive. There may be less conscious awareness of praying; but if it is by an effort of will that they submit to the prescribed communitary activity and if they try to see its difficulties as significant tokens of the difficulties of charity then they are indeed praying and, moreover, praying in a way which is relevant to their own situation. This is what the Mass is for, the offering of the life one really leads, not just of vague good intentions. It is not an escape from reality; it gives our lives their significance within the mystical body.

All this may seem unbearably tortuous to those who positively enjoy ceremonial participation. So often one hears it said: The Church wants it, so everybody has got to do it. The ability to see human problems in so straightforward a way as this must simplify life to a considerable, though hardly an enviable, degree. It is of course admirable that people should enjoy the liturgy. Those who do should not make the mistake of thinking that this necessarily means that they are worshipping as they should. Their particular temperament may be an even greater obstacle to true participation than that of the person who has to master himself if he is not to give way to his distaste for mass demonstrations; but again it too can promote genuine worship. Even more important, since this concerns the welfare of others, those who enjoy ceremonial participation should not be intolerant of the hesitancy of their fellow-parishioners. In order to get everybody "to do it" and to make it true worship a great deal of patience and common-sense is necessary. Enthusiasm is tolerable only when it is backed by intelligence and human understanding. Full ceremonial participation in the liturgy is desirable only if it promotes authentic community worship. It will do that only if the faithful realize what they are doing and are persuaded, individually if need be, to want to do it.

OUR LADY AND THE MASS

There is another theme to be woven into the fabric of our theology of the Mass: the part that our Lady plays. Her role in redemption is still a matter of discussion among theologians. While it is accepted by all Catholics that she joins her intercession to that of her Son in favour of men, there are theologians who do not admit that she had any part in that act by which Christ redeemed the human race, restricting her role in the scheme of salvation to the distribution of graces won by him. As far as recent published works go, it may be said that this represents a minority opinion. Most modern theologians teach that Mary cooperated with Christ on Calvary, meriting with him and making reparation for men. Within this group there are differences of opinion on the precise effectiveness of her intervention. Accepting this teaching here without entering into the arguments on which it is based, and abstracting from the elements of the opinion still discussed, we wish to make some attempt at describing its significance for the Mass.

MARY'S ROLE IN REDEMPTION

⏉ The sense of the role assigned Mary in the act of redemption must first be made clear. Mary herself was redeemed by Christ and it is impossible that she should have merited this for herself. Her corredemptive function at Calvary was confined in its scope to others. Nor did she add anything to the merit of Christ or to his reparation. As with our own merits and reparation, hers were based on Christ's mediation; and, again like ours, far from taking away from the supremacy and uniqueness of Christ, her merit and reparation manifest his power. Not only did he redeem humanity; he did this so perfectly that he raised up a simple human being, though one who was his mother, to be his associate in the redemption of the rest of the human race. He did not need his mother's help; it was for her honour and our comfort that he made Mary in the fullest sense possible "mother of all the living" in the order of grace (cf. *Gen.*, 3:20).

The chief objection proposed to this teaching argues that Mary's acquisition of grace presupposes as complete Christ's redemptive act which, though later in time, already benefitted her at her immaculate conception; and to say that she subsequently had a part in this act is like saying that a person could hold up the platform on which he is standing. This is, of course, true as far as Christ's own redemptive action is concerned; this is the foundation of all merit on the part of humanity, including Mary's. But what is meant by corredemption is that Mary, using freely the grace won for her by Christ's act, merited with him, by her own act, the graces to be given the rest of men. Our grace, accordingly, has been won for us on two titles, by Christ as principal mediator and by Mary in virtue of Christ.

Granted that this was Mary's role at Calvary, her part in that sacrifice can be more clearly defined. There is a perfect analogy between her cooperation in the sacrifice of Calvary and the participation of the faithful in the Mass. She offered the redemptive sacrifice through Christ and with him.

Firstly, she offered through Christ. As his associate, she formed with him a redemptive community of which he was the priest. He performed the specifically priestly action of designating his death as the sacrificial expression of his self-offering to the Father. She was redeemed by this sacrifice—though she enjoyed its fruits from the first moment of her conception—and accordingly she offered it by faith through her Son of whom she was a member by grace. As in the case of the faithful at Mass, the expression "to offer through Christ" is simply a restatement in specifically sacrificial terms of the dependence of the redeemed on Christ's unique redemptive act. The same may be said of St. John and the holy women, of the good thief and of the centurion, assuming that he had supernatural faith in Christ; it may be said of all who in succeeding ages believe in Christ. But there is a difference between Mary's offering through Christ and that of all others. Only she was Christ's associate in redemption; only her offering merited supernatural life for all men. Others who offer Calvary through Christ by living faith may merit grace for their fellowmen; but not with the universal efficacy of Mary, nor by the same title as hers. She alone is established by God as Mother of the whole Christ, Head and members, and she alone was moved by God to act in subordination to her Son to make the rest of men worthy of grace by her merits.

If all men can offer Calvary through Christ, only Mary as she stood at the foot of the cross offered the sacrifice with him. Once again, the part of the faithful at Mass illustrates her role. The baptized in virtue of their sacramental character can adopt the eucharistic Victim as the sign, made sacrificial by the celebrant, of their own self-offering. It is the character which gives them this right over the sacramental body and blood. On Calvary Mary possessed rights over the body and blood of Christ; she was his mother who had given him his body and blood. When he as Priest of that redemptive community designated his sufferings and death as the sacrifice of the New Law, she who was his associate in redemption and his mother was able to adopt the Victim as the sacrificial sign of her own self-offering.

MARY'S EXTERNAL ASSOCIATION WITH THE MASS

Mary at Calvary is the perfect model of the Church of the faithful assisting at Mass. There is the same complete dependence on the one priest both for grace and for visible sacrifice. What the offering of the Victim meant for Mary in terms of a complete surrender of herself to the divine will it should mean likewise for the faithful. Her involvement in the sacrifice led to her compassion, the suffering of mind and emotions provoked by the sight of her Son's passion and death and by her knowledge that it was sin that had made them necessary. The offering of the Mass with Christ must draw the Church into Mary's compassion; this is the Pattern, repeating itself, as it will repeat itself under infinite variations until the fullness of Christ's body is achieved.

Our Lady is, then, the model of the faithful's participation in Mass and as well, since she is Corredemptrix, its source under Christ and God. This implies that Mary is involved in every Mass that is offered at least in external fashion; she is, in technical terms, the exemplar of the faithful's offering and the meritorious cause both of their spiritual submission to God and of the very existence of the Mass as a sacramental reality belonging to the Church. It is a natural question to ask further whether she is directly involved in the Mass. It is not our intention to propose any definitive answer to this question but we should like to suggest a line of thought.

THE PROBLEM OF HER DIRECT ASSOCIATION

If theology, to be genuine, must be penetrated throughout with the revealed word of God, it still remains that one of its functions is to essay the construction of a whole scheme of thought. Parts of this scheme will necessarily be speculative in the sense that they cannot be verified by reference to immediate revelation; but they may nevertheless claim a certain provisional validity to the degree that they are in harmony with what is held as certain. That this exploratory method has been abused, and perhaps nowhere so much as in the field of Mariology, is something of which theologians are acutely conscious. But the revealed mysteries, besides holding out an invitation to prayerful acceptance, will always present a challenge to the inquiring mind of the believer. It is indeed our acceptance which urges us to seek for deeper understanding. By the very fact of bringing ourselves to the point where we must acknowledge our incapacity to grasp the full implications of the mystery we heighten our appreciation of revealed truth.

The problem is whether our Lady actually offers the Mass. Evidently the question has full significance only for those theologians who admit such an offering for Christ. For if we grant that in the act of transubstantiation Christ's priestly act is brought to bear on the eucharistic body and blood and actually offers them to God as sacrificial sign of Christ's worship then it is natural to enquire whether Christ's associate in redemption offers the Victim with him as an expression of her own worship. The theological method being followed is that of comparison of the mysteries among themselves. If the Mass is the sacramental representation of Calvary and if Mary cooperated in the sacrifice of Calvary, must we not look for her intervention in the Mass? Likewise, if the Mass applies the fruits of the passion to the Church and if Mary with Christ merited these fruits, must she not have a part in the Mass in subordination to Christ, analogous with her part in Calvary? Her intercession for mankind continues in heaven as does that of Christ. If his is expressed by the Victim of the Mass should not that of his associate be also expressed?

It is not acceptable to say that Mary can exercise over the eucharistic Victim the maternal rights in virtue of which she offered the sacrifice with Christ on Calvary, and that therefore from heaven she could adopt directly the sacrifice of the altar as hers. This would be to confuse the two distinct orders of sacramentalism and natural reality. Offering of the sacramental Victim must itself be sacramental, as was said earlier about Christ himself. Nor may we say that our Lady after the assumption enters the sacramental order in the way that the baptized do, in virtue of her baptismal character. The function of the character is to enable members of the Church on earth to express their faith by sacramental signs and its use is directed towards increase of grace. If Mary does offer the Mass she must do so through a bodily representative belonging to the visible Church through whom her act of adopting the sacrificial symbol is signified and is applied to the Victim.

THEORY CONCERNING MARY'S INTERVENTION IN THE SACRAMENTS

We are led in this fashion to consider a theory proposed by a minority of Thomists regarding our Lady's part in the sacramental system and in the giving of grace generally. It has been suggested that Mary not merely intercedes for grace but is also used by ·God, in subordination to the humanity of Christ, as a physical or direct instrument for producing grace in men.[4] The principal passage in Scripture indicated as hinting at this is the account of the visitation in which Elizabeth says: "As soon as the voice of thy salutation sounded in my ears, the infant in my womb leaped for joy" (*Lk.*, 1:44). Certainly the coming of our Lady and her words brought about the sanctification of John the Baptist; and it is on accounts of similar episodes that the Thomistic theory of Christ's physical causality is based. As well, Mary's physical union with Christ, her unique relation to his body through which all graces come to us, and her bodily

---

4. The most recent defender of this theory is R. Spiazzi, O.P., in **Causa salutis. Maria santissima nell'economia della salvezza**, Ed. Mame, Rome, 1961, ch. XI.

assumption, all prompt the idea that her association with him in redemption would be most fittingly complemented by her instrumental intervention in giving grace. But the step from "it was fitting" to "it was done" is one that can only be made to the accompaniment of the jeers of theologians who demand with justice that nothing may be asserted as factual in the mystery of salvation if it is not shown to be revealed. Nor does it seem likely that any clear indication of Mary's instrumental intervention in the giving of grace will be found in the sources of revelation. We are, however, entitled, on the basis of such slight positive indications as we have, to claim, not that "it was done," but that "there are some indications that it has been done." It might be suggested that the scant regard paid the theory even by Thomists stems from an insufficient appreciation of the significance of the body as part of the person. If Thomists are to be faithful to their teacher's anthropology they should be quick to grasp the incongruity in the notion that Mary's mediation as exercised in heaven is purely spiritual. The case is different with the other saints in heaven; she alone is Corredemptrix. If she is to fulfill this function in an integrally human fashion then her body should be involved in the giving of grace; and this can only be if she is an instrument of God subordinated to Christ.

APPLICATION TO THE MASS

To go on to apply this hypothesis to the Mass is not, as might at first appear, to emulate the circus artist who, after doing a handstand on an unsupported ladder, proceeds to lift off one hand. On the contrary, a further verification of the hypothesis will be supplied if it can suggest a fashion in which the integral sacrifice of Calvary might be reproduced sacramentally in the Mass. If Mary is used as a physical instrument in subordination to the humanity of Christ in the act of transubstantiation then, just as Christ's priestly act is applied to the Victim on the altar through the celebrant, so too Mary's act by which she adopts the Victim as her own would be applied through the celebrant.

This may seem a simple enough idea but it is mined with theological booby-traps. Our Lady is not a priest. She could not make Calvary a sacrifice and she cannot make the Mass a sacrifice. Christ did the first, the ordained priest as Christ's minister does the second. Having this in mind, if we are to admit, even as a hypothesis, that Mary intervenes in the Mass as an instrument subordinate to Christ but superior to the celebrant, two difficulties at once present themselves. Firstly, does not this put us in the position of affirming that Mary relays, as it were, Christ's priestly act to the celebrant and consequently is herself responsible for the Mass being a sacrifice; and is not this to attribute to her a priestly function?

This is a real difficulty but it can be overcome if we define carefully the limits of the intervention attributed to Mary. She, like Christ, would be the instrument of God in the action of transubstantiation. It would be divine power that would apply to the Victim Christ's priestly act and Mary's act of offering, each of these acts being, it will be remembered, acts of the practical intellect, that of Christ designating the Victim as sacrificial, that of Mary adopting the sacrifice as a sign of her own worship. Mary would thus be the channel through whom Christ's priestly act is transmitted, but her function should be described as mediatorial, not as priestly; for she, unlike the celebrant, does not perform the liturgical sign-action of offering the sacramental species. Christ is the principal priest of the Mass because his priestly act is applied to the eucharistic Victim; the celebrant is a ministerial priest because he performs the ceremonial sacramental offering; but Mary's intervention, in the hypothesis we are considering, falls in neither of these categories. Her act, like Christ's and presupposing his, is applied to the eucharistic Victim by divine power so that she can offer with Christ.

We have described Mary's instrumental intervention as mediatorial. This defines precisely its character, for Mary is by her merits the source of the Church, not only as assembly of the faithful, but also as endowed with the means of salvation. In subordination to Christ she has merited the institution of the sacraments, among them the Mass; she has merited the ministerial priesthood of the Church. The function that the ordained priest performs at the altar constitutes one of the means of salvation; as such it comes from Mary and whatever it achieves she has already achieved in a different but higher fashion. There is accordingly no incongruity in the notion of her being also the instrumental cause of the Mass.

The second difficulty is closely allied to the first. According to the hypothesis, the priest at the altar would represent in the liturgical assembly Mary as well as Christ; and this appears to involve a confusion of sacramental function. Only Christ the Priest can be symbolized by the sacramental sacrificer; the symbol of Mary, supposing that there were one, must be one who merely offers the sacrifice with Christ. Again the difficulty is serious but, it may be suggested, one that leads to a deeper understanding of the function of the ordained priest. It must not be forgotten that the priest of the Church is not the High Priest of the New Alliance; he is a sacramental representative of the one Priest. The fact that the priest is himself one who stands in need of redemption is no scandal to the Catholic, accustomed as he is to making the distinction between the individual and the office. What is not so quickly recognized is that there is a profound ambivalence in the priest even in terms of his official position. He represents Christ but he is also a priest of the Church, the Spouse of Christ. The whole Church, comprising the assembly of believers and the hierarchical institution, is set over against Christ, distinct from him because brought into existence by him as the fruit of his sacrifice. The priesthood of orders, being an office in the visible fabric of the Church, does not transcend this distinction. Certainly we must say that the priest, in so far as he is used by Christ as an instrument of sanctification or as a minister of sacrifice, is drawn into the sphere of Christ as Head of the mystical body. But he remains a priest of the Church, and this even in his office. His function is both redemptive, in the sense that he applies the fruits of redemption, and is itself the fruit of redemption. It is both mediatorial and a gift procured by the one mediator. The Church, as institution of salvation, provided with the organs of grace, is in fact like Mary.

Mary is the type or model of the Church, both redeemed and redeeming, taken from the world of sin and mediatrix, creature and mother of Christ. Mariologists are at present engaged in exploiting the richness of this biblical and patristic theme. The relation between Mary and the priest has long been recognized, at least in terms of bringing Christ to the world. At Mass the

254 *Meeting Christ in the Sacraments*

celebrant offers the sacrifice as minister of Christ but also as one who holds office in the Church. It is the Church's act of worship into which Christ enters. Through the priest the Church makes her response of faith to Christ's command at the last supper; when Christ transforms her sign of faith, making available to her in bodily form his sacrifice, he does not make her action any less a sign of faith. His presence gives new richness, new reality; the Church, represented by the priest, remains his Spouse, distinct from him, though she cooperates with him in the exercise of his headship. It is evident that Mary and the Church have their separate functions in the economy of salvation. Mary, by reason of her maternal association with Christ and her fullness of grace, gave the world its Redeemer and with him redeemed the rest of mankind. The Church as institution of the means of salvation cooperates with Christ in bringing his redemption to men through preaching and the sacraments. Nevertheless there is an analogy between the two functions based on common dependence on Christ combined with participation in his redemptive mission. And just as Mary was the type of the Church, so the Church carries the likeness of Mary into the world, being the mother of Christ's fullness. In the celebrant of the Mass, accordingly, precisely as he is priest of the Church, we may see the symbol of Mary. His form of cooperation with Christ, being sacramental, means that he is also the symbol of Christ. There is no confusion of function here but rather a recognition of the two-fold significance of the sacraments as acts of the Church and as acts of Christ.

CONCLUSION

To draw a conclusion from all this: it does not appear impossible that Mary should offer the Victim of the Mass through the celebrant with Christ. She could do this if she were used by God as an instrument, subordinated to the humanity of Christ, in the action of transubstantiation. There are certain hints in revelation which could be interpreted as indicating that Mary does fulfill such a function. The idea that she does is fully in harmony with St. Thomas's anthropology and may be said to be a legitimate development of his Christology in the light of the Church's growing understanding of Mary's place in the economy of salvation. In particular, Mary's role at Calvary suggests to us that she should have a similar role in the eucharistic representation of the sacrifice. The whole development of this notion cannot be said to be more than a hypothesis. At the same time it should not be thought that it represents an illegitimate attempt to devise new prerogatives for Mary in the style formerly adopted by some theologians. If Mary is Corredemptrix her part in the Mass would add nothing to her essential role. For the Mass belongs to the scheme of means left the Church by Christ for giving effect to Calvary. If Mary does offer the eucharistic Victim then the body and blood of Christ on the altar symbolize sacrificially, as they did in their natural state on Calvary, her worship as well as Christ's. Then, united by faith with the redemptive sacrifice of Christ and Mary, the baptized offer the sacramental representation with these two. Mary offers the Mass with Christ as his principal member, redeemed by him and herself saving the other members. The baptized offer together with her but in subordination to her, imitating her response to Christ's gift, and receiving from her the means of imitation.

Whether Mary actually offers the Mass or not, she provides the answer, at once simple and profound, to the problem of the faithful's role in the Mass. They must act as she acted on Calvary.

10 Marriage: Conjugal Love in Christ

The Church is incurably romantic about marriage. Her belief in the essential goodness of the married state and the happiness and fulfillment that are to be found in it has not been shaken by the saddening experience of years or by the confidences she has received from those who have discovered only disillusion and embitterment in the unsuspected burdens of married life. She greets each new bride and bridegroom with fresh joy: "You are come today to seal your love for each other before God and in the presence of these witnesses" (Irish Ritual, 1960); and in that greeting she holds out to them the hope she cherishes for them and reveals her own confidence in human nature redeemed by Christ.

MYSTERY OF FAITH

REVEALED BY GOD

What the Church is romantic about is not the marriage of the "true-love" magazines. She cannot isolate any human experience from that greater love-story in which she and all mankind are involved, the mystery of God's love for men. Her romanticism is a world apart from the shallow sentimentalism that passes for idealism in those whose ideas about marriage are nourished on commercial and journalistic exploitation of man's inborn yearning for a "happy ending." It is a world apart because it is of another world than that of any purely human estimate of the possibilities of happiness in marriage. The Church recognizes only one truly happy ending; and what she thinks about marriage and teaches about it is a mystery of faith. She does not rely on any merely human experience; what she has to say can be accepted only by faith. She is romantic about marriage as redeemed by Christ.

This supernatural origin of her teaching needs to be stressed, not only for non-Catholics but for Catholics themselves. Married laymen are increasingly apt to be a little condescending when it comes to priests talking about marriage. The relationship between husband and wife, so the argument goes, is so personal and intimate that one who has no experience of its subtle variations is condemned to being irrelevant if he should speak about it. The reason for this reservation about the priest's competence in marriage questions is precisely lack of awareness that the Church teaches a revealed doctrine on the matter. Everybody has to live his own life, whether he is single or married. Husband and wife have their own personal life in common to work out together. But the Church has a revelation from God not only about individual lives, but also about married life. This is the supremely relevant message she has for those who are married.

This is something too that apologetes of Church law on marriage should not lose sight of. In its essentials this law is a statement of divine revelation on the nature of marriage. The attitude of the Church to divorce or birth-control does not rest on the arguments put forward by her theologians. That these arguments are valid in their own sphere and that they develop the meaning of marriage is not being called into question; but, because they are arguments of human reason concerning a natural institution, they are incapable of expressing all that the Church knows about marriage. These arguments derive from natural ethics and as such have their own demands to make on human reason. They show how the teaching of the Church is a defence of human nature and of the dignity of man. But they fail utterly to give the compelling reason why the Church's teaching is what it is. Those who do not accept her authority as guardian and interpreter of revelation are incapable of appreciating the divine certainty of her doctrine on marriage. It is part of her mission to try to convince the unbeliever by rational argument. For her own children she has a greater treasure and she exacts from them, in virtue of her divine mission, a greater obedience, the obedience of faith which holds fast to the word of God even when unaided reason would hesitate. For the Church there is only one true happy ending, the face-to-face vision of God. She is romantic about conjugal happiness only when it means that the story will end in heaven.

A SACRAMENT OF THE WORLD

If the light that the Church sheds on marriage derives from another world, the sacrament itself is unique among the seven in the degree of its involvement with earthly reality. The nature of a sacrament requires that common objects of daily use be endowed with spiritual symbolism and be made spiritually fruitful through the intervention of Christ in the Church. What distinguishes marriage from the other six is that, unlike them, it possesses a great deal more than its spiritual significance. Take away from baptism its function as profession of faith introducing a new member into the Church of Christ, and nothing is left but a very summary ritual washing; and the like may be said of the other sacraments. But marriage fulfills an essential role in society quite apart from its sacramental function. In this case Christ did not institute a completely new liturgical ceremony or give new significance to an existing ritual; he adopted a natural human institution as a sacrament of his Church.

Because it is a sacrament marriage has a part to play in the Christian life. In common with all the sacraments, it promotes the worship of God in the Church and heals the wounds of sin. But the genius of this sacrament lies in the fact that a purely natural human association, making its own contribution to the life of temporal society, has been directly incorporated into the Christian life. The human couple, man and woman, in all their affective and bodily faculties, have been introduced into the Kingdom of God.

Even before any further consideration is given to marriage it should be apparent how significant is its admission to the scheme of Christian living. With this sacrament is brought to its logical conclusion that orientation, implicit in the sacramental system, towards the sanctification of ordinary human activity and through this of society. Marriage reveals the pedagogy of all the sacraments. The others could be misread in a purely formalistic sense as having no direct relevance to daily life; but the sacramental status of marriage is a mighty protest, springing from the depths of human nature, against formalism in the liturgy and in Christian living. For, while the other sacraments constitute a more or less arbitrary, or at least formalized, system of sacred signs whose significance for day-to-day life must be consciously sought out and consciously applied, in marriage it is the day-to-day life itself, with all its human joys and sorrows, which is sacramental. Here the transformation of human values brought about by the Incarnation is revealed with undeniable clarity to the eye of faith. A man and a woman, living together with their family, earning their living, watching television, going shopping, talking to the neighbours, a man and a woman fulfilling each other, praying together, planning for their children—this is not something which has to be blessed to make it good, this is Christianity because it is lived in conformity with an agreement between the man and the woman which Christ has made a sacrament. A truly Christian marriage proclaims how meaningless it is, since the coming of the Word into human nature, to make any sort of practical division of human activity into sacred and profane. And the same utterly sincere giving of oneself that is involved in true conjugal union, the same unguarded friendship with another, is involved in all the sacraments; but there the Other is God. The sacramental nature of marriage demonstrates that the reign of Christ extends to all that is human. Its theological lesson is that all that is human must be consecrated to Christ through the sacraments.

Here too lies the theological significance—whatever may have been the immediate historical occasion—of the Church's condemnation of theories put forward by supporters of state jurisdiction over marriage. According to these theories the sacrament is separable from the contract of matrimony, the latter being the exclusive concern of the State. The sacrament, insisted the Church, is not just a liturgical flourish added to a civic agreement; and for this reason the minister of the sacrament is not the priest who conducts the service. The sacrament is the contract itself; and consequently the ministers are the bride and bridegroom. It is this most natural and intimate agreement between a man and a woman that constitutes for the two a new way of entering into the mystery of Christ. These two people are members of Christ; all their actions have relevance to the fact of their belonging to him; but this particular action, when they give mutual consent to marriage before an official witness of the Church, has a special relevance and has been made by Christ a privileged source of grace in their lives.

THE PROBLEM OF SACRAMENTAL STATUS

Why should Christ have made this particular human institution a sacrament? Calvin, who, like many of the Reformers, had a knack of getting to the heart of theological problems and giving them incisive expression, declared that he could see no more reason for this than for farming, shoemaking, building or shaving being made sacraments. He claimed that by withdrawing matrimonial legislation from the jurisdiction of the clergy he had "stripped these asses of their lion's skin." The example of farming, in the light of the history of religions, has more significance than perhaps Calvin intended.

For primitive societies the fertility of the earth and of the human race were closely linked, first of all by symbolism, but also at a deeper level where the influence of some other-worldly force was instinctively recognized as the source of life. Both farming and marriage were invested with a sacred quality, as human activities in which man could not act alone but must wait upon the intervention of the gods for fruitfulness. That the mythical nature-gods were imagined as producing life in human fashion, and that the fertility rites of primitive religions degenerated accordingly into orgiastic liturgies, may be evidence of the corrupting influence of original sin; yet at the same time the religious sense, however warped, implicit in the pagan cults reveals the instinct innate in human nature to refer the mystery of life to a transcendent being. Certainly, the primitive pagans, for all their excesses, showed greater humanity than their modern counterparts who appeal to the mystery of science to silence whatever human instinct remains in them.

It is only in the light of revelation that the mystery of the source of life and the sacredness of marriage can be truly appreciated; for only God can make known the fullness of His design for the human couple within the context of His plan for bringing men through Christ to Himself. Only God can indicate to us the goal towards which the pagan cults were obscurely and vainly striving; only He can say why marriage is a sacrament. We find His word in the Scriptures.

REVELATION OF THE MYSTERY

THE ORIGINAL COUPLE

The idyllic setting of the first two chapters of *Genesis* forms the background for the basic revelation concerning marriage. The mythical form of Chapter Two contains beneath its symbolism the account of the creation and original state of the first man and woman. It provides for Christians, as it did for the Jews, the ideal of marriage in the People of God. Later revelation will build on this.

"Yahweh said: It is not good for man to be alone; let us make him a help like unto himself" (*Gen.*, 2:18). Set above the beast because he was made in the image of God, destined for friendship with Him, Adam could find a companion only in one who was specially fashioned for him by God (*ibid.*, 2:19-22). The editor of the text, putting *Genesis* together at a period when woman's position in society was degraded, when she was considered one of man's material possessions, stresses that in God's plan she was meant to hold a position of dignity in the family as the cherished and unique companion of her husband.

"Adam said: This now is bone of my bones, and flesh of my flesh. . . . Wherefore a man shall leave father and mother, and shall cleave to his wife; and they two shall be one flesh" (*ibid.*, 2:23-24).

The perfect conjugal concord of the two is expressed, again symbolically: "And they were both naked . . . and were not ashamed" (*ibid.*, 2:25). Before their sin the two lived in grace, their wills fixed upon God as the supreme arbiter of their lives and actions; and in that original paradise grace permeated their whole being to the extent that all the inclinations of their nature moved in perfect harmony with their state as children of God. St. Thomas almost betrays the amusement that he must have felt at the suggestion that were it not for sin the human race would have been propagated in some fashion other than at present.[1] Human nature remains what it always was according to the design of God; but in the original state it enjoyed without effort what it now acquires only with discipline, control of all its passions, and in particular control of sexual desire. While his will remained subject to God Adam enjoyed the perfect freedom of his nature, untroubled by disordered concupiscence. Adam's sin, when it was committed, could not have been one of the flesh; his was the graver sin of pride and disobedience.

But after they had sinned, Adam and Eve "perceived themselves to be naked" (*Gen.*, 3:7). The perfect harmony of their nature was lost irrevocably; for them and their offspring concupiscence of all kinds would present a moral difficulty and a trial. The association of the human couple was involved in this fall. It no longer moved in the atmosphere of innocence; from this time onwards it would be marked with sin. It was not that marriage or the reproduction of the species had become sinful in themselves; but human nature was wounded; its natural functions had won a perilous emancipation from the rule of reason and grace. This is one aspect of divine revelation that must necessarily colour the Church's attitude, not simply to sexuality,

---

1. Cf. **Summa theol.**, I, q. 98, a. 1; **ibid.**, a. 2, ad 3: "There would have been nothing praiseworthy about continence if Adam had not sinned. In our present state it is praised, not because it is unfruitful, but because it removes the occasion of disordered sexual desire."

which is only one element, but to all the impulses of human nature. Goodness she recognizes everywhere in divine creation, but only when the order of that creation is preserved or restored. The science-fiction fantasy of the revolt of the machines mirrors exactly the Christian view of sexual activity which has broken away from the control of the human person and which is not regulated by reason and by faith. Man and woman must meet each other as persons and as children of God, not as means of mutual sensual gratification only. The book of *Genesis* pictures vividly the disturbance of original harmony when sin disordered human nature. The woman lost her position of dignity in relation to the man, a dignity that had been given by grace and can be restored only by grace, not by social reforms alone.

The results of the corruption in the relations of the human couple are amply recorded in the Old Testament. Polygamy and divorce were only two of the vices which contaminated their association, even among the Chosen People. Yet it was to this same corrupt society that the ideal of *Genesis* was proposed as representing God's design for marriage. It would have been an impossible ideal, a utopian dream springing from man's unquenchable nostalgia for the earthly paradise, were it not that in divine revelation another theme began to assert itself, a theme which had always formed a muted counterpart to the revelation on conjugal union, but which from now onwards will gradually build up in volume until it dominates the theme of the human relationship, giving the key to its interpretation.

MARRIAGE AND THE ALLIANCE

The promise of redemption from sin follows close on the account of the Fall. Vague and uncertain at first, it gathers definition as the concept of the Alliance between God and Israel, initiated at Sinai, takes a firmer hold on the mind of the Chosen People. Misunderstanding there certainly was among the mass of the people as to the spiritual character of the promised restoration; but there was a constant effort on the part of the prophets to purify the nation's concept of the future messianic kingdom. It is with Osee (8th cent. B.C.) that divine revelation concerning the Alliance and that concerning marriage are seen clearly to flow together to form a harmony and to manifest by their newly-discovered mutual relation the place of each in God's supernatural Providence.

The marriages of Osee with a "wife of fornications" (*Os.*, 1:2) and with an adulteress (ibid., 3:1) express symbolically the fortunes of the Alliance between Yahweh and Israel. The nation has proved herself unfaithful to her divine Spouse, turning from His service to the nature cults of the Chanaanites, "for she said: I will go after my lovers, that give me my bread, and my water, my wool and my flax, my oil, and my drink" (*ibid.*, 2:5). But the image of the patient, forgiving husband reveals the merciful kindness of God towards Israel; He will send her purifying punishments, but when she returns to Him He will receive her with love: "I will espouse thee to me for ever; and I will espouse thee to me in justice, and judgment, and in mercy, and in commiserations" (*ibid.*, 2:19).

The symbol of marriage, which is taken up as a traditional theme by the later prophets (*Ezech.*, 16; *Is.*, 50:1-3; 54:1-6), is used in the Old Testament primarily to illumine the relations between Yahweh and Israel, introducing the lyrical note of the divine loving kindness. But the institution of marriage in its turn receives a reciprocal illumination from the concept of the Alliance. That this interpretation of the symbol in terms of the reality, of the human association in terms of the union between God and His people, is not pure literary artifice is later to be affirmed by St. Paul in the famous passage in *Ephesians*. Nor, indeed, could it be otherwise for precisely by indicating marriage as a human image of union with God by grace the Scriptures make a statement about marriage itself. It must not be forgotten that in Christian marriage the symbolism is constituted, not by any sort of arbitrarily chosen ritual, but by the natural, inter-personal association itself. It is this conjugal union, with all the richness of human experience contained in it, which is a natural institution in its own right, that is pointed out by revelation as an analogy which will bring home to us the meaning of God's relation with His people. And primary among the points of comparison singled out by the prophets are the faithfulness of the partners to one another and the permanence of their union despite all shortcomings or betrayals.

It is here that the true supernatural basis is found for the unity and indissolubility of marriage. Arguments of a social character can be found for these tenets of the Church; but specious counter-arguments of the same kind can be put forward against them, claiming that, at least in exceptional circumstances, the greater good of society and of the individual requires that an impossible union be dissolved, or that no great harm is done by occasional lapses from faithfulness to one's partner. These counter-arguments may be objectively invalid but the extent to which people are guided by reason in these matters is at least debatable. The primary stand of the believer is on faith. It is the divinely-revealed harmony linking marriage with the Alliance which makes known to the believer that divine design for marriage which is defended by the Church. God in the wisdom of His creation has willed that the union of husband and wife should be faithful and perpetual because such is the union which binds Him to His people.

It is the prophets too who indicate the sole hope for the human couple, wounded by sin as they are in their association. The Alliance will be re-established only by the Messiah; the faithfulness of Israel to Yahweh will be won only by him: "I will draw them with the cords of a man, with the bands of love" (*Os.*, 11:4). Though the Mediator's mission will be to restore the human race to friendship with God and therefore will be concerned with bringing all human activity under the rule of grace, his coming will nevertheless have a special significance for that basic unit of human society which most closely mirrors the Alliance. Christ will redeem the human couple; only he can sanctify their union and supply them with the means to make the hard journey back towards the ideal of the earthly paradise of *Genesis*. By restoring grace to the individual, he heals at its root the disease which corrupts human relations. Yet the weakness brought on by sin is left. The man and the woman must look beyond this earth for paradise.

FULFILLMENT OF THE ALLIANCE

In the person of Christ, the Alliance between God and man is brought to undreamed-of-fulfillment. Its terms have now undergone a radical transformation. The human parties to the agreement are no longer held together simply by common nationality or even simply by faith in the divine saving initiative. Those who enter the New Alliance become identified mystically with Christ, the personal embodiment of the Alliance; they are incorporated into his body by faith and baptism and so share in his love for his Father and in his unshakeable faithfulness to Him. Through Christ the conjugal harmony of Eden is restored to the relationship between man and God; this is a restoration of the harmony which was reflected in the idyll of Adam and Eve. The Church is the New Eve, Christ's Spouse, bone of his bone, flesh of his flesh, taken from his side as he slept on the cross (cf. *Gen.*, 2:23; *Jn.*, 19:34). The Church is the body of Christ because she receives all her graces from him and stands justified before the God of the Alliance, made worthy in His sight through the merits of Christ. The Church is the Spouse of Christ because in him the eternal love of God for mankind has become incarnate so as to make possible the Church's response of love.

St. Paul reinterprets the marriage theme in terms of this new intimacy given the Alliance through Christ. It is almost by accident, as he outlines the obligations of married Christians, that he is led to this restatement of the prophecies in the light of their fulfillment. He gives new formulation to the ideal of conjugal union. The model is no longer the preliminary, symbolic harmony of the original couple in the earthly paradise of innocence; it is now the association between Christ and the Church, marked on his side by redemptive love, on the side of the Church by repentant faithfulness. If the serenity of the conjugal perfection of the the first couple is beyond the grasp of redeemed humanity, there is now a higher perfection to be won, a fullness of union with God, by the very living of its human image, marriage, with all its richness and with all its frustrations.

"Husbands, love your wives, as Christ also loved the Church, and delivered himself up for it." "As the Church is subject to Christ, so also let the wives be to their husbands in all things" (to the extent, that is, that the husband is the reflection of Christ; *Eph.*, 5:25, 24). The degradation of woman consequent on sin is here seen to be foreign to Christianity; the relations of the sexes are restored to nobility by the mission of Christ. But St.

Paul develops further the parallel, going beyond the range of simple metaphor and moral teaching. The theme of the prophets comes to his mind and the centre of his thought is transferred from marriage to the nuptial relation of Christ and the Church. He quotes Adam's praise of Eve: "For this cause shall a man leave his father and mother; and shall cleave to his wife, and they shall be two in one flesh" (*Gen.*, 2:24); and goes on: "This is a great sacrament; but I speak of Christ and the Church" (*Eph.*, 5:31-32). This is the final and most complete revelation on the nature of marriage within the context of God's saving plan. It is not said explicitly that marriage is one of the seven sacraments (this is "insinuated" according to the Council of Trent); it is the traditional idea of "image" that is foremost in St. Paul's mind. The explicit reference to Adam's love song and its interpretation in terms of the mystery of Christ suggests that marriage, the relation of the sexes, was established from the beginning in function of the redemptive Incarnation, as a natural image, that is to say, of the union of Christ and the Church.

Thomists especially must give this last statement a very subtly nuanced explanation. It must not be understood as prejudicing in any fashion the absolute distinction which obtains between the natural order and the supernatural. The marriage contract as the basis of a natural institution has its own intrinsically natural purpose in the propagation of the human race and the conjugal association of man and woman. The union of Christ and the Church belongs to that scheme of things freely willed by God to bring men a wholly gratuitous share in the life of the Blessed Trinity, a life which lies utterly beyond the natural aspirations of humanity or of any creature. Accordingly, it is not being suggested that marriage as such demands to be fulfilled by a higher union of love between God and mankind; marriage is not essentially an image of the mystery of Christ. Likewise, there is no implication that the order of nature as such (abstracting, that is, from God's free choice to elevate man to the order of grace) demands to be crowned by the Incarnation of the Word, as though without this the universe would lack something of its due perfection. But, while holding firmly to these basic Thomistic tenets, we may still maintain that in the present dispensation of divine Providence marriage is indissolubly linked with the Alliance. For the Incarnation was not an afterthought of God; it was from eternity an integral part of the divine plan for creation. Thomists will rightly insist that the sources of revelation indicate that the "motive" for the Incarnation is redemption; what they mean by that is that only by permitting man to sin could God's wisdom justify the Word's becoming man. But the whole plan, with all its parts, is willed by God in a supremely simple act which coordinates all the diverse elements entering into the history of creation. The order of nature was designed by God as one which in man would be raised from sin by a redemptive Incarnation; the perfection to be given creation by the Christian economy was in view when God made men to His own image and when He made them male and female. The first Adam was from the beginning, before time began, the type of the second Adam, reproducing as head of the human race what Christ was to be as Head of the mystical body. Marriage, as a natural institution, designed for the transmission of human nature, reproduced at its own level the characteristics of the Alliance between God and mankind which was to propagate that sharing in the divine nature given by Christian grace. Human love, the image of divine love, was to be fruitful in children, sharing the nature of the father. The fatherhood of God is the supreme model of all fatherhood; from it "all paternity in heaven and earth is named" (*Eph.*, 3:15). The image of Himself which the Creator has reproduced in marriage cannot but be an intimation of the fatherhood which He extends to His adopted sons. The love which binds husband and wife must hint at the love which God has for His chosen people.

A SACRAMENT

MARRIAGE AND THE ALLIANCE IN NEW HARMONY

Between the time of Adam's sin and the coming of Christ, marriage and the Alliance, in spite of their similarity of structure, were at cross-purposes. In the state of innocence there would have been perfect co-ordination, the child of human love being born in grace, an adopted son of God; but this harmony of the natural and the supernatural was disrupted by sin, just as was the interior harmony of the individual. The child was born in sin, and only among the Chosen People, as a foreshadowing of what was to come with the Church, was he destined to become a son of God by means of a ceremony which formed part of the ritual of the religious society of his parents. With Christ's establishment of the Church the co-ordination of marriage and the Alliance is restored, though not in the perfect fashion of Eden.

As members of the Church by baptism, the partners of Christian marriage have entered the New Alliance with God in Christ. As individuals they have risen with Christ and, in spite of failings, until they renounce faith in him they remain members of the society of salvation, orientated by their baptism towards eternal happiness. Their marriage is consequently one of members of Christ's body. "Know you not," demands St. Paul when reproving sexual licence, "that your bodies are the members of Christ? . . . Or know you not that your members are the temple of the Holy Ghost, who is in you, whom you have from God; and you are not your own?" (*I Cor.*, 6:15, 19). Marriage belongs to Christ. The natural function of Christian marriage, the propagating of the human race, is elevated to the role of building up the mystical body. It is for this reason that the natural contract has been made a sacrament, one of the seven rites of the Church directed towards promoting the worship of God. It is true that the children of Christian marriage are still born in original sin so that human love is not the immediate instrument of that divine love which makes the child of man a child of God. But when this marriage is seen in its full context as a function of the Church entrusted to two of her members then it is realized that it is the Church, the mother of all the living, who is the true mother of the child. It is she who, through the two sacraments of marriage and baptism, bears the child into the New Alliance, into the fullness of life, both human and divine. The love of husband for wife and that of Christ for his Church are made fruitful in one child, an adopted son of God.

Christian marriage is a great sacrament, not simply because it reflects the relationship between Christ and the Church, but as

well because it co-operates in making the love of Christ for his
Bride effective. By making it a sacrament and thus part of the
structure of the Church, Christ restored to it a participation
in the perfection of marriage in the earthly paradise (cf. Pius
XI, Encyc. *Casti connubii*, CTSE ed. § 14). Children born of a
sacramental marriage are already directed sacramentally towards
baptism. Whether this is sufficient for their salvation when baptism cannot be administered is a question which occupies theologians at the present time. It is hardly necessary to add that the
partners of a true Christian marriage do not contribute mere
physical existence to the birth of a child of God. They too belong
to the Church who gives grace through baptism and bear their
child again by faith in the baptismal font; and theirs is the task
of nurturing their "godchild."

THE GRACE OF MARRIAGE

The partial return to the harmony of Eden is not confined
to the bearing of children of God, though this constitutes the
primary end of Christian marriage. The conjugal association of
man and woman is itself raised by the sacrament from the corruption attached to it when the interior harmony of human
nature was lost through Adam's sin.

"He that loveth his wife loveth himself. For no man ever
hated his own flesh; but nourisheth and cherisheth it, as also
Christ doth the Church" (*Eph.*, 5:28-29). A new, wholly supernatural sense is here discovered in the "two in one flesh" of
Genesis. The mutual assistance of husband and wife extends
into the world of grace, for both are members of the body of
Christ and are united with one another there. As ministers of
the sacrament, they give themselves, each to the other, as a
grace from Christ. There is something eucharistic about the
sacrament in the sense that each partner finds in the other the
permanent presence of a sanctifying gift from God. Husband
and wife are for one another an abiding external grace, that
is to say, an occasion of drawing closer to God; and this is
something which remains true whether their association is one
that men would judge happy or not. It is normal that this external grace of the sacrament be accompanied by interior sac-

ramental grace to make holy their union. Besides this, their official position in the visible structure of the Church orientates all the graces they receive towards the life they live in common. Their sacramental grace has a special conjugal quality, regulating and ennobling the whole range of their mutual relations. The tendency of this grace is to restore progressively the interior harmony of the person, at once eliminating sinful concupiscence and promoting the habitual subordination of sensual desire to the rule of Christ. This is a tendency only; if it is to develop all its potentialities there must be responsible cooperation on the part of the man and the woman. They are called on often enough to make agonizing decisions in their married life; what may appear to the unbeliever as an intolerable renunciation will be recognized by the eye of faith as growth in true conjugal perfection. The union of the couple is consummated at its highest level in charity which must permeate human love in all its manifestations. Here the marriage merges wholly with the Alliance and, even if childless, is fruitful in building up the body of Christ.

The Church has another external grace to offer her married children: the religious orders and congregations whose members have renounced marriage. The place of honour given dedicated virginity in the Church, very far from casting any reflection on marriage, is a constant witness to its holiness. Those who have renounced marriage for the sake of Christ have as their exclusive ideal that conjugal association between Christ and the Church which forms the basis for the sanctity of Christian marriage. The mystery of charity which religious are attempting to live underscores the values of conjugal love in the Christian family. The wedding-dress of the nun as she goes to receive the habit is not just a concession to feminine sentimentality; hers is to be a true marriage, one that is at the centre of all marriages and one that proclaims to the world the qualities of faithfulness and indissolubility which belong to all marriages. The vow of chastity bears witness to the reality of the infused virtue of chastity given by Christ to all his members who are united to him in charity. Chastity is the virtue of the married as well as of the unmarried; it brings conjugal union as well as celibacy under the rule of Christ. It is the power that God gives to those united to Him, enabling them to give sexuality its proper place in the life of a child of God. Chastity cannot but mean renunciation, not of any truly human values, but of all inhuman use of sex and of all that is contrary to the inspirations of the Holy Spirit. The total renunciation involved in religious life is a powerful assertion of the Church's belief in the strength and nobility of chastity. One function of the religious orders is to bring this profession of faith before the eyes of those who are married. The same ultimate ideal is set before all Christians. Religious life is a constant reminder of what lies at the heart of Christian love. If we recall what has been said about the character of confirmation it will be seen how the power of Christ works through this public witness of religious so that it is an active influence in the Church preserving the sanctity of the married state.

MARRIAGE AND THE PASSION

The Church is romantic about marriage because she knows its place in the love story of God and humanity. But she knows too a great deal about the way in which grace works and the effects of original sin. If she is romantic about grace she is aware too of the rigour of its demands on weak humanity. She knows the torments of a divided conscience; she realizes with compassion how few of her children understand that the happiness she speaks about in marriage is a prize to be won, not a gift at the altar-rail. Christian marriage is made in heaven for it is a sacrament; it must be lived and can be broken on earth. It is a part of the Christian life and demands the same patient effort, the same struggle to be integrally human, as any practice of virtue. St. Paul's picture of the Christian family is not reproduced by a stroke of the pen on the marriage register; it must be painted in, detail by detail, in a lifetime of dedication.

Marriage is a sacrament; this means that those who receive it enter in a new way into the passion of Christ. St. Thomas comments that this is by reason, not of the pain of Calvary, but of the love manifested by Christ there. But the love of Christ was one that accepted suffering and rejection; marriage may make a like demand. The Christian family is dedicated to the suffering Heart of Christ by the sacrament itself. His was a heart that knew how to love with all the powers of human nature, emotional as well as spiritual—"See how he loved him," said the Jews when he wept before the tomb of Lazarus, his friend (*Jn.*, 11:35-36); but the joys of human companionship shared a place in his heart with the sorrows that his friends and brethren brought him.

If human love should fail in marriage, the sacrament remains with all its demands of fidelity and permanence. Human reason alone will never understand this; only by revelation do we see that it has meaning in terms of God's unfailing love for mankind. In the light of that revelation we may discover too a spirituality even for the separated partners of a broken marriage. There is a union to be sought with the God of the Alliance, abandoned by the Chosen People, stern in condemnation of wrong-doing, but eternally faithful to His promises. "In a moment of indignation have I hid my face a little while from thee, but with ever-lasting kindness have I had mercy on thee, said the Lord thy Redeemer" (*Is.*, 54:8). "Thou shalt wait for me many days; thou shalt not play the harlot, and thou shalt be no man's; and I also will wait for thee" (*Os.*, 3:3). There is a call here to enter, in spite of past failings, beyond the ruins of the earthly image to the reality of the all-encompassing love of God. It is the sacramental grace of marriage that will make this heroic virtue possible.

This is a great sacrament; but a sacrament for the confirmed Christian, one who bears the character of confirmation and is deputed by the Church to bear witness to Christ.

11 Penance: Sorrow in Christ

One of the simplest and the best ways for a person to discover whether he appreciates the doctrine of the mystical body, not just as an abstract idea, but as a guiding influence in his life, is for him to question himself on his attitude to confession. It does not matter if he finds the telling of his sins to a fellow-man distasteful; if he did not, there would probably be something unbalanced in his character. The test questions are, firstly, whether he realizes why Christ instituted such an apparently difficult way of reconciling the sinner to God, and, secondly, whether he makes use of the opportunity given him by the sacrament to enter seriously and whole-heartedly into living the doctrine of the mystical body. It is one thing to slip into the confessional and to get the business over with the minimum of trouble, another to take part in the sacrament with a full awareness that the ceremony forms one of the most typical and potentially one of the most fruitful activities of the Church.

CONFESSION AND THE MYSTICAL BODY

STRUCTURE AND INTERIOR LIFE

Confession is one of the most typical activities of the mystical body precisely because of that character which makes it one of the least attractive of the sacraments. It requires that the most intimate secrets of the Christian's life be brought out into the open, and confessed to a minister of the Church. There is nothing particularly Christian about the unattractiveness of this; what is important is the externalization of what is interior. This is the logical consequence of the form that Christian life has been given by its founder; it is a life flowing from the Holy Spirit who is given only through the visible structure of the Church. It is not a "spiritual" life in the sense that it can be reduced to a lonely communion between the soul and God; it must always be humanized, finding its bearings by reference to an external norm and seeking for expression in official ceremonies. The study of the other sacraments has shown that this applies to the beginning of the Christian life, to its growth and to its perfection on earth; it applies also to its restoration when it has been lost by sin.

It is this constant link which must be maintained between what is interior and what is visible in the Church that makes the mystical body what is it. The nature of this body is, then, misunderstood if either of its elements is divorced in practice from the other. Nowhere is this more clearly seen than in the sacrament of penance. The liturgical ceremony does not dispense with sincere interior sorrow and repentance; but neither, on the other hand, is the interior return to God sufficient of itself; it must be externalised, ratified and stabilised by the sacrament.

While this point may be appreciated, a lurking suspicion may remain that perhaps logical consistency has been preserved throughout the whole scheme of Christian life at the expense of sympathy for man's natural repugnance to reveal his faults. In the view of the majority of Protestants the reconciliation of the sinner with God takes place in the hidden places of a man's heart where no other creature has the right to intrude. In so far as there is widespread belief outside the Church that the sacra-

ment is considered by Catholics as a substitute for interior conversion, this insistence on the need for a sincere return to God
is not only understandable, but commendable also for it represents a certain truth of Christianity. But for the Church the
added necessity of the sacrament is also a revealed truth which
cannot be set aside simply because it is not very attractive or because its usefulness is not immediately apparent. The task that
the sincere Catholic must set himself is the discovery of the advantages that are his by reason of Christ's insistence that he seek
forgiveness of his sins through the visible Church.

HOW IT BEGAN

The details of the Gospel description of the institution of
penance indicate very clearly the attitude to the sacrament that
Christ wished to encourage in his disciples. The scene is the
supper room in which the Eucharist, the sacrament of love, had
been given to the Church; the day is Easter Sunday. The whole
setting speaks of the richness of the messianic age and of the
loving mercy of God. The risen, glorified Christ comes among the
disciples though "the doors were shut" (*Jn.,* 20:19). It is no more
than an accommodated sense, yet we might take the closed doors
which present no barrier to the risen Saviour as a symbol of the
unimportance of the human difficulties that surround the practice
of confession. The possible shortcomings of the minister of the
sacrament constitute no obstacle to Christ's entry into the soul of
the penitent. With the power that is now his he can make use even
of an unsympathetic confessor to bring peace and comfort to
the sinner. "Peace be to you" is the greeting of the risen Christ
and, as he extends to his apostles the mission which he himself
has received from his Father, he breathes on them: "Receive ye
the Holy Ghost."

It is by means of this visible mission of the Spirit that the
apostles receive the power to judge sinners in the name of Christ
and to forgive them their sins. Now the apostles share in Christ's
power to give the Spirit. When they and those whose priestly
power derives from them pronounce the words of absolution
the love of God will be breathed into the sinner, restoring him
to his lost divine sonship.

The sacrament must be seen against this Easter background as the instrument of divine love. Its use may involve difficulties; however distasteful they may make it, they have been devised by God in His love to serve His Providence for His children.

ANALYSIS OF THE SACRAMENT

THE SIGN-ACTION

Simple though it is in its administration, the sacrament of penance poses some very subtle problems for the theologian who attempts to analyse its structure. The history of its theology is bewildering in the variety and complexity of opinions put forward and constitutes a specialized field in itself. Here nothing more will be attempted than to outline St. Thomas's approach to the sacrament, using this as a basis for certain practical suggestions.

Penance is like baptism in that it is responsible for justification, the transit of a person from the state of sin to friendship with God based on grace; but while baptism is intended primarily for first justification, that is, liberation from original sin, and for entry into the Church, penance restores the member of Christ to grace after personal sin for which he now has sorrow. This sets penance apart from all the other sacraments, including baptism, as regards both its effect and its sign-structure. Its purpose is not to bestow a richness of grace or confer an ecclesiastical office; it achieves reconciliation of the sinner to God. What is primarily signified in the other sacraments is a new divine initiative which brings advancement in the life of the mystical body through a new divine gift to man: increase of grace, function in the Church, a marriage partner. Consequently, the principal element in the visible structure of these sacraments is the handing over of a symbolic object to the recipient or the action of the minister on his body. Penance is more complicated. Its ceremonial structure must represent symbolically the extremely complex interplay of divine and human actions which enter into the justification of the adult sinner who is already a member of Christ by baptism. Exactly the same spiritual process is involved in the justification of an adult through baptism; but in baptism the sacramental sign-action focuses on the gratuitousness of incorporation into Christ. In penance, on the contrary, the focus shifts to the willing return of the sinner to God. Justification remains the work of God; but in no case does it dispense with the responsible adult's whole-hearted co-operation; and it is this human aspect which is emphasized in penance. Accordingly, the ceremony, which reflects the inward event, is made up of actions of both minister and penitent, each contributing an essential element which corresponds to his own part in the interior restoration of grace.

The priest's role in the specifically sacramental moment of confession is to speak the words of absolution. Here he acts as the intermediary through whom God and Christ in his humanity give sanctifying grace to the repentant sinner. This is the sacramental representation and realization of the divine initiative in justification.

The penitent's part is to provide for the ceremony such external actions as signify his interior preparedness for the gift of grace. He must show signs of sorrow; he must confess his sins verbally or by some other sign; he must indicate his willingness to make some kind of recompense for his wrong-doing. This is the sacramental representation of human co-operation in justification. Obviously, if the sacrament is to be effective, the penitent must be sincere about these external acts; but the sacramental ceremony (*sacramentum tantum*) is formed of the external acts as such.

The whole sacrament, the visible sign of justification, is in this way built up from the words or other perceptible signs of both priest and penitent. At this visible or audible level, where the interior event of grace is symbolically acted out, the structure of the sacrament is quite clear. Since in justification the divine intervention is primary, the words of absolution are·called, by analogy with the other sacraments, the "form" or determining element of the sign, while the penitent's three acts are termed the "matter," that is, the element of the sign-action which draws its full significance from the "form." The relationship which obtains between "form" and "matter" on the level of signification corresponds to that between the action of God and the co-operation of man at the level of grace. As preparation for this essential sacramental moment of justification when the priest imparts absolution there is a preliminary judicial process during which the minister determines the extent of guilt, on the basis of the penitent's confession, and assigns a fitting punishment.

ATTRITION AND CONTRITION

While the visible sacrament is constituted by external actions of the penitent and the minister, it is clear that, if it is to be fruitful, it requires sincerity on the part of both. Apart from the intention regularly required of the minister and recipient of a sacrament, this implies authentic sorrow for sin in the penitent. Now, while psychological awareness of sorrow will vary widely from individual to individual, ranging from an intensely felt horror of sin as an offence against the goodness of God to a quite unemotional recognition of the penalties attached to it and a consequent determination to renounce evil, there are in fact only two possible objective states in which the penitent can find himself. Either he is in the state of grace or he is not. In the opinion of the medieval theologians the former case is of more frequent occurrence; and this seems reasonable enough if we think of the sincere Christian who, as soon as he is aware of having sinned gravely, turns to God with repentance, begging His forgiveness, and makes up his mind to go to confession as soon as possible. Nevertheless, the model case for a theological explanation of the sacrament is that of a conscious penitent in mortal sin; this case serves to illumine the other which, if not in fact more frequent, is certainly more commendable.

There is an essential difference in quality between the sorrow of one who is in the state of grace and that of a person in a state of grave sin. The first is inspired by charity; the second cannot be for, lacking grace, there is no charity in the sinner. It is on this basis that Thomists distinguish between contrition and attrition, the former implying charity, the latter not. Other theologians make the same distinction in terms; but many of them base it on a diversity of motives, contrition being defined as sorrow for sin arising out of a sense of God's offended goodness, attrition as sorrow springing from fear of punishment. While these two ways of expressing the distinction may come to the same thing, the Thomistic formulation, by indicating the fundamental and objective difference between the two forms of sorrow, avoids the vagueness necessarily attendant upon a distinction based on psychological factors. What is accepted by all theologians, because taught by the Council of Trent, is that attrition is sufficient for approaching the sacrament of penance worthily. This is the case of the sinner who submits to the sacrament sincerely. The external actions of such a penitent signify his imperfect sorrow; and this is sufficient on his part for ensuring that the sacrament is efficacious.

INTERMEDIARY EFFECT (RES ET SACRAMENTUM) AND FINAL EFFECT (RES TANTUM)

Pursuing our examination of the model case, we can develop the mode of efficacy of the sacrament by analogy with the other sacraments. In them there is an immediate or intermediary effect (*res et sacramentum*) and a final effect (*res tantum*). The clearest example is baptism where the intermediary effect is the character and the final effect is the grace of regeneration. Having this framework of sacramental signification and causality before his mind, St. Thomas states that the immediate effect of penance is contrition, or perfect sorrow, flowing, that is, from charity, and that the final effect is forgiveness of sin. Still maintaining the sacramental point of view, he goes on to relate the three levels in terms of causality. The sacrament (*sacramentum tantum*), that is, the words of absolution and the external acts of the penitent, is the cause of the perfect contrition (*res et sacramentum*); and these two together are the cause of forgiveness of sin (*res tantum*) (*Summa theol.*, III, q. 84, a. 1, ad 3).

At a superficial reading it may appear that St. Thomas has yielded here to the temptation to force the event of sacramental forgiveness into preconceived and artificial categories. In particular, to say that perfect contrition is the cause of forgiveness of sin looks suspiciously like putting the cart before the horse. But superficial reading will not do when St. Thomas is the writer. What is essential to grasp, first of all, if there is not to be confusion is that St. Thomas is working out the meaning of penance by analogy with the other sacraments; and consequently he singles out an immediate effect of the sacrament corresponding exactly to the symbolism of the visible ceremony, and this he makes responsible, in unison with the visible sacrament, for the final effect. Now, the external rite is composed of the penitent's profession of sorrow for the sins confessed and the minister's words of absolution; the sacrament, that is, focuses on the validating of the penitent's sorrow. It is quite true that the penitent's sins cannot be forgiven unless grace is granted to him, and this, accordingly, is the final effect of the sacrament. Nevertheless, grace is, as it were, filtered to the penitent through the sacrament; the effect is produced in conformity with the symbolism of the external rite. This means that the emphasis of the grace given, its salient aspect, is the power which it gives to the penitent of making an act of perfect contrition. Without the gift of grace there cannot be perfect contrition; yet at the same time this contrition has a part in procuring the justification of the sinner. Hence it may be said to act with the visible sacrament as a cause of grace; but what this means can be discovered only by further investigation.

The next step is to try to penetrate to the real happening St. Thomas is talking about. What he is doing is very easily explained: he is relating the process of justification to the structure of the sacrament. He wants us to see how the sacrament achieves justification by bringing the power of Christ to bear on the penitent's capacity to make an act of contrition. Confession is a sacrament of forgiveness, yes; but it achieves its purpose by making a responsible adult genuinely repentant. The human person, with his freedom and moral responsibility, is the central figure in the sacrament. Certainly, it is God who, in His mercy, draws the sinner back to Himself; but He does draw Him, respecting the nature which He has given him. We lose all the profundity of St. Thomas's insight into the intimate assimilation of grace into human liberty if we are content to think of grace being "restored" to man, as it were by brute force, from above, without any regard for the kind of being man is. On the contrary, man's sorrow for sin is indispensable; it is an essential and positive element in forgiveness.

The theology of justification which forms the background to the present problem has been seen in Chapter Six. There the mutual dependence of grace and the movement of free will in the conscious adult was explained and the necessary qualifications were introduced to account for worthy reception of the sacraments by those incapable of an act of charity or perfect contrition. Without perfect contrition of some kind sin cannot be forgiven; or, looked at in another way, forgiveness of sin implies perfect contrition, for sin is forgiven only when grace is infused; and the presence of grace means that sorrow for sin is inspired by charity. Such sorrow *is* contrition. When a penitent approaches confession worthily he infallibly receives grace and therefore contrition. It may be that, for one reason or another, he does not make an *act* of contrition when the words of absolution are pronounced; but the habit is certainly infused. As has been noted in Chapter Six, a conscious adult recipient, if he is to personalize the gift of charity must sooner or later make an act of charity. The ideal situation, and the one immediately envisaged by the sacramental structure of confession, is that this act should be made while absolution is being given. This in fact is the case with the sincere penitent who is not distracted at this moment.

Accordingly, in the model case of penance which we are considering, where the penitent approaches the sacrament with mortal sin but with attrition, and where all the necessary conditions are fulfilled, the sacrament infallibly justifies the sinner. The sacrament, applying the power of Christ's saving mysteries, brings sanctifying grace to the penitent; but it does this in a manner proportioned to the symbolism of the ritual and to the individual moral responsibility of the penitent. The grace is given in such a way that the penitent has true perfect contrition; and this contrition, though an effect of sanctifying grace, and though, consequently, presupposing forgiveness of sin, still enjoys a certain priority over grace. It is prior in so far as contrition is the subjective disposition for receiving grace and in so far as the sacrament is focused on effecting forgiveness of sin through this disposition. This is what is implied in St. Thomas's designating perfect contrition as the immediate effect (*res et sacramentum*) of penance.

The obligation of confession is meant in the first place to introduce the Christian to an instinctive grasp of the truth which

lies at the heart of this abstruse theological reasoning. No effort
of will can suffice of itself to turn the sinner back to God. The
simple fact of having to seek absolution from Christ's earthly
representative brings home this deep truth of the primacy of
divine grace in the Christian life. At the same time, the necessity
of genuine sorrow for sin in confession puts in simple terms the
mystery of God's mercy. God gives His gift in absolute freedom;
it is one aspect of His gift that His creature should freely respond to the call of His love and by so doing make himself
worthy of the gift.

With the giving of grace the sacramental ceremony becomes
the outward sign of the mercy of God meeting with the interior
repentance of the sinner. This moment represents the activity
of the mystical body in one of its ideal phases. Particularly
when the penitent actually makes an act of contrition during the
absolution, there is an instant of absolute harmony between the
inner life of the Spirit and the visible fabric of the Church, the
sacrament of Christ. It is meaningless here to speak of substitut-
ing purely formal ceremonial for sincere repentance; one merges
wholly with the other, the ritual throwing into clear relief the
co-operation between God and man which is at the heart of the
sacrament.

Thomists have sometimes been accused of rigorism because
of their insistence on the necessity of perfect contrition in the
sacrament of penance. It should be clear from our analysis of
justification that there are no grounds for such a charge. With
equal justice one could accuse a cook of being a rigorist because
he insists that eggs are needed to make an omelette. The source
of the confusion about penance is that non-Thomists define perfect contrition in psychological terms as sorrow which is mo-
tivated by love for God. They rightly stress that not every
penitent need be conscious of such sorrow. Thomists do not disagree with this; they simply state that forgiveness of sins necessarily implies perfect contrition—actual or habitual—because it
is brought about by an infusion of charity. The sorrow of one
in charity, we repeat, *is* perfect contrition, no matter how little
such a person is aware of his love for God as a conscious motive.

Nor do Thomists see any advantage in setting aside St.
Thomas's clear perception of the relative primacy of perfect con-

trition among the effects of penance in favour of identifying the immediate effect (*res et sacramentum*) as reconciliation with the Church. Not only does this alternative concept destroy the subtly-fashioned harmony established by St. Thomas between the reality of justification and the sacrament; it also deprives the sacrament of any real causality in respect of grace. The sacrament may well reconcile the sinner with the Church; but it is the visible ceremony (the *sacramentum tantum*) which has this juridical effect. Many theologians, it would appear, are led to reject St. Thomas's teaching because they think there ought to be something in penance corresponding to the character of baptism—a *res et sacramentum* which is not grace but in some fashion calls for grace. This is to confuse the analogy which certainly exists between the sacraments with strict reduplication. St. Thomas himself passed through this stage of theological thinking when, in his twenties, he was a young lecturer in Paris. But when he had reached his full development he was quite ready to acknowledge the extraordinary diversity of the seven sacraments existing within their common characteristics. He was nearing the end of his life when he wrote that section of the tract on penance which closes his unfinished *Summa theologiae*. His teaching on the immediate effect of the sacrament represents his mature thought. It is besides a general norm for reading St. Thomas that when he says something unexpected it is worth while to take the trouble to search out patiently his point of view.

THE PENITENT

The recitation of the act of contrition normally supplies the penitent's external participation in the central moment of the sacrament; but in exceptional circumstances any sign of repentance will suffice. Probably, though this is not certain, even the mere bodily presence of an unconscious person who has been baptized and who has at some time indicated his desire for the sacrament constitutes adequate external participation. The element of doubt raises some question about the efficacy of absolution of an unconscious person; for this reason it is important that in such a case, when there is danger of death, the sacrament of anointing be administered for it does not require the same active external participation as penance.

The attitude of mind required in the penitent at the moment of absolution is summed up by the word "repentance." St. Thomas points out that this means more than sorrow for sins; charity would be sufficient for that. What gives repentance its own character is the readiness to make reparation which it implies in addition to sorrow, for there are requirements of justice to be met by the sinner who has offended his Creator. To be repentant means that one is prepared to make satisfaction for the offence (III, q. 85, a. 3). Since the only adequate satisfaction ever made for sin was the suffering of Christ, Christian repentance must call upon the resources of the passion. Only if we believe that we can benefit from the reparation for sin which was offered by Christ can we be truly repentant. Without this faith in Christ our repentance would be either hypocrisy or illusion, for we would be promising to do something utterly beyond our powers. It is only because we are conscious of our union with Christ that we dare to say we are repentant, ready to make atonement through his sufferings.

The sacrament of penance assists faith in this, providing a new means of union with Christ, granting us a new way of sharing in his infinite reparation. The sacraments always provide such a new and life-giving link with that great work of Christ which is the sinner's foundational claim on the justice and mercy of God. As we have seen already with each of the other sacraments, the sacramental link with Christ presupposes that of faith, giving to it a new richness because providing the believer with corporeal contact with the saving mysteries. It is because the penitent is confident that Christ has already restored the order of justice in man's relations with God, has atoned for all the sins of the world, that he can presume to enter the confessional with the certainty that his sins will be forgiven if he is sincerely sorry for them. The sacrament is founded on this belief. There is, consequently, nothing ludicrous about the trifling penance imposed in confession. Any penance, no matter how severe, would be trifling, would be infinitely inadequate, in comparison with the offence. The three Hail Marys or the round of the beads are simply token damages; it is the Church's appeal to the passion of Christ that makes the sinner's act of repentance feasible. The confessional is a unique seat of judgment. Here Christ is judge; but he also speaks for the defence and himself undergoes the punishment.

NECESSITY OF CONFESSION

It is in the light of this link between the sacrament and the passion of Christ that we must try to understand the teaching of the Church that mortal sin cannot be forgiven independently of penance. True enough, if we were left to work out our own theology and had not to have recourse to revelation, we might well suggest that faith alone in the atonement of Christ could suffice to validate the penitent's desire to make reparation. But the Church insists that it is a revealed truth that such a claim may be entered against Christ's sufferings only if—to use a bureaucratic metaphor—it is put through the proper channels, referred in some fashion, that is, to the sacrament of penance.

It is not hard to discover the harmony between this revealed teaching and what we know of the structure of the mystical body. To share in the life of this body faith alone never suffices; by the decision of Christ when he gave over administration of the body to earthly representatives faith must always be sacramentalized, expressed, that is, and nourished through the ritual of the Roman Catholic Church. Accordingly, just as original membership of the body necessarily implies submission to baptism, either actual or in desire, so, and for a like reason, repentance is ineffectual unless brought about by sacramental confession. As in the case of baptism, where adults are concerned, it frequently happens that God grants or restores grace before the sacrament is received. This cannot happen, however, unless the sinner has the intention of submitting to the sacrament when the opportunity is given and of confessing mortal sins not sacramentally absolved. Restoration to grace has been tied, by the will of Christ and in conformity with the condition of fallen mankind, to the sacrament so that forgiveness is absolutely unobtainable without some desire, explicit or implicit, of the sacrament. This is another aspect of the principle: Outside the Church there is no salvation. Wherever a sinner is reconciled to God, the sacrament of penance enters in, even if only as an unrecognized object of desire, implicit in the wish to do all that God requires for salvation.

When the sacrament is received by a person who has already been reconciled with God by an act of perfect contrition none of its efficacy is lost. It brings an increase of grace to the devout penitent; but above all it gives the largest possible measure of security that sin has in fact been forgiven, for its immediate effect is to evoke perfect contrition and to associate the penitent with the atonement of Christ. This is something which is achieved by the sacrament even when the penitent is guilty of no grave sin and confesses only venial faults. Here we have one of the firmest corroborations of the Thomist explanation; for it is difficult to understand what account can be given of such confessions of devotion—in which only venial sins are confessed —by those who see in reconciliation with the Church the immediate effect of the sacrament. No such reconciliation is called for when no grave sin has been committed. By recognizing that the notion of immediate effect (*res et sacramentum*) is an analogical one, and by assigning to penance as its immediate effect something pertaining to virtue, St. Thomas is able to account for any case of sacramental confession that occurs.

ADVANTAGES OF CONFESSION

GUIDANCE

While the essential benefit brought by the sacrament is the security which it gives that sins are forgiven, it has other helps to offer the Christian which derive from those aspects of it which are usually experienced as difficult. The weak or confused conscience can find in it firm and inspired guidance. Even on the most critical judgment, and supposing a total lack of sympathy on the part of the confessor, his words of advice, mechanical though they may sound, represent the accumulated wisdom of the Church, which loses only little of its salutary power when passed on by unheeding lips. But it was Christ's intention that his mercy should be made known to men through the human understanding of his ministers; and it is not to be doubted that the grace of ordination is at work in the confessor, guiding him to find the words which Christ would speak.

The confessor cannot fulfill his role as healer of spiritual illness if the penitent does not, at least when advice is particularly needed, make a sincere manifestation of conscience; and it is here again that the obligation of the sacrament can help: it gives self-knowledge.

SELF-KNOWLEDGE

The examination of conscience required as preparation for confession is meant to open the Christian's eyes to his own state of soul. The necessity of making a detailed presentation of faults leaves no room for any vaguely formulated, summary review of lapses. There is something very realistic about this obligation; it reveals the divine pastoral care, and a father's shrewd understanding of his children; for there is little doubt that getting to know our own faults is not a task which many of us relish and we would be content with a very general review of our sinfulness were it sufficient to turn to God in repentance in the secret of our hearts. After confession we are supposed to know fairly clearly how we stand with Christ. That assumes evidently that we have made a responsible examination of conscience. While confessors may judge it prudent to advise in exceptional cases that a penitent should dispense with a searching examination, this is not the rule for the normal Christian. It might be doubted whether manuals of devotion which counsel brief examination of conscience and prolonged attempts to arouse contrition present a true picture of confession. Many of their authors have been influenced, directly or indirectly, by a tradition of rigorism which demanded psychologically perfect contrition of the penitent.

That contrition—or attrition—must be sincere may be taken for granted; but part of the genius of sacramental penance lies in the opportunity it gives for making a detailed, objective appraisal of just how well we are living the Christian life. Though we may not be objective with ourselves, the priest may usually be trusted to help us to become so. This aspect of confession needs to be stressed for those who receive the sacrament frequently and have venial sins only to confess. What they should look for in their examination of conscience is not material for lengthening their litany of faults; they should be making an honest, grown-up assessment of their response to Christ. The litany of sin is something that was got off by heart from the First-communion manual and it will begin to tick over in our mind as a reflex action when we kneel down outside the confessional. It is almost inevitable that this becomes with habit a surface phenomenon of consciousness in which we are not really involved as persons. An adult should be satisfied only with a mature investigation of his Christianity. This means, more than anything else, discovering the deeper motives behind the silly sins which register almost automatically on our conscience. To tell a confessor that one has been uncharitable or impatient is from this point of view as useful as telling a doctor that one has a temperature. Something is obviously wrong; but so far only a symptom common to a variety of maladies has been reported. Not much in the way of useful advice may be expected from such a superficial confession. What the penitent should be trying, with the help of the priest, to discover is his own dominant fault, his attitude to God or to his fellows which determines his actions towards them. Perhaps we shall discover that we have no attitude to speak of at all and that we do not much care about the interests of others. In confession the Church herself examines her conscience for we are her failures, all of us who must kneel for absolution. This sacrament is her safeguard against activism, the veneer of apostolicity that covers a profound unawareness of the meaning of Christianity. Once again, without any polemic intent, we may be permitted to wonder whether the layman's new consciousness of his role in the Church is accompanied by heightened appreciation of the functions which he already fulfills, and in particular, of his role as penitent.

HELP OF CHRIST

By instituting the sacrament of penance, Christ has revealed his deep understanding of the needs of human nature. Confession, if properly used, calls into play all the elements which form the human, personalized and individual side of Christianity. Turn the coin, and these same elements are seen to be sacramental and ecclesial also, forming part, that is to say, of the chain of created things through which God intervenes in the individual's life, taking over for Himself the initiative. There is no more striking object-lesson of the theology of grace or of the nature of membership of the Church to be found in the liturgy.

The sacramental side of confession guarantees the human side. It guarantees especially the part played by the minister. Though the priest may sometimes not be equal to the demands made on him for advice or encouragement, Christ, sacramentally present and active, never fails. The grace that he gives in penance is a grace adapted specifically to the individual penitent who presents himself to this sacrament precisely as burdened by his own particular temptations and weakened by his own particular faults. The confession of these faults is a component part of the "matter" of the sacrament; it enters into the construction of the liturgical sign-action; consequently it modifies the sanctifying grace given the penitent. The grace is "tailor-made" for the individual penitent. It is here that the value of frequent confession, even of venial sins only, is primarily to be sought. This is the sacrament which applies the power of the passion of Christ to the moral weakness of his individual members.

12 Anointing: Suffering and Dying in Christ

Something very like a public opinion poll is being conducted at present among theologians on the issue of the sacrament of anointing. The question being canvassed is whether this is a sacrament of the dying or of the sick. The two ideas are obviously not mutually exclusive in all their extension; a sacrament of the sick will be a sacrament of the dying. The point on which theologians are being asked to declare themselves is whether anointing is not meant also for those whose sickness is not such as will normally lead to death.

Lying behind this question about the recipient of the sacrament is a more basic one concerning its effect. The Church affirms that anointing can restore bodily health. While, accordingly, all theologians have incorporated this notion into their accounts of the sacrament's effects, most of them relegate it to a secondary place. But, objects a number of modern writers, does this do justice to the scriptural revelation on anointing in the *Epistle of St. James* (5: 14-15; cf. *Mk.*, 6: 13) and to the usage of the early Church? There the stress was laid on the healing power of the sacrament; and, the argument goes on, the reason why Catholic theology has shifted the emphasis to the spiritual effects of the sacrament, and in particular, to the assistance it gives at the hour of death, is a purely historical one, having nothing to do with the belief or dogma of the Church; theologians have been unduly influenced by a disciplinary prescription which restricts administration of the sacrament to those in danger of death. The suggestion is accordingly put forward that adequate recognition be given the healing effect of the sacrament and the hope is expressed that the Church will modify her present discipline, permitting anointing even when there is no obvious danger of death.

It is of some importance in this discussion to distinguish between the historical research that has led to certain conclusions concerning the practice of the early Church and the inferences drawn from this material by individual theologians. The problem in the terms in which it has been stated has been formulated at this second stage of the theological process.

ANOINTING IN THE EARLY CHURCH

CONCLUSIONS OF HISTORIANS

The principal conclusion which emerges from the historical inquiry is that no evidence can be found that anointing formed part of the rites for the dying before the period of the Carolingian reform (centred on 800). Only one ritual from this period is extant but, since it has only recently been discovered, no account has yet been taken of it by historians in their judgment concerning the period.[1] Positive evidence on early usage is gleaned from texts giving the rites of consecration of the oil and

---

1. Cf. E. Testa, **Scoperta del primitivo rito della Estrema Unzione in una laminella del primo secolo** in "L'Osservatore Romano," January 31, 1963. Bought in January, 1963, from the Bedouins who discovered the scrolls of Qumran, the sheet of silver, dated by the author of the article 70-90 A.D., bears a Judaeo-Christian ritual of the anointing of the sick. The The rite is described as applied to a particular case, that of a man who has gravely injured himself by falling over a cliff. The anointing is by aspersion and the effects are described as physical healing and pardon of sins. The rite closes with a reference to Christ's coming as judge.

from rare references in ancient biographies and in the writings of the Fathers. These all point to a predominant belief in the healing powers of the anointing, in accordance with the passage in *James* on which the practice is based.

From the Carolingian period onwards evidence is abundant; but now anointing has become part of the rites for the dying, linked with penance and viaticum. B. Poschmann explains this development as a consequence of the introduction of a rite of anointing in the reconciliation of a penitent. The reluctance of the faithful to undertake the rigours of the medieval public penance and the consequent postponement of confession—and hence of the possibility of receiving the other sacraments—to the time of death led to a fusing of this penitential anointing with that of the sick so that in the popular mind the latter was connected with the undesirable consequences of the former. A general unwillingness to receive the anointing of the sick was the result. This false idea, in spite of opposition on the part of the Church, held sway particularly from the eleventh to the fifteenth century, so that the name of "extreme unction," introduced in the tenth or eleventh century, was widespread from the end of the twelfth century.[2] Although the text of the ritual retained, and still retains, its emphasis on the healing function of the anointing, actual use of the sacrament became fixed as a prelude to death; and theologians have developed their accounts of the sacrament accordingly. The Council of Trent, in considering the anointing primarily as a help to the dying, conclude the historians, simply accepted the current practice of the Church, while at the same time, by the silences of its decrees, leaving the way open for a return to the earlier tradition.

THEOLOGICAL RELEVANCE OF THESE CONCLUSIONS

Theological interpretation of the sacraments can gain much light from the history of their use in the Church. Proved historical conclusions, however disconcerting at first sight, can only lead to a richer understanding of modern liturgical prac-

---

2. Cf. B. Poschmann, **Busse und Letzte Olung**, Freiburg im B., 1951, pp. 131, 132 (**Handbuch der Dogmengeschichte**, ed. Schmaus etc., B. IV, Fas. 3).

tice. Moreover, when historical specialists pronounce themselves satisfied that their conclusions have been proved as far as available evidence permits, it would be at least imprudent for those engaged in the systematization of revealed truth to reject their thesis out of hand simply because it does not appear to square with present-day practice. While this is so, it cannot be said that the results of the historical enquiry into anointing are wholly satisfying.

The lack of early rituals and the dearth of clearly formulated theological commentary leaves an uncomfortable historical void throughout the first seven centuries and a half. For the believer, and hence for the theologian, this gap in historical evidence is of no immediate concern as far as the existence of the sacrament and its institution by Christ go, since the present teaching of the Church guarantees this much. But when it comes to deciding the precise nature of the early usage it does appear that certain questions remain unanswered by the historians. They admit that several of the documents they bring forward to illustrate practice in the first eight centuries, particularly from the fifth onwards, refer to anointing by the laity.[3] The theologian must assert at once that this could not have been the sacrament; either it was an abuse that had grown up in imitation of the sacrament, or it was a sacramental, as are such lay anointings at the present time.

This difficulty is a radical one for it brings to light a constant source of ambiguity in early references to several of the sacraments. It was not until the twelfth century that the Church had sufficiently reflected on her traditional ritual to be able to formulate clearly the distinction between a sacrament and a sacramental. When agreement was reached that a sacrament is to be defined as a sign of grace, causing grace, it was possible to complete definitively the list of the seven, eliminating several symbolic rituals which could not be said to cause grace. Now, in the case of anointing, when it is clearly considered as a sacrament reserved to priests, after the Carolingian reform, it is

---

3. Cf. P. Palmer, S.J., **Sources of Christian theology**, vol. II: Sacraments and Forgiveness, Westminster, 1959; London, 1960, pp. 283-285, where some of these texts are translated.

shown as a ritual for the dying. This does not exclude the possibility that previously it was something more; but the mere fact that there existed in those early centuries an anointing for all kinds of sickness does not give evidence that it was the sacrament which was so used. It might quite well have been a simple sacramental. Since a sacrament of the dying is now in possession in the practice of the Church, the burden of proof rests on those who dispute this practice.

On the other hand the rituals of consecration of the oil, where there is clearly question of the sacrament, do suggest strongly by their emphasis on the theme of bodily healing that the sacrament was not considered as one to be administered only when death is immediately at hand. This appears to be the most significant conclusion which emerges from the work of the historians.

The question that we are left with is this: even granting the historians' claim that the sacrament of anointing was originally used more widely than at present, what were the limits of its use? Is there sufficient evidence to show that the sacrament itself, and not a sacramental, was used in cases where sickness was not grave? Account must be taken of the state of medicine in the early centuries. An illness which nowadays is a matter of routine treatment would then have meant certain death. In short, though we admit that anointing was not delayed until a Christian was in the death agony, is there any justification for supposing that it was normal practice to administer it when there was no danger of death? The newly-discovered ritual of the first century, with its example of a typical case, points rather in the other direction.

NEED FOR A NEW THEOLOGY OF ANOINTING?

When we come to the second stage of theological enquiry, where inferences are drawn from the evidence supplied by historians, considerable prudence is called for. It is to be regretted that some of the popular presentations of the results of this historical research are notably lacking in this respect. A few writers, untroubled by the dogmatic problems involved, have succumbed to the temptation to pour scorn on the present practice of anointing and on the traditional theology built round it. The majority of theologians who discuss the matter, however, has been more concerned to review the present practice in the light of the suggestions of the historians. One benefit has already emerged from this. Attention has been drawn to the fact that, even when administered to the dying, anointing is a sacrament of sickness, not of death. The unexceptionable conclusion has been drawn that it should be administered, not when a patient has already lapsed into unconsciousness, but at a time when it may be of assistance in suffering. But even among these more prudent writers the suggestion is evident that there is need to elaborate a new theology of anointing to displace that of the traditional theology. The great Scholastics of the thirteenth century are dismissed as having nothing to offer because, it is explained, their entire concept of the anointing derived from the prevailing practice of administration at the latest possible moment.

What recent writers have in mind when they condemn the thirteenth-century theologians and their successors is their teaching that anointing is a sacrament which wins the Christian immediate entry into glory after death. Following on the publication of a book at the beginning of the present century drawing attention to it, this medieval notion enjoyed renewed success and popular writers made much of the idea that anointing could exempt the Christian from Purgatory. On its face value it would be hard to think of anything more opposed to the concept of a sacrament of the sick and this perhaps explains why, now that the reaction has set in, we read sweeping condemnations of anybody who ever subscribed to the theory. But it is surely regrettable that the development of theology should be governed by the same laws as the pendulum. Revelation is the source common to theologians of all centuries; what has been achieved in the past will always be relevant to present problems. In particular, as we hope to show, St. Thomas's account of anointing retains its validity in the context of the new awareness of the sacrament's function during sickness.

Let it be said at once that St. Thomas does teach that anointing is an immediate preparation for heaven. This was the teaching of his predecessors and his contemporaries and he accepted it as harmonizing with the medieval practice of delayed death-bed anointing. But he was very far from teaching that exemption from Purgatory is an automatic consequence of receiving the sacrament. Such a conclusion is wholly foreign to his concept of the sacraments as acts of the Church, adapted to the state of faith; and not only is he aware that they can directly affect the Christian only while he belongs to the Church on earth but, as will be apparent from all that has been said about the other sacraments, he constantly insists on the determining role played by the recipient's devotion. The fact is that St. Thomas's theology of anointing is the theology of a sacrament of the sick. That it was coloured by medieval practice and looked towards death is undeniable; nor, as we have seen, has it yet been proved that there is anything wrong about this. But at the same time it was centred on the sick person precisely as a suffering member of Christ. St. Thomas's is a theology of suffering in the Church; it may be applied either to the suffering which precedes death—in which case it must take account of the Christian significance of death—or to any grave illness. The first application, corresponding to the modern as well as the medieval practice of the Church, St. Thomas makes for us himself; the second, should it ever become necessary as a result of an extension of the use of the sacrament by the simple procedure of eliminating the reference to death. The emphasis which is nowadays being placed on sickness even when the sacrament is administered to those in danger of death is already to be found in St. Thomas. Indeed he clearly envisages as normal that the recipient should be fully conscious when anointed. The ideal situation for him is when the sick person can receive the sacrament with the actual devotion that is called for when going to communion (*Summa theol.*, Suppl., q. 32, a. 4). Anointing is, in fact, a preparation for worthy communion (III, q. 65, a. 3). Without doubt, for St. Thomas this meant the viaticum[4]; but his remark is equally valid when there is ques-

---

4. The Dominican ritual retains viaticum in its original and more correct place as the last of the sacraments of the dying. Several of the new regional rituals approved for the Roman rite return to this order, abandoned since the twelfth and thirteenth centuries. The Second Vatican Council makes a general prescription in this sense (Vat. II Const., ch.3, art. 74).

tion of ordinary communion of the sick. His criterion for judging when the anointing should be administered is as liberal as any proposed by modern theologians. He does not require that death should be objectively at hand; his rule is primarily subjective: the anointing should be given when in the common estimation of men death is approaching (Suppl., q. 33, a. 1, ad 2). It will be understood accordingly why it can be suggested that the new awareness of the role of anointing in sickness can receive light from St. Thomas's teaching. We shall attempt here to give some account of what that teaching is. To appreciate it properly it is necessary to grasp the outline of St. Thomas's theology of sickness and death. With St. Paul he sees them as an integral part of the Christian mystery, drawing their significance from the act of redemption.

REDEMPTION OF THE WHOLE MAN

THE SCANDAL OF SUFFERING AND DEATH

St. Thomas recognizes in the *Summa* only two objections to the existence of God; the first, that there is no need for a Supreme Being; the second, that the fact of evil is incompatible with the existence of a loving divinity. Even the convinced Christian can be brought up short by the second objection when he discovers for himself that personal experience of suffering and death does not square with comfortably vague ideas about God and Christianity. The question must be faced whether pain and mortality are not in conflict with the very idea of redemption.

Perhaps this does not appear to be a problem at all. If we think of Christianity as a spiritual life, then we will be quite prepared to say that Christ redeemed men's souls and to consider bodily suffering and death as irrelevant essentially to progress in Christian perfection. This attitude may promote stoical acceptance of these evils and, since God's sanctifying power is not limited by our failure to understand it, may quite well result in heroic virtue; but intellectually it is a parody of Christianity, a way of life which has nothing to do with stoicism.

If Christ is our Redeemer at all it is because he has saved us from death; and to restrict the sense of death to sin, as though bodily death were a matter of no importance to us, is not simply to misunderstand the meaning of redemption; it is dishonest humanly speaking. Normal people are repelled by the prospect of suffering and death. Christ himself has taught us by his agony in the garden that it is natural to pray that the chalice may pass. Redemption of humanity must mean liberation from bodily death as well as from sin. The plain fact that men are still suffering and dying is a difficulty which is basic to the Christian idea; it is the scandal of Christianity, for it is the apparent proof of the failure of Christ's essential mission.

HEALING OF THE BODY

Christ's miracles of healing, worked while he was on earth, are a manifestation of the humanism of salvation. We are inclined to consider them simply from the apologetic point of view as proofs of his divine origin; but the command, "Take up thy bed and walk," reveals as much about Christ's mission as does "Thy sins are forgiven thee." When he sent his disciples to preach during the period of his own earthly mission, "going forth, they preached that men should repent, and they cast out many devils, and anointed with oil many sick people and healed them" (*Mk.*, 6:13). Repentance for sin and bodily healing go hand in hand; the two belong to the mission of the apostles of Christ as well as to that of Christ himself. The Council of Trent selects this passage from Mark as hinting at the sacrament of anointing because of the reference to oil; but any of the New-Testament accounts of the gift of healing possessed by the followers of Christ serves to reveal the fuller implications of salvation.

Christ's bodily resurrection sets the seal on the message of redemption. Faced with the tendency of his Greek converts to interpret Christianity in exclusively spiritual terms, so much so that they thought they had already come to the Kingdom of God (cf. *1 Cor.*, 4:8), St. Paul insists on the primitive message of Christ's resurrection and demonstrates its relevance for every Christian (*1 Cor.*, 15). Rejecting the false contrast of body with spirit, St. Paul points to Christ's resurrection as the model of Christian salvation (*Rom.*, 8:23, 29-30; *Phil.*, 3:21; etc.). Christ's glorious body rising from the grave begins a new era for humanity; what God has begun in Christ, He will complete in all Christ's members (*1 Thess.*, 4:13; *1 Cor.*, 15:20, 23). More than that, the risen Christ is established with the power to complete the divine plan of resurrection (*1 Cor.*, 15:21-22; 6:14). Christ has proclaimed in his own resurrection his dominion over the body and his mission will be fulfilled only when death and all that belongs to death have been overcome (*1 Cor.*, 15:54-57).

BAPTISM AND BODILY SALVATION

ST. PAUL

A difference of perspective is noticeable between the Gospel accounts of the healing ministry of Christ and his disciples on the one hand and St. Paul's expectation of bodily restoration only at the return of Christ on the other. St. Paul was familiar with the charismatic gift of healing enjoyed by the early Church, but his view of Christianity looks beyond this extraordinary phenomenon to the essential plan of human salvation: "In Christ all shall be made alive. But every one in his own order: the first-fruits Christ, then they that are of Christ in his coming" (*1 Cor.*, 15:23). The Church's mission of salvation, because it concerns the whole man, body as well as soul, is of its nature eschatological; its fulfillment is deferred to the end of time when Christ will come personally to bring its achievement. In the Church on earth the body is always one step behind the soul in the journey towards final union with Christ.

St. Paul's teaching on baptism reflects this view of the economy of salvation. Though the Christian's conformity to the death of Christ is complete because baptism marks a definitive liberation from the slavery of sin, St. Paul does not go so far as to describe the life of grace as a resurrection with Christ: "We are buried together with him by baptism into death, that as Christ is risen from the dead by the glory of the Father, so we also may walk in newness of life" (*Rom.*, 6:4). The risen Christ communicates his life to the Christian when he sends the Spirit of grace; but the closest approach St. Paul makes to saying that this

is a life of resurrection is in *Ephesians*, 2:5: "God who is rich
in mercy, for his exceeding charity wherewith he loved us, even
when we were dead in sin, hath quickened us together in Christ,
by whose grace you are saved." Resurrection in the proper sense
of the word is something which affects man in his whole being
and is not yet within grasp of the Christian though in a transferred sense the life of grace has been named by Christian tradition a life of resurrection.

Between baptism and the return of Christ lies the testing
time of the Christian and his period of waiting for the fullness of
salvation. St. Paul's personal experience and the history of the
Church in the years through which he lived convinced him that
this intervening period is a time of suffering and tribulation. He
sent Timothy to the Thessalonians to preach the sense of faith
in Christ: "That no man should be moved in these tribulations;
for yourselves know that we are appointed thereunto" (*J Thess.*,
3:2-3). St. Paul glories in the Thessalonians' patience and faith
during persecution and suffering "which you endure for an example of the just judgment of God, that you may be counted
worthy of the kingdom of God, for which also you suffer" (*JJ
Thess.*, 1:5). This experience has made them "followers of us
and of the Lord, receiving the word in much tribulation, with joy
of the Holy Ghost" (*J Thess.*, 1:6). "Unto you it is given
for Christ, not only to believe in him, but also to suffer for him"
(*Phil.*, 1:29).

Suffering for Christ is also suffering with him. The period
of trial and expectation is a period of preparation during which
the Christian becomes like Christ, fitting himself for bodily resurrection. The love of God, active through Christ and made effective in baptism, grants to Christians a participation in Christ's
divine sonship: "And if sons, heirs also; heirs indeed of God,
and joint-heirs with Christ; yet so if we suffer with him, that we
may be also glorified with him" (*Rom.*, 8:17). Full resurrection
lies for the Christian, as it did for Christ, beyond the sufferings
of earthly life and beyond the grave. Pain and death, though con-
quered by Christ, still remain to be overcome by the Christian.
The word of Christ which heals bodily ills, though it may be
anticipated in exceptional circumstances, at it was anticipated

during his years on earth, cannot be spoken for the whole mystical body until the mystery is achieved. The loss of all earthly goods means nothing to St. Paul if only he may gain Christ "that I may know him and the power of his resurrection, and the fellowship of his sufferings, being made conformable to his death, if by any means I may attain to the resurrection which is from the dead" (*Phil.*, 3:8-11). The mystery of Christian suffering becomes a vital influence in his apostolic life; it is the source of the fruitfulness of his preaching: "Death worketh in us; but life in you" (*II Cor.*, 4:12; cf. *I Cor.*, 2:1-5; *Col.*, 1:24-29; *Eph.*, 3:1 f.). This is the paradox of the Christian life, a life in which we only participate here on earth, which is to be fulfilled in the future: it is a life in which death works.

ST. THOMAS

St. Thomas does not fail to grasp St. Paul's paradox. In one of his most perceptive insights into the economy of the Christian mystery he writes: "Baptism has the power to take away all the hardships of our present life—hunger, thirst, sickness and death —but it does not in fact take them away during the present life. When the just are finally liberated from them in the general resurrection it will be through the power of baptism" (III, q. 69, a. 3 and ad 2). These words, taking account as they do of one of the principal embarrassments which threaten the composure of the unreflective Christian, penetrate beyond the over-simplified, accepted formulas which are sometimes used to sum up the teaching of Christ. They acknowledge the true meaning of salvation and at the same time admit its present limitations.

While it is natural for man, a material as well as a spiritual being, to die and before that to suffer sickness, the dignity of divine sonship granted to Adam in the earthly paradise was such that it carried with it the gift of bodily immortality and freedom from pain. Christ's restoration of fallen humanity to grace ought to imply the restoration of this gift also. By atoning for sin Christ removed the obstacle forbidding divine love to give that fullness of spiritual and physical life which Adam first enjoyed.

This being so, baptism, the sacrament which incorporates

the individual into Christ as a member of the High Priest who has made full recompense for sin, ought not only to restore divine sonship; it should bring with it the gift of bodily immortality and freedom from suffering which, in the eyes of God, is the fitting state for His adopted sons. St. Thomas recognizes the force of this line of argument and asserts at once that baptism has the power to do all this precisely because it extends to its recipient the life-giving power of Christ's sacrifice. This is one of the least acknowledged and at the same time one of the most significant aspects of baptism. The sacrament draws us into the sphere of Christ, the sphere of redeemed humanity; and Christ redeemed us body and soul. Anything further from stoicism, from toleration of the body and its weakness for the sake of the soul, it would be hard to imagine. By reason of baptism the body is sacred, claimed by the sacrament for Christ.

Yet Christ refrains from asserting his claim; the Christian's body is left subject to the law of sickness and death established by sin. The adopted son of God must bear a congenital weakness of nature and must prepare himself to face a supreme crisis of belief when his faith in Christ will encounter the incontrovertible fact of death, apparent proof of the dominion of evil over his own person.

St. Thomas resolves the paradox in the same fashion as St. Paul, in terms of the mystical body. "By baptism a man is incorporated into Christ and becomes one of his members. We can, accordingly, grasp how reasonable it is that what was borne by the Head should be borne by the member incorporated into him. Now Christ, from the first instant of his conception, was full of grace and truth; in spite of this he had a body subject to suffering which, now that it has passed by the way of the passion and death, has been raised up to the life of glory. In similar fashion the Christian at baptism receives grace in his soul but his body remains subject to suffering, so that in it he may bear suffering for Christ; it too will finally be raised up to immortal life" (III, q. 69, a. 3; cf. *Rom.*, 8:11, 17). In bearing the sufferings of the present life and by conquering the sinful tendencies of his wounded nature the Christian merits for himself the reward which Christ has won for him (ibid.).

SIN AND SUFFERING

The tragedy of suffering and death in Christ and in his members reveals the hidden drama of sin. Christ rejects the over-simplification of the disciples when they ask him about the man born blind: "Who hath sinned, this man or his parents, that he should be born blind?" (Jn., 9:2-3). But though Christ makes it manifest in his own person that the innocent can suffer, sin is at the root of all pain.

Wherever there is suffering there is evidence of the disruption introduced by sin into the original harmony of creation. It was Adam's sin which forfeited for all men the gift of bodily immortality and released the mystery of suffering and death. It was Christ's passion and Mary's compassion which revealed the mystery of atonement for sin. Suffering and death are a punishment that must be borne by the human race; and this is the primary sense that they have for the Christian.

Man's sin cannot touch the infinite perfection of God's happiness; but it is an offence against Him because it implies a rejection of His law and a frustration of His design for creation in the measure that a man can frustrate it. It is in fact man himself who is destroyed by sin; it is his own happiness that he undermines; it is the fulfillment of God's plan in himself which he frustrates. If the mercy of God raises him up from his sin the order of justice must still be restored; there is a penalty to be paid. It is not that God can receive anything from man, or that He finds pleasure in the punishment of His creature. It is man who must be put back into just relations with God. The sinner is like the component of a machine, which has been twisted out of shape in an accident. The part must be bent back to its original form if it is to fit back into its socket and fulfill its proper function in the movement of the machine. The self-indulgence of sin must be counter-balanced by accepted privation; the withdrawal of submission to God must be compensated for by the prompt obedience and the more fervent charity that bears suffering as atonement for sin. These are repairs that have to be carried out on man after he has damaged himself by sin. The mystery of Christ and Mary reveals the wider implications of this damage; the whole mystical body is involved in the sin of the individual members. The suffering of one can help another, lightening the burden of his punishment; for no man stands alone in his relations with God. There is one mystic person who goes to the Father in Christ. The mystery of Christ's unmerited suffering continues in his chosen members.

Yet St. Thomas warns us not to interpret all the ills of humanity as punishment for sin. What we sometimes call evil—poverty, for example, and sickness—has a constructive part to play in the design of divine Providence which looks to the salvation of men. These are indeed evils, but they are not in themselves human evils; for the only truly human evil is separation from God. A man, says St. Thomas, is sometimes deprived of lesser goods by God so that he may grow in authentic human goodness. Our modern awareness of social evils makes us slow to accept this point of view or at least makes us reluctant to acknowledge that we accept it. But if we are prudent enough to renounce with St. Thomas all generalizations about the influence of social conditions on genuine human values we will appreciate his argument. Human nature, he points out, has been corrupted by original sin—in a sense that will be explained below—and "it happens sometimes" that a man advances in virtue only when he has to support the burdens of poverty or illness or any other kind of suffering (I-II, q. 87, a. 7). Because mankind has been disorientated by original sin and has to take positive steps to recover a balanced judgment of the relative value of created goodness, deprivation of those things on which men set their hearts to the exclusion of God can serve to convince the individual that true happiness is to be found in God alone. Divine Providence uses shock tactics, leaving an individual with only one source of happiness but this the true Source; or, as the medieval Scholastics put it, God administers the bitter medicine which is for the good of a wounded nature. This is the second sense that suffering has for the Christian.

The close Scholastic analysis of suffering, the outlines of which we have sketched out, must not be seen as arid speculation indulged in for its own sake; this is the sort of charge that is brought against it by those who have lost sight of the great beacons of revelation that constantly directed the investigations of theologians like St. Thomas. This analysis is a fearless meditation on the mystery of the love of God, an intellectual search that will not be content with conventional cliches but probes into the appalling mystery of the love of a Father who "spared not even his own Son" (*Rom.*, 8:32). Suffering has its place in the life of union with God because of God's love; it is a penalty which, if accepted in a spirit of union with Christ, is transformed into atonement for sin which removes the obstacles to love; it is a cure for the more deeply rooted disorder of egoism. But if either of its ends is to be achieved man's attitude to it must be Christian, Christ-like. And here is the dilemma: the effects of sin are purged through suffering; yet these effects are such as to vitiate the healing power of suffering. The twisted metal shrinks from the blows of the shaping hammer; the wound rejects the medicine. As the sacrament of anointing is given us so that we may be able to resolve this dilemma the reason for the rejection must be looked at more closely.

THE WOUNDS OF SIN

THE CORRUPTION OF HUMAN NATURE

As a consequence of sin, both original and actual, man's nature is attacked by corruption. Catholic teaching refuses to admit that any disease has infected the fundamental goodness of this nature. Man remains a creature of God, made in His image, basically capable of regulating his life by reason and, by grace, directing all his activity towards developing that image and thus growing towards the union of heaven. The corruption is there, nevertheless, in the sluggishness which weighs down upon man, making virtuous action appear unattractive and burdensome beyond measure. All of man's powers should respond readily to the directing light of reason; his whole person should move in harmony with his higher aspirations. It is the lack of ready response in these powers, their unwillingness to submit to the discipline of harmony, which constitutes the corruption of nature. Man's natural inclination to virtue, St. Thomas phrases it, is diminished or weakened as a result of indulgence in sin (I-II, q. 85, a. 1).

The source of this weakness may be traced to the obstacles which sinful action places in the way of subsequent attempts to act virtuously. The sinner, even after conversion, is attracted by pleasures without regard for the moderating rule of reason and he is repelled by the difficulties involved in virtuous action (ibid., a. 2; II-II, q. 123, a. 1). There are accordingly four wounds inflicted on human nature by original sin and aggravated by actual sin. Reason itself is slow and hesitant in determining the course of action to be followed; it loses its sensitivity for what is truly human good and compromises with material interests. The will becomes pathologically self-seeking, absorbed in asserting the individual's own rights and blind to the rights of others. Man's sensual powers which should cooperate with and make more profoundly human the decisions of the virtuous man initiate a separatist movement and seek for autonomous satisfaction; where they should provide vigorous emotional reaction to the difficulties of virtuous action they show themselves weak and timorous, protesting at the first sign of hardship; where they should be content with moderate bodily pleasure they flare up in unruly desire and sweep aside all restraint (I-II, q. 85, a. 3).

When sin is forgiven and grace is restored this weakness of nature remains. Grace does provide a pick-me-up; but the violence done to our moral constitution by sin is too far-reaching to be repaired without a long period of convalescence and training. The virtues are like so many injections which assist the return of full health. Prudence enlightens the reason in its control of action; justice begins to deflate the growth of egoism and makes the will ready to respect the rights of others; fortitude stiffens the sensual powers to face up to the rigours of Christian living; temperance moderates their craving for inhuman satisfaction. But the after-effects of sin are not so easily expelled; the good resolutions of the morning after cannot cure the still throbbing head. While grace retains control the poison is held in check; and as grace grows the influence of the after-effects is progressively neutralized; but they remain a constant threat to moral well-being. In times of crisis, especially, when temptation is strong or when circumstances make the task of conformation to Christ more than usually difficult, the old wounds make themselves felt again and the delicately held balance of forces becomes precarious.

THE CRISIS OF ILLNESS

One of the principal crises which the Christian has to contend with is precisely ill-health. When it is serious it needs more than the attention of a doctor; it is a crisis of the whole person, affecting his entire outlook. Not only is there a natural disinclination to accept suffering as a means of atoning for sin; as well, the depression which goes with sickness casts a shadow of unattractiveness over the normal duties of the Christian life, calling up a positive tendency to revolt against the will of God.

Fortitude and its associated virtues, like N.C.O.'s in a demoralized army, resist this movement of surrender. The virtue of patience is assigned the task of rallying the other virtues to their duty when the new and unexpected difficulty of suffering makes its appearance, a hazard for which their own specialization has not prepared them. Constancy has to cope with the particular problems raised by a prolonged campaign. If these subordinate virtues do their work well the way will be open for the higher virtues of charity and repentance, cooperating with the gift of fortitude, to exploit the situation created by ill-health and to lead the sufferer to the glories of victory.

It is at this point in the Christian life that the sacrament of anointing is inserted. It brings reinforcements when the Christian's own defenders are wavering and when the opportunity to win a great victory may slip from his grasp.

THE SACRAMENT OF ANOINTING

Our introduction to the sacrament has led us through a long discussion of the meaning of suffering for the Christian. A summary of our conclusions will help to show their relevance in indicating the function of the sacrament.

Though the risen Christ communicates the life of grace to his members through baptism, salvation of the whole man is a reward which the Christian looks for at the end of the present era when Christ returns in glory. Meanwhile suffering and death form an integral part of the Christian life. Though Christ at times anticipates the use of his power of bodily restoration, the established rule of divine Providence is that the penalties of the present life should be used by us as opportunities for growing in likeness to Christ whose suffering was a condition of his glorification. Because the Christian has been rescued from sin his newly-restored union with God requires that he make reparation for past faults, his own and those of his fellow-members in the body of Christ. Suffering, too, in common with other burdens of life, provides a school in which the true values of human existence may be learned by those whose natural inclinations have been warped by sin. But this very weakness of human nature, the legacy of sin, protests against the opportunities offered for atonement and for learning the lesson of Christ. Grace, working especially through the virtue of fortitude, strengthens this weakness; but when bodily strength is failing the threat of collapse is constantly impending.

It is against this background of the Christian mystery of suffering and death that St. Thomas sees the sacrament of anointing. Like any other sacrament, its purpose is to promote Christian life at the same time as healing the wounds of sin. It is at once apparent that in this framework of thought the sacrament's power of restoring bodily health, acknowledged by St. Thomas and taught by the Council of Trent, will be relegated to a secondary place. True, physical sickness is itself an effect of sin and falls within the sphere of Christ's saving power; but the sacraments belong to the intermediate phase of the Christian mystery, the time of preparation for the parousia. The first objective of their healing power is the interior wounds of sin. If anointing should restore bodily health, it will be only in the measure that this benefits the life of grace.

BODILY HEALING

St. Thomas's explanation of anointing follows the model of his explanation of the other sacraments. Taking baptism as the simplest example and recalling that in it there is a bodily washing which brings about spiritual cleansing, he makes a parallel analysis of anointing. Here there is the application of a sub-

stance used for medicinal purposes which procures interior healing. The application of the oil is the sign-action (*sacramentum
tantum*), the interior healing is the effect (*res*). Now comes a
decisive and illuminating step in St. Thomas's exposition. He
compares anointing's power of restoring bodily health to the
baptismal water's property of bodily washing. There is, of course,
he hastens to add, a difference. Washing is a natural property of
water; the oil used in anointing has no intrinsic capacity to restore bodily health; on the occasions when it does so it is by
divine power. This explains why this effect is not always brought
about. A thing's natural properties are always activated when
it is applied to a suitable object; but God acts according to His
wisdom and accordingly sacramental anointing restores bodily
health only when He wishes it to do so (Suppl., q. 30, a. 2).

What is interesting about this explanation of St. Thomas is
that it locates the power of bodily healing, not at the level of *res*
or sacramental effect, but at that of *sacramentum tantum* as an
occasional element of the sign-action. Even without it the sign-
action is adequate for symbolizing and causing the principal sacramental effect; all that is needed for that is a token application
of bodily medicine. But since this is the particular sign-action
chosen by Christ in view of the gift of interior healing, it is understandable that sometimes it should become more than a token
of medical care and should actually restore health. If this does
not happen it does not mean that the sacrament has been only
half-successful; we do not make such a complaint about baptism
if the water does not in fact clean the child's head.

To grasp the full significance of St. Thomas's approach the
general structure of sacraments should be recalled. They are acts
of the Church, possessing their own validity as signs of faith and
rituals of worship independently of the symbolism and efficacy
attributed to them when Christ enters with his saving power. In
anointing, this action of the Church which forms the efficacious
symbol of spiritual healing includes prayer for the bodily health
of the suffering Christian. This theme is dominant too in the rite
of consecration of the oils. In other words, the strictly sacramental moment comes within the context of a ritual of prayer for
the sick. Granted that the recipient participates adequately in
the sacramental action—to the extent permitted by his illness—

the strictly sacramental effect will infallibly be procured. But the ritual, the sacramental sign, retains all its own significance; and it is a prayer not only for the spiritual well-being of the recipient, but also for his recovery from sickness. The efficacy of this prayer of the Church for the sick is governed by the normal providential laws which determine the efficacy of all prayer; though the official character of this ritual will enhance its impetratory value.

St. James presents the healing power of anointing in the same light. "The prayer of faith shall save the sick man; and the Lord shall raise him up" (5:15). It is to prayer such as this that Christ himself attributed the power of working wonders (*Matt.*, 21: 21 f.; *Mk.*, 9:23; 11:22-24; cf. *Matt.*, 7:7 f.; *Lk.*, 11:9 f.; *Jn.*, 3:22; 5:14-16). Both Christ and St. James make unconditional promises. Christ had said: "These signs shall follow them that believe.... They shall take up serpents; and if they shall drink any deadly thing, it shall not hurt them; they shall lay their hands upon the sick, and they shall recover" (*Mk.*, 16:16-18). Yet not all prayers are answered in the sense in which they are offered for a silent condition is always understood: if the object of prayer is in conformity with the will of God. "This is the confidence which we have towards him: that whatsoever we shall ask according to his will, he heareth us" (*I Jn.*, 5:14). Now the whole glory of the sacraments is that they ensure infallibly that Christ will grant the worthy recipient the effect symbolized. The healing power of anointing is not attached to the ritual in this certain fashion; and consequently it is to be considered formally as an effect of the act of Church worship which has its own intrinsic value as prayer, independently of the value given to it when Christ uses it as a means of conveying salvation to men.

If this development of St. Thomas's teaching is accepted it will be understood that the charismatic gift of healing granted to the early Church has, for normal circumstances, merged with the sacrament of spiritual healing. The disciples' ritual of healing described by St. Mark (6:13)—which according to Trent hints at anointing —has, in virtue of Christ's act of institution, developed into the sacrament. Its principal function now is to serve purely as a sacramental symbol; but it has not lost its original significance and may have its own efficacy, distinct from the infallible sacramental effect.

The extent to which restoration of bodily health is actually achieved by the sacrament is obviously impossible to determine statistically; all the more so because recovery need not be effected in miraculous fashion. It may quite well be that medical science could indicate the physical factors responsible for the cure; but this normal, though often unexpected, functioning of natural or secondary causes, far from excluding the intervention of God, is an indication of His providential care; and the teaching of the Church concerning anointing makes it clear that administration of the sacrament is one of the supernatural factors that influence physical health. It must in addition be stressed that no sacrament is concerned with bodily health as such; the Church makes no claim to supplant the medical profession. Sacraments are for the promotion of Christian worship of God. If anointing effects bodily health, it does so only in so far as sickness derives from sin and influences the recipient's Christian life. It follows that physical recovery will be obtained through the sacrament only when this is advantageous either for the recipient directly or for the Christian community as a whole. It would of course be quite unjustifiable if recovery were to be attributed exclusively to the recipient's lack of preparation for a Christian death.

INTERIOR HEALING

The principal and infallible sacramental effect of anointing worthily received is interior healing. This much is indicated by the symbolism of anointing; what is not so clear is the exact nature of this healing. Absolution of sins could be so described; yet this cannot be the specific effect of anointing for there is another sacrament, penance, for that purpose. The Council of Trent, reproducing the traditional Scholastic teaching, assigns to anointing a role supplementary to the sacrament of penance. Anointing "is considered by the Fathers as perfecting not only penance but as well the Christian's whole life which ought to be a continual exercise of penance" (sess. 14: Extreme unction; Denz.-S. 1694). As is clear from the chapter on confession which

precedes the introduction of this phrase and from the slight play
on words in the phrase itself, what is primarily envisaged is the
function of perfecting the virtue of repentance, activated in the
sacrament of penance and characteristic of the life of the Christian as a sinner who seeks to atone for his faults. What form
this perfecting takes is more clearly stated later: "The effect
(*res*) is the grace of the Holy Spirit whose anointing removes
sin, if any remains to be absolved, and the after-effects of sin,
and as well lightens and strengthens the spirit of the sick person,
awakening in him great trust in the divine mercy, so that the
invalid is raised up and is able to bear more readily the incon-
venience and burdens of his sickness and to resist more easily
the temptations of the devil who lies in wait for his heel" (ibid.,
c. 2; Denz. - S. 1696).

The Council echoes here St. Thomas's teaching on the sacrament. For him also the anointing is directed primarily against
the after-effects of sin (Suppl., q. 30, a. 1); but in his pages
this cryptic formula takes on all the significance of a key-phrase
in his exposition of the meaning of Christian suffering. He too
recognizes that the sacrament can absolve sin should the recipient
be guilty of any. This is not the purpose for which the sacrament
was primarily instituted; but it is more convenient to consider
this aspect before dealing with the specific function centred
on the after-effects of sin.

ABSOLUTON FROM SIN

Should the recipient be in a state of grave sin, and granted
that he has such sorrow as is compatible with this state—that is,
attrition—anointing will bring him absolution. The normal case
envisaged here is that of an unconscious Catholic and it is in this
situation that anointing enjoys a decided advantage over penance.
It is not certain that penance can benefit an unconscious person
since, although the required imperfect sorrow may be present, it is
not clear that it can be externally manifested as the sacrament requires. Anointing does not demand such active external participation of its recipient and consequently its efficacy in the case
proposed is assured since it may be assumed that Catholics have
at least an implicit intention to receive the sacrament. It is for

this reason that every effort should be made to ensure that anointing is administered in danger of death.[5]

REMOVING THE AFTER-EFFECTS OF SIN

The situation just considered is an extreme one. It is normal that sin should have been absolved in penance before anointing. The specific function of the sacrament is to bring the spiritual assistance which is needed in the crisis of grave sickness. It is directed against those defects which weaken the patient's Christian life and impede his adopting a Christian attitude to suffering; in so far as it does this it completes the work of the sacrament of penance and promotes the activity of the virtue of repentance.

These defects, as we have seen, are precisely the after-effects of sin which sap the vigour of the Christian; foremost among them is the disinclination to confront the burdens of suffering as a means of conformation to Christ. St. Thomas describes this disinclination, when he is speaking of anointing, as "a certain weakness and incapacity left in us by actual or original sin" (Suppl., q. 30, a. 1). This has nothing to do with bad habits left by sin; these are not directly affected by the anointing so that, should the sick person recover, he will retain whatever evil tendencies he had before unless he has meanwhile uprooted them by prolonged practice of virtue (Suppl., q. 30, a. 1, ad 2). It is question of that more radical corruption of nature which is the inheritance of sin, that "spiritual weakness of the mind" which we have seen St. Thomas identify as an inborn lethargy, aggravated by personal sin, in man's inclination to virtue. When this is overcome man is less inclined to sin because virtuous action is easier for him, even though all the bad habits he has formed previously remain untouched (ibid.).

In contrast to the spiritual weakness of mind which threatens the sons of Adam particularly in sickness, the effect of the virtue of fortitude is described by St. Thomas as "strength of mind"

---

5. On the assumption that cessation of breathing does not constitute true death, moral theologians generally counsel that anointing should be administered conditionally to those apparently dead who have not received the sacrament: within half-an-hour if there has been long sickness, within two or more hours following on a sudden accident.

(II-II, q. 123, a. 1). The sacramental grace of anointing brings a special vigour to this virtue, lending to it something of that perfection which belonged to it in the state of original justice or in Christ. A parallel quality belongs to the grace of marriage, the tendency of which is towards the due subordination of bodily desire to the rule of reason and grace.[6]

It is as a consequence of the strengthening quality of its grace that anointing has an effect on the penalty of temporal punishment to which even the reconciled sinner is liable. The sacrament does not remit anything of this penalty; but by stiffening the patient's Christian resolve and arousing his love of God it makes the same punishment appear lighter (Suppl. q. a. 1, ad 2).

Here, then, is the function of anointing as a sacrament of the sick. It enables the Christian to incorporate ill-health into the life of the Church. For not only does it make suffering meaningful and profitable for the individual; through his acceptance of pain the Church takes on more vividly the characteristics of Christ and is made more perfect as his sacrament in the world. When the patient has received the sacrament of confirmation his suffering in Christ acquires new apostolic significance and efficacy, as did St. Paul's. "My grace is sufficient for thee; for power is made perfect in infirmity. Gladly therefore will I glory in my infirmities, that the power of Christ may dwell in me. For which cause I boast of my infirmities, of reproaches, of necessities, of persecutions, of distresses, for Christ. For when I am weak, than am I powerful" (*II Cor.*, 12:9-10).

SACRAMENT OF THE DYING

While anointing strengthens the Christian in sickness, its full significance appears only when its role in relation to Christian death is brought to light. Though it may not be possible from the medical point of view to draw in practice a sharp dividing line between these two states, with the result that a person considered to be dying may in fact recover, or one whose illness has been diagnosed as not serious may in fact be dying, there is

---

6. In Scholastic terminology, the grace of marriage perfects the concupiscible appetite, the grace of anointing the irascible appetite.

nevertheless a new threat to be met in the Christian life when a person becomes aware or apprehensive of approaching death.

At this moment the instinct of faith itself is to protest against the deprivation of life: Lord, if thou hadst been here, my brother would not have died (cf. *Jn.*, 11:32); for the promise of Christ is fullness of human life. The insistent memory of personal sin which troubles so many death-beds is, it might be said, the conscious expression of a deep-seated recognition of the victory of sin implicit in death. The powerlessness of the mind to overcome the inborn weakness of the body is paralleled by the life-long difficulty with which reason, even with the aid of grace, controls sinful tendencies.

When the frightening memory of past sins, heightened by present weakness and a premonition of imminent death, tempts the Christian to despair, the priest brings the healing oils to anoint the senses which have so often led to sin. Though there has been some development and there still exists some freedom in the ritual as regards the parts of the body to be anointed, the present practice of the Latin rites brings into focus the intention of the Church in the sacrament. The anointing is directed against the after-effects of sin; and what is principally envisaged are the ravages left by faults deriving from the bodily senses, occasioned, that is, by the passions unbridled by sin. The prayer of the priest looks directly to the anguish of mind of one who has sinned and who fears the judgment of God: May God in His infinite mercy and by means of this holy anointing pardon your offences of sight, hearing, smell, taste and touch. An appeal is made to the mercy of God, that divine attribute which enfolds the whole mystery of Christ. This is an appeal which looks beyond all human failures, beyond remiss use of the countless means of salvation offered in the Church, and directs the gaze of the dying Christian to the dominant theme of the Christian message. The grace of the sacrament is coloured by this symbolic act so that, besides strengthening the sufferer, it moves him to trusting reliance on the mercy of God. For this reason anointing is the sacrament of hope, the virtue which gives personal confidence in God's merciful design for oneself, and the sacrament of peace of mind, reinforcing penance, by the gift of "clarity of conscience" (Suppl., q. 29, a. 4, ad 1).

It is in order that the recipient may participate fully in the sacrament and in this way cooperate consciously with the grace it gives that St. Thomas recommends that anointing be administered when the dying person is still capable of appreciating it. This particular sacrament, he argues, since it is framed in the form of a prayer, gains greater efficacy from the devotion of the recipient and from the merit of the minister and the whole Church; the recipient should approach with the same devotion that is called for when receiving the Blessed Eucharist (Suppl., q. 32, aa. 3 and 4). Nevertheless, the sacrament is not without effect even when the recipient is unconscious; but clearly in such a situation, at least as long as the recipient remains in this state, there is little more for the sacrament to do than absolve the sins which may remain, granted that the dying person has attrition.

IMMEDIATE ENTRY INTO GLORY?

The widely-held medieval opinion that the anointing wins for the Christian immediate entry into glory after death must be interpreted within the context of the whole theology of the sick. It is based on the assumption that the recipient participates fully in the sacramental action and cooperates whole-heartedly with the interior grace it gives and with the external grace of suffering. When we recall that St. Thomas describes the effect produced by the Eucharist as "inebriation with the goodness of God" we are more ready to appreciate the sense of his teaching on the efficacy of anointing. He himself suggests that we should draw this parallel in the place just noted. The present reaction against exaggerated presentations of the medieval teaching on anointing should not induce us to reject as wholly absurd the much more moderate suggestion of the Scholastic theologians themselves. If the Eucharist is to achieve the kind of union with Christ which St. Thomas describes with such unaccustomed fire it must be received, as he received it, with the devotion of a saint. It may seem impractical to suggest that anointing must be received in the same way if the Christian is to enjoy its full benefits after death. But it is not impractical to recognize the splendour of the sacraments of Christ and their transforming power when they are used with devotion. Made members of Christ the Priest by baptism, Christians are united to him by anointing in his suffering and death when he was himself the Victim offered to the Father. His passion was for him a baptism where he was submerged in pain and death. The anointed Christian, offering himself as a victim, accepting his own suffering and death in conformity with Christ, can find in them a new baptism from which he will rise up, as Christ did, to glory.

————

As to the opinion poll referred to at the beginning of this chapter, we prefer to be counted among the "Don't knows." We cannot know with certainty whether anointing is meant for the sick who are not considered to be in danger of death unless the Church declares this to be the case. The presumption at present is that it is not, for the practice of the Church, corroborated by such formal teaching as she proposes, including that of the Second Vatican Council, is decisive.

Whether or not the Church introduces any modifications in her practice, what is clear already is that the popular notion that the sacrament is a last-minute ritual, so that to say of a person that he has been anointed is synonymous with saying that he is at the point of death, has no foundation either in the teaching of the Church or in the authentic traditional theology. We have already drawn attention to St. Thomas's rule for administration; he leaves the judgment on the proximity of death to the common estimation of men (Suppl., q. 33, a. 1, ad 2). Since the modern Canon Law is more liberal, the rule should now be rephrased to permit anointing when on a commonsense judgment there is danger of death (cf. can. 940). And since the whole emphasis of St. Thomas's discussion of the sacrament is on the active participation of the sick person and on his co-operation with the graces he receives, it is clear that the earliest permissible moment should be chosen for administration. The Second Vatican Council states:

"Extreme unction," which may also and more fittingly be called "Anointing of the Sick," is not a sacrament intended only for those who are at the point of death. Accordingly, as soon as any of the faithful begins to be in danger from sickness or old age, the suitable time for receiving the sacrament has certainly arrived (Vat. II Const., ch. 3, art. 73).

A cloud of fear which is not free from superstitution has obscured the true nature of the sacrament. Even if no changes are possible or forthcoming in the law of the Church this cloud should be dispelled. Anointing is a sacrament of sickness and of preparation for death. It is not a sacrament of death. It promotes the worship of God in the Church through suffering borne in union with Christ.

13 Sacramentals: Daily Life in Christ

Most passengers feel more confident with a competent driver than with one who displays an image of St. Cristopher on the dashboard and looks to the saint to cover up his mistakes. There is sound theological backing for this commonsense judgment. Can the same be said for a motorist's decision to carry the image? Perhaps "decision" is too ponderous a word to use in this context; it hardly appears likely that much thought is given to the matter. Catholic drivers, or some of them, feel vaguely that it is the right thing to do. Probably there is a fleeting act of faith involved, though without very clear understanding of what is implied; add to this the likelihood that the image will serve as a reminder to the driver—or his passengers—to say a prayer when starting on a journey—and not even the most finicky theologian could object very strenuously to the practice. What is interesting about it all is the example it provides of the shading-off of genuine sacramental piety into the realm of superstition. Here there is a no-man's-land where only subjective attitudes determine whether faith or superstition holds the upper hand.

SUPERSTITION AND REMEDY

CHRISTIAN LIFE: CENTRE AND PERIMETER

It is superstitious to look to a material thing for benefits which go beyond its natural usefulness. We are more conscious of its threat to Christianity when we think of the proliferation of religious objects and prayer-formulas over the centuries. The minor devotions which have found a passing popularity and have surrounded themselves with their own little liturgies appear to later generations like curios hoarded up by a collector of unperceptive taste. With the wind of reform blowing vigorously through the Church there is no shortage of critics at the present time ready to complain that the same compulsion to accumulate devotional lumber is still at work in the Church. The principle is being enunciated that the further popular devotions and practices are from the letter of the Scriptures, the less do they represent the authentic Christian spirit and the greater is the danger of their assuming autonomous existence somewhere on the border-line between faith and superstition.

It is certainly true that some of the most popular devotions are those which, if not theologically unjustifiable, have at least outstripped actual theological justification; nor is it always the case that theologians are blind to the true needs of the faithful. Sentiment shrugs off fine distinctions and what might be legitimately incorporated into Catholic practice as a subordinate devotion reflecting the richness of the Christian mystery becomes for the unwary the central and formative element of their religious outlook. No doubt good will speaks louder in heaven than bare theological precision; but there is a dominant mystery which Christ commissioned his apostles to preach, not only to theologians, but to all men. Members of religious congregations, in particular, though not suspect of superstition, must be on their guard against overstressing devotional practices characteristic of their own tradition. Fidelity to the spirit of a founder or foundress does not have to extend to every detail of spiritual ob-

servance; and this is especially true of post-Reformation foundations lacking a theological tradition. Individualism and variety
bring vitality and strength to the Church; but any sort of par-
ticularism or exclusivism can lead only to sickly growth, cut off
from the main life-stream of the Christian tradition.

The sole importance of the liturgical movement with its attempt to establish the liturgy as the consciously recognized hub
of Christian life is that it reaffirms the mystery of Christ's death
and resurrection as the supreme efficacious revelation of the
saving action of the Blessed Trinity in the world. In accordance
with this intuition we should envisage the Christian life in all
its manifestations, both communitary and individual, as something like a great wheel which turns on the paschal mystery as
its centre, with devotion as the spokes and devotions as the
perimeter. Then we shall see that there is a two-fold influence
at play throughout the whole structure. From the centre, moving
outwards, there is the fact of the Incarnation, influencing all of
material reality, seeking to draw it into the sphere of Christ;
and from the perimeter, attempting to move inwards, there is a
materializing influence tending to falsify the principle of incarnation and to distract attention from the hidden mystery of God,
directing it instead to the bodily shapes in which He reveals
Himself, as though they had value in themselves.

This means that the threat of superstition is not just a problem that makes its appearance at the circumference of the
Church's life where the uninstructed faithful place more trust
in the Miraculous Medal than in the Mass. To concentrate the
fire of the guns of orthodoxy on this area brings a cheap local
victory—on paper at least—but it does not defeat the enemy;
and, even worse, it is indiscriminate and does nearly as much
damage to friend as to foe. The fact is that sacramentalism, beginning with Christ, the sacrament of God, is a divinely-planned
corrective to superstition, to that tendency innate in the de-
scendants of Adam to materialize whatever is spiritual. This
implies two things. The first is that superstition represents a
threat to the whole structure of Christianity; the second that
Christianity has a mission to absorb and reorientate all human
attraction for a mystique of materiality.

THE THREAT OF SUPERSTITION

It is not always recognized by writers on the liturgy that sin has had a decisive influence on the structure of the Church. In St. Thomas's view there would have been no need of sacraments if Adam had not sinned (*Summa theol.*, III, q. 61, a. 2). As in the question of the motive of the Incarnation, with which the present question is intimately connected, St. Thomas is concerned, not with pointless speculation about unrealized hypotheses, but with bringing to light the precise validity of the elements which go to make up the present situation of the Christian. The harmony of man's nature before sin, with its perfectly ordered hierarchy of faculties, was such that man's spirit would have been perfected in union with God without reliance on corporeal realities. Spirit would have communicated with Spirit and sanctification of man's body would have followed as a natural consequence. After sin, with the gift of original justice withdrawn, union with God is necessarily a work of reconstruction of the wreckage of human nature; and it is in this state that man finds God in material reality. It is still God who communicates Himself to man; but He does this in a manner adapted to man's wounded nature. He comes Himself in the shape of a man and He continues His work of salvation through corporeal realities. Man learns the mystery of God through signs perceptible to the senses, in the words of the preacher and the actions of the sacraments. He finds in the material realities to which he has transferred his affections the source of renewed intimacy with God; and from this he should learn the humiliation of sin which has so materialized his relations with the Blessed Trinity. His superstitious attachment to material symbols is purified by placing in his hands objects which will lead him to God (III, q. 61, a. 1; cf. q. 1, a. 2).

The sacred symbol is redeemed by Christ, purged of its corruptive influence on faith. The human shape that man can hardly refrain from giving to God is ratified and guaranteed by the humanity of God incarnate; the mystic rite evocative of the intervention of God in human affairs becomes a life-giving extension of the saving humanity of God, an authentic means of incorporation into the Redeemer.

But while the Incarnation transforms in this way the central area of belief and liturgy, the human appetite for symbols which will lead to Christ remains unsatisfied. The imagination can get its teeth into clearly depicted representations only. The eye must always see something; the hands must hold something. The humanity of Christ is not enough; we can no longer see or touch it; though we can construct its image, the reality has passed into the realm of faith. The sacraments are a help; but they are rare occurrences when compared with the length of a lifetime and, except for the Eucharist, they are brief in duration. Yet nothing is more embarrassing for a human being, burdened by the consequences of Adam's sin, than to be called upon to enter the world of the spirit in the nakedness of his mind. He will go to almost any lengths to cover his beliefs with clothing that can be seen and touched. Things like the sacraments are what he needs and, unless he is forced by faulty education into a mould of sophistication which is accurately described as inhuman, he will do his utmost to stretch the sacramental idea as far as it will go. Since all this is done by instinct rather than by calculation, the step from legitimate representation to superstition is a slight one and it is not always easy to determine whether it has been taken or not.

Superstition can creep into use of the sacraments, as it does if it is thought that they give grace whether the recipient is properly prepared or not. But the strict control which the Church exercises over administration of the sacraments and the constant instruction she gives on them very largely obviate the danger; once this closely-guarded area has been left behind, the likelihood of ambiguous attitudes increases. When the choice of religious symbols and devotional aids is left to individual preference, guided often by a very sketchy grasp of Christian teaching, there is no lack of exhibits suitable for a theological chamber of horrors.

As long as such aberrations remain within the field of sacred art, as long, that is, as their function remains a purely symbolic one, probably no great harm is done unless to good taste, though there is an obvious danger that cheap-jack art will open the way for inferior, if not positively erroneous, ideas about God. Superstition begins only when people start believing that their private symbols can obtain for them spiritual or temporal advantages.

MISSION TO MATERIALITY

The Church, whose own structure is sacramental, cannot close her eyes to the attraction exercised by religious symbols on her children. Evidently she must restrain them from attributing supernatural power to material things; but she would be denying the principle of incarnation on which she is based if she were to demand that the faithful should be content with the essentials of sacramental practice. Nor is it sufficient for her to warn against superstition. While a very satisfactory law could easily be drawn up simply condemning superstitious practices, this would go as far towards solving the consequent human dilemma of the faithful as any legal prohibition; a complementary programme of reorientation is called for.

Christianity does not condemn anything that is authentically human; the Church's moral code is based on the premise that only by control and the harmony which results can human goodness be achieved. The Church recognizes that the sacraments and indeed the whole liturgy are inadequate to satisfy the normal person's desire to reach God with his eyes and ears and hands. She understands the fascination that superstitious practices have. Her role as Christian educator is not only to instruct her children on the errors of superstition; she must as well direct into orthodox channels the genuinely human instincts which prompt people to be superstitious. She is confronted with the results of sin and she will not be browbeaten by any theologian into liturgical snobbery. Her task is not the purely negative one of rooting out evil; she must draw all that is human into Christian living.

Sacramentals are the means she chooses. She provides these as necessary complements to the sacraments, having learned by experience that her children have religious needs left unsatisfied by the central rites of the liturgy. The Church envisages the sacramentals as developments of the sacraments. This is a phase of the outward movement from the central mystery of the

Church; it belongs to the process of incarnation of Spirit in matter. The closer this movement of the Church's life comes to the perimeter, the greater the danger of superstition or other eccentric tendencies in the individual faithful; but it is poor theology to settle on these peripheral aberrations and to use them to demonstrate the undesirability of all that is non-liturgical. The use of sacramentals and minor devotions needs to be discouraged only when they develop, as they can very well do if not controlled, into a substitute for authentic Christian worship.

In order to maintain a balanced view of the sacramentals and of the devotions connected with them they must be seen as the medieval theologians saw them, from the centre of the Christian mystery, as assisting and completing the sacraments' work of bringing Christ to the world. The modern Code of Canon Law, being concerned only with a juridical description, does not quite preserve this theological view. It defines the sacramentals as "objects or actions used by the Church in a certain imitation of the sacraments to obtain by her prayer principally spiritual effects" (can. 1144). The stress is here laid on the autonomy and multiplicity of the sacramentals rather than on their unifying principle, their dependence on and derivation from the sacraments. This reflects an historical development in the practice of the Church and in theology which have both tended to minimize the connection with the sacraments and to grant an increasingly independent existence to sacramentals. A certain amount of house-cleaning of the kind already begun with the simplification of the liturgical calendar and the reform of parts of the ceremonial would be a good thing. This has, in fact, been prescribed by the Second Vatican Council which, however, though stressing the connection between the sacramentals and the sacraments, retains the Canon-Law definition (Vat. II Const., ch. 3, arts. 60, 79). An effort must be made to cast the spotlight on the central mystery of the Church and to clear away whatever obscures the structural connection between peripheral devotions and the centre. To promote this effort we cannot do better than attempt to recover the view of the sacramentals taken by the medieval theologians. The majority of their modern successors prefers to adopt the straightforward and practical view of the Canon Law. In order to coordinate these divergent approaches we shall look first at St. Thomas's teaching, then at that of the moderns. This is a slightly unwieldy procedure and involves a certain amount of overlapping of one account with the other as there is agreement between the two approaches on several points. But whatever disadvantages this may entail appear to be outweighed by the opportunity of recapturing the medieval mentality and showing its relevance to the present practice of the Church.

THE THOMISTIC APPROACH

CEREMONIAL OF SACRAMENTS

The only sense in which St. Thomas uses the term "sacramental" is that of "something connected with the sacraments." He describes in this way, for example, the preparations for baptism: the catechism or interrogations of candidates, the exorcisms, and the blessing of the water (III, q. 67, a. 3, ad 2). The recently introduced order of baptism for adults, which is divided into seven distinct steps taken progressively as the instruction of catechumens proceeds, illustrates clearly in modern practice this concept of sacramentals (cf. Decree of S. Cong. of Rites, 16th April, 1962; Vat. II Const., ch. 3, art. 64). The explanatory paragraphs to be inserted in the Roman Ritual read as follows:

The whole ritual is divided into seven steps:

The first step is concerned in its introductory parts with the spiritual preparation to be undertaken by the priest who is in charge of catechetical instruction and with that of the faithful whose obligation it is to give spiritual help to the catechumens by their prayers and by the example of mature and responsible Christian living. On this follow the first ceremonial naming of the catechumens, the basic catechetical instruction, the acts of renunciation of evil and of turning to God, and the first solemn signing with the Cross, this last being also the fundamental exorcism, that is, the radical subjugation of the power of the demons.

The second step contains the very ancient ceremony of the tasting of salt, which symbolizes the growing delight of the catechumens in Christian teaching.

The third, fourth and fifth steps consist in the thrice-repeated solemn exorcisms, the effect of which is to impress deeply upon the catechumens a sense of the struggle involved in whole-hearted conversion to God and a sense of the tenacious opposition set up against such conversion by the enemy of the human race.

The sixth step incorporates the ceremonies immediately preparatory to reception of baptism. These derive from very ancient practice and are rich in signification.

Following on the solemn entry of the catechumens into the church there is the delivery of the Creed and the Lord's Prayer, the final exorcism and the rite of opening the ears. Finally, after a further renunciation of Satan, the catechumen is anointed with the oil of catechumens and is enrolled as a soldier to fight against the powers inimical to Christ and to his Church.

The seventh and final step leads to baptism itself.

Once again the name is given; there is a profession of faith, a request to be baptized, the administration of baptism and the anointing with sacred chrism, this signifying the grace of the Holy Spirit received in baptism. Finally come the presentation of the baptismal garment and the lighted candle and the dismissal of the newly baptised (cf. *Acta Apostolicae Sedis*, 54 (1962), pp. 312-3).

The mentality revealed in this commentary represents a return to the medieval idea of sacramentals. The whole ritual is composed of a series of sacramentals, chief among which are the exorcisms, the tasting of salt, the interrogations and the anointings. These lead up to, or follow on, the central rite of baptism itself and develop its significance. As far as psychological indications go there is nothing to distinguish the sacrament from the supplementary rites; this fact recalls to mind the prolonged uncertainty in the Church about the nature and number of the sacraments, which was not resolved until the twelfth century.

Though the teaching of the Church is now explicit on the question of what constitutes the essential ritual of the sacrament, this homogeneity of ceremonial is a matter of capital importance for liturgical training since it makes very clear the fact that the recipient of a sacrament is performing an act of worship, indistinguishable as such from any other act of worship.

TWO-FOLD PURPOSE OF THE SACRAMENTALS

The distinction between sacraments and sacramentals is indicated first of all by their effects. Sacramentals, says St. Thomas, are not sacraments because they do not bring grace; their function is rather that of disposing or preparing for the sacraments (III, q. 65, a. 1, ad 6). As the quotation from the addition to the ritual of baptism shows, this preparation in the first place concerns the faithful, not only those who are presenting themselves for the sacrament but also the Christian community as a whole, including in particular the priest who is in charge of instruction and the people of the parish. In addition there are other sacramentals the purpose of which is to prepare the materials used in administration of the sacraments. In the case of baptism there is the blessing of the water with its preliminary exorcisms; for the Eucharist there is a much more complex system of consecrations and blessings of the vessels and vestments used and of the church building itself. All of these preparatory rites, both of people and of objects, are directed towards the sacraments in one or other of two ways: either because they remove obstacles to the achievement of the sacraments' effects or because they provide an ambient suitable to the dignity of the sacraments (III, q. 65, a. 1, ad 6). St. Thomas develops both of these ideas.

PREPARATION FOR SACRAMENTS: REMOVING OBSTACLES

Exorcisms. The ritual of baptism, at the heart of which occurs the essential sacramental moment when Christ enters the ceremonial to give grace, expresses symbolically the struggle between God and the forces of evil; the solemn exorcisms show the Church repulsing evil and opening the way for the grace of Christ. Similar exorcisms appear in the blessing or consecration of materials used in Christian worship, in the blessing of baptismal water, for example, in the making of holy water and in the consecration of a church.

These exorcisms do not carry the same implications as those employed in the case of a person "possessed" by the devil, though there are obvious similarities. Whatever be the precise meaning of diabolic possession, the present practice of the Church appears to indicate that it is an extraordinary phenomenon. The exorcisms connected with the sacraments are rather a recognition of the existence of evil forces at work within creation until redemption has produced its full fruit. If Christ is not in possession, whether of persons or material reality, evil is. The ritual exorcisms call upon God and upon the power of Christ to expel the demons so that the salvation of Christ may enter. It is sanctifying grace essentially that brings the sinner out of the power of Satan; but the preliminary exorcisms are not without positive effect. Acting on the promise of Christ (*Mk.*, 16:17), the Church exercises the power she has received from him to protect the faithful from the assaults of the demons. It may be noticed in the extract from the baptismal ritual already reproduced that only to the first exorcism is attributed the subjugation of the evil powers; the succeeding three are explained rather as admonitory exhortations addressed to the catechumens. The new rubrics for these baptismal exorcisms introduce to the Latin rite the novelty of leaving room for an alternative ceremony where local custom would find unacceptable the normal one of breathing in the face of the catechumens; on this point the Holy See anticipated a more general decision of the Second Vatican Council regarding liturgical ceremonies.

For St. Thomas holy water finds its place in the sacramental system as an extension of the baptismal exorcisms. He suggests two ways of attaching this sacramental to the liturgy. Either we may think of holy water as protecting the Christian from external attacks of the demons, while exorcisms protect from interior temptation; or we may relate the use of holy water to the baptismal exorcisms in the same way as we relate confession to baptism, that is, as a means of recovering the original immunity of the Christian (III, q. 71, a. 2, ad 3).

Forgiveness of venial sins. In addition to repelling the powers of evil, sacramentals prepare more immediately for worthy reception of the sacraments by procuring forgiveness of venial sin (III, q. 65, a. 1, ad 6). From the point of view of pastoral liturgy this is the most interesting thing that St. Thomas has to say about the sacramentals. As well as providing a further example of his insistence that genuine sacramental practice demands the fullest cooperation on the part of the recipient, it brings to light the fact that there is an essential role for the sacramentals in the liturgy. Their function is to establish ideal conditions for reception of the sacraments. Accordingly we find them woven into the text of the liturgy. The text is primarily a prayer of the Church but some of the prayers are sacramentals. The clearest example is the *Confiteor* and subsequent absolution which appear in the prayers at the foot of the altar at Mass as well as in certain parts of the divine office, in the administration of the last rites and on many other occasions. Closely associated with this general confession of sin are the sprinkling with holy water in the *Asperges* before High Mass, and the action of striking the breast prescribed in the Roman rite before communion (III, q. 87, a. 3).

These and similar sacramentals are said to forgive venial sin because they cannot be used properly by the faithful unless they are made the expression of an act of true repentance (*ibid.*). Venial sin does not involve that complete rejection of God and His plan for man which characterizes mortal sin; it corresponds rather to the occasional falling-out of a happily married couple who, in spite of a temporary cooling of affection, remain substantially bound to one another in the depths of their persons. Venial sin reflects the complexity of man's personal commitment to God. Surrender to God is not something which is achieved at one blow by grace; precisely because it is personal it permits of all sorts of hesitations and doubts and contradictions while preserving its basic acceptance of God's saving love. Minor acts of unfaithfulness reveal the limitations of charity's hold on the Christian even while he remains in the state of grace. They are forgiven when charity reasserts itself as the absorbing motive of a Christian's whole life or when, under the prompting of charity, there is specific recognition of the imperfection of one's response to God accompanied by rejection of whatever impedes full union with Him. Sacramentals such as the *Confiteor* nudge the faithful into making acts of charity or repentance. They do this more effectively than, for example, an act of contrition read from a prayer-book because of their status as sacramentals in virtue of which, as will be explained below, they call upon the resources of the whole mystical body in order to help those who use them. Here once again the communitary character of the Church is discovered. Not only is the individual Christian supported by his fellow-believers at the central moment of the sacrament; he is sustained by them in his preparation. The holiness of the hidden saints of the Church is active throughout the whole body, communicating its light to all the members who are open to it.

PREPARATION FOR SACRAMENTS: RELIGIOUS AMBIENT

For the Blessed Eucharist, even more than for the other sacraments, a suitable ambient must be prepared by the Church. The holiness of this sacrament requires that all that surrounds it be holy. The ritual of consecration brings this holiness to whatever is immediately associated with the Eucharist: the church building, the altar, the chalice and paten, as well as the bells of the church which call the faithful to the sacrament. Less solemn blessings are used for the other sacred vessels and for the priest's vestments. The central and transforming consecration of the bread and wine demands these subsidiary consecrations which, while leaving unchanged substantially their objects, relate them exclusively to the Eucharist so that they are placed in a state of permanent service of God. These things are called "holy" in a derived sense. Strictly, holiness is a quality of God which is communicated to those who are united to Him by charity. The furniture of worship is holy because of the part it plays in the commerce of holiness between God and man. It is given over by the Church exclusively to liturgical use and it assists the faithful in paying worship.

In the field of worship consecration serves a two-fold purpose (III, q. 83, a. 3). Firstly, the fact that certain material objects are dedicated exclusively to the Eucharist expresses the reverence in which the Church holds this sacrament and, at the same time, impresses the faithful with a like sense of reverence. The sacred vessels of the Mass are indued with an air of mystery and apartness; they take on the quality of sacredness which properly belongs to God and in which they share because they are used when man approaches Him. In addition to this—and here is its second purpose—consecration attributes to the ambient of the Eucharist a symbolic value so that the material furnishings of the Mass represent the holiness of those who take part in the sacrifice. In particular, St. Thomas notes that the consecration of the altar represents the holiness of Christ, while that of the church building represents the holiness of the whole Church (*ibid.*, ad 4). This theme is taken up and developed in the breviary's office recited on the anniversary of the dedication of a church. The holiness of the consecrated building is seen as a symbol of the inner holiness of the mystical body which will be revealed when Christ returns. The hymns of the office— which must be heard in their plain-chant setting to be fully appreciated—create in the material building the image of the Church of Christ being built up with living bricks, to construct the city of the blessed: Holy city of Jerusalem, called the Vision of Peace.[1]

The aura of holiness which surrounds the consecrated church, as a natural consequence of its representing the holiness communicated to the Church by the passion of Christ, signifies the holiness required in those who offer the Mass and receive communion (III, q. 83, a. 3, ad 2). Here the sacramental quality of the building takes on new realism for, in St. Thomas's eyes, there is a positive assistance given to worship in this place, deriving from its consecration. He speaks of a "power" given to the building, similar to, though clearly not of the same nature as, that which is at work in the sacraments (*ibid.*, ad 3; cf. q. 87, a, 3, ad 1); and in explanation he recalls that consecration is a work, not only of man, but of God also (III, q. 83, a. 3, ad 4). As a consequence prayers offered in this place have an added efficacy (II-II, q. 84, a. 3, ad 2) and it is probable that

---

1. Cf. **Towards a theology of church architecture**, "Doctrine and Life," 11 (1961), pp. 194-208.

those who enter it win remission of venial sins (III, q. 83, a. 3, ad 3) in the fashion already explained.

Theologians are not at one in their interpretations of St. Thomas's thought on the nature of this "power." It seems clear that any suggestion of God's using the church building as an instrumental cause of sanctification is to be excluded for this is the prerogative of the seven sacraments. On the other hand it is inadequate to appeal simply to the "devotional" atmosphere of a church since this is something purely psychological and varies widely according to individual sensibility. It is not without significance that the consecration of a church is reserved to the bishop who represents Christ as ruler of the Church assembly (III, q. 82, a. 1, ad 4). As will be seen below when the theology of blessings is developed, the ordained priesthood has power to bring down the favour of God on persons and things; and as a consequence the rite of consecration, besides engaging the prayer of all the faithful in favour of those who enter the building, places the church in a special relation to God so that He may be said to be present there in a unique way, exciting devotion in His worshippers. Clearly, the focal point of such devotion is the Blessed Eucharist reserved in the tabernacle and the sacrifice of the altar. It is in fact this sacrament which forms the centre of St. Thomas's thought on the sacramentals, as it does for his whole sacramental theology. This eucharistic mentality is characteristic of the medieval view of the sacramentals.

THE MODERN APPROACH

While St. Thomas develops the notion of sacramentals as sign-actions of the Church associated with the sacraments, the subsequent theological tradition began to take a broader, less unified view. Among the most famous classifications is one which lists the following sacramentals: Praying (the Our Father and other prayers recited in the name of the Church in her ceremonial), Sprinkling (with holy water, oils), Eating (of blessed food), Confessing (the *Confiteor* at Mass and in the divine office), Giving (alms-deeds carried out according to the indications of the Church) and Blessing. Modern theologians, on the contrary, have tended to restrict the field of sacramentals, excluding ceremonies, prayers and pious works such as alms-deeds. The juridical view expressed in the Code of Canon Law has imposed the most widely-accepted modern classification which distinguishes broadly between sacramentals which are *objects*, having stable existence, and those which are *actions*, namely, consecrations, simple blessings and exorcisms. Attempts have been made to break away from this untheological convention and lists have been drawn up in which the sacramentals are grouped round the various sacraments; but, while this procedure is partly satisfactory, an element of artificiality makes itself evident at a certain point. It seems preferable, while maintaining St. Thomas's point of view as regards liturgical ceremony, to recognize that sacramentals have established for themselves an independent right of citizenship in the Church and have staked out claims beyond the immediate context of the sacraments. If, however, we are to preserve a theological view of the sacramentals we must be careful not to interpret this independence as a complete divorce from the sacraments. As developments of the sacramental idea which have evolved under the supervision of the Church, the sacramentals extend the area of sacred signs which mark the life of the Christian and bring to its regular rhythm, as well as to its outstanding events, the beneficent influence of the Church. It is along these lines that we must look for the link between the medieval and the modern approaches.

MODERN CLASSIFICATION

The basic distinction between objects and actions is clear, at least from the juridical point of view. Sacramentals which are objects are those which remain for the specifically religious use of the faithful after an action of the Church, normally a blessing, is ended. Holy water, blessed candles, palms and ashes are examples. So too, it would appear, are blessed rosaries, statues and other articles of devotion, though this point could be discussed. The contrasting term "action" is self-explanatory; under this head are classified two broad groups: exorcisms and blessings.

Blessings form the largest group of sacramentals. There are two types. The one most commonly used is the simple or prayer-blessing (*benedictio invocativa*). This is applied to people or to things people use, its purpose being to win the favour or blessing of God for those who believe in Him. The more solemn form of blessing is reserved for those persons or things dedicated exclusively to the service of God. This is the dedicatory or constitutive blessing (*benedictio constitutiva,* cf. can. 1148 § 2; 1150); and once again there are two degrees of solemnity. When the sacred oils are used the blessing is a consecration. If there is a simple formula with no anointing the dedicatory blessing is termed "verbal." [2]

A brief examination of the two types of blessing will help to clarify their nature and to place the modern classification in relation to St. Thomas's mentality. This will prepare the way for an investigation into the source of the sacramentals' efficacy.

DEDICATORY BLESSINGS

Consecrations. The most solemn form of blessing, consecration, is still applied in modern practice to the church building, altars, chalices and patens and church bells. The consecration of churches, in particular, is regarded by the Church as an event of considerable importance and is carried out according to a complex ritual, being preceded by a day of fasting. Here the medieval view of the sacramentals is preserved at the centre of the modern system.

The classification of consecrations as blessings reveals the two-fold movement implicit in every act of worship which has already been discovered in the sacraments. Consecration as such, in so far as it is the dedication of an object to liturgical use,

---

2. Thus the modern classification of sacramentals is as follows:
    Sacramentals:
                    — objects
                    — actions:
                                — exorcisms
                                — blessings:
                                            — dedicatory:
                                                        — consecrations (oils used)
                                                        — verbal
                                — simple or prayer-blessings

consists in transferring human property to the service of God. In spite of the renunciation which this implies, it is man who benefits from the action. It is he who needs the support of material things when he pays worship to God. By investing the immediate ambient of the Eucharist with the sacred quality of consecration the Church places these sacramental supports within the realm of God so that they become sources of divine help and blessing for the faithful who take part in the liturgy. We have already seen how real this presence of God in the furniture of the Eucharist is for St. Thomas.

Verbal dedicatory blessings. The less solemn form of dedicatory blessing, in which the holy oils are not applied, is used for the faithful who devote themselves wholly to the service of God. The tonsuring of clerics and the blessings of abbots and virgins are typical examples. Monastic and religious profession, while centred on the contractual agreement of the vows, may also be inserted here though, in some forms of profession at least, the idea of blessing plays a small part as far as the text of the ceremony goes. In all of these examples the connection with the Blessed Eucharist is easily discovered; and it would appear to be in conformity with St. Thomas's view of sacramentals to insist on this aspect. Dedication to the service of God in the Church is essentially eucharistic; the blessing called down upon those who dedicate themselves in this fashion will have the same orientation.

The coronation of a king appears to belong to the present context. The ceremony is certainly a sacramental and takes the form of a dedicatory blessing. In addition, the holy oils are used which would suggest that it is a solemn consecration. The Christian king received his royal anointing from the Church and therefore from Christ; he shared thereby in Christ's temporal kingship. But the use of oils implies, according to the practice of the Church, a relation to the Eucharist, in this case obviously only indirect. While changing times have rendered the sacramental largely obsolete, the concept which inspired it does not derive exclusively from medieval ideas on the relation between Church and state and remains significant for Catholic politicians.

SIMPLE BLESSINGS

When the faithful ask for blessings for themselves or their property it is normally a question of the simple or prayer-blessing. The blessing of people includes the blessing given by the priest at the end of Mass or at other times, the nuptial blessing, the blessing of the sick and the blessing with the Blessed Sacrament at benediction.

The extraordinary number and variety of blessings contained in the Roman Ritual for the material possessions of the faithful provide a remarkable insight into the desire of the Church to sanctify daily living; it is regrettable that the text of these blessings is not readily available for lay people. There are blessings not only for the obvious articles of devotion such as rosaries and images, but also for printing machines, libraries (where fire is mentioned as the principal threat), archives, fishing boats, railways and trains, cars, planes (compared to the House of Loreto), fire-fighting appliances (significantly, stress is laid on human skill as supplementing the efficacy of the blessing), seismographs, bees, silkworms, sick animals, telegraphic equipment, pests (with the reservation that their destruction should be limited to the requirements of human well-being); and this is only a brief sampling. In each case the text of the blessing provides an apt commentary on the usefulness of the particular object in the Christian life and formulates a suitable prayer for God's favourable care. Always it is clear that the blessing is for the benefit of those who use the object; nowhere is there any trace of a magic incantation purporting to give supernatural power to an inanimate being. Blessed objects have meaning only within the context of the life of the faithful.

It is in the light of this last consideration that it appears legitimate to suggest that the modern distinction between objects and actions has only a limited validity. The concept of "object" is a product of the juridical mentality which has transformed the major sacraments into things possessing their own independent existence and, as far as this way of talking about them is concerned, in some quasi-magical fashion causing grace. On the contrary, apart from the Eucharist reserved in the tabernacle, the sacraments are actions of the Church and of Christ. A similar adjustment of juridical categories is called for in the case of sacramentals. They are an expression of the life of the Church; they are symbols of the communion in holiness which binds together all the members of Christ; and this implies that they function as sacramentals only when they are caught up into the movement of life which animates the mystical body. It would, accordingly, appear more correct theologically to say that in the use of the faithful certain objects are sacramentals, for the attitude or dispositions of the user are all-important. When a blessed candle or rosary or any other religious object is used devoutly the prayers of the individual are assisted in some measure by the effects of the blessing. It seems necessary to insist on this "dynamic" view of sacramentals in order to avoid the danger of religious objects being considered good-luck charms. Sacramentals are not talismans possessing magical power; they are signs of the communion of the faithful in charity. It is this inward mystery of the sacramentals which must now be considered; it provides the basis for coordinating the medieval and modern approaches to this aspect of the life of the Church.

SOURCE OF EFFICACY

PRAYER OF THE CHURCH

Unlike the sacraments, sacramentals are instituted, not by Christ himself, but by the Church in virtue of power given her by Christ. While not enjoying, accordingly, the fullness of power proper to the seven sacraments which derives from the direct sanctifying intervention of the risen Christ in the liturgy, they do possess a certain intrinsic value so that their use can achieve results which go beyond the normal efficacy of a private act of religion. This is because the sacramentals, in virtue of their institution by the Church, draw upon the merit not only of the individuals who use them but also, and primarily, of the whole Church.

As far as the individual is concerned this means that the sacramentals enjoy an efficacy which is in part independent of his personal merits; and in this sense they must justly be said to work *ex opere operato*, it being understood that the individual brings some devotion to his use of them. There is, however, an evident ambiguity in the employment of this term in the present context since theologians have agreed to reserve it to describe the unique mode of efficacy possessed by the sacraments and, as a result, it has come to connote the direct sacramental action of Christ. In order to make it clear that the efficacy of the sacramentals depends on the charity of the Church and not solely on that of Christ, a new term is found. The sacramentals are said to work *ex opere operantis Ecclesiae*, in virtue of the merit of the whole Church, "inasmuch as the Church is holy and acts in the closest union with her Head" (Pius XII, *Mediator Dei*, CTSE ed. § 29; cf. *Summa theol.*, III, q. 82, a. 6).

It is evident that behind the merits of the faithful who make up the Church on earth there is Christ in his paschal mystery, imparting and maintaining the life of the Church, united with his members in worship of the Father (cf. Vat. II Const., ch. 3, art. 61). Consequently the sacramentals draw their efficacy from Christ, interceding for his Church in heaven and living by grace in his members. By reason of the charity which unites them, the Head and members hold their supernatural possessions in common. This does not make the Church a classless society; there are clearly marked grades of individual sanctity; but it does mean that the prayer of the whole Church is not something which can be calculated mathematically by adding up the "value" of the prayer of the individual members. It is the whole Christ who prays. It means also that the individual can benefit from the holiness of all the members and from the infinite holiness of the Head. In addition, the divinely-appointed rulers of the Church on earth can make certain provisions concerning the particular fashion in which the common possessions of the faithful will be placed at the disposal of individuals. The practice of the Church indicates that this may be done not only for the prayer of the whole body but also for the reparation which the members offer. Hence derives the efficacy of sacramentals and of indulgences.

We are perhaps tempted nowadays to picture this in terms of the welfare state; but a system of social security based on compulsory taxation is only a feeble imitation—though quite possibly one that is valid in its own sphere—of the communion of the saints which is based on charity and is controlled on earth by the hierarchy. In the eyes of God—and prayer, merit and reparation must be placed in this perspective—the unity brought to the faithful by union with Christ through charity and by participation in God's own life is of greater significance than the distinction which separates one human individual from another. It is this that lends universal validity to the passion of Christ; it is this too that gives the meritorious actions of one person a similar, though less radical, validity in respect of others. Whereas political society must deprive one person of his surplus wealth in order to assist less fortunate citizens, in the mystical body of Christ the individual can assist others without thereby losing anything himself. This sharing of Christian wealth never exempts those who benefit by it from personal effort; rather it makes personal effort possible. It is a constant phenomenon in the life of the mystical body; what happens in the special case of the sacramentals is that the Holy See, the only competent authority, decrees that the religious use of approved ceremonies or objects will bring to bear in favour of the user the prayers and good works of the whole Church. This act of hierarchical authority is an intervention of Christ through his vicar in the life of his body.

RESPONSE OF GOD

The mode and degree of efficacy of the sacramentals are now clearly definable at least in general terms; they are determined by the same factors as those which govern the efficacy of an individual's prayer for others, the only difference being that the sacramentals draw upon the prayer of the whole Church and form part of the activity proper to the mission confided to the Church by Christ.

The combination of the two elements, prayer and official mission, is something which is characteristic of the sacramentals. The efficacy of the major sacraments is guaranteed exclusively by the Church's mission and constitutes the direct application to the faithful of the power of Christ's passion; the prayer of the Church is here relegated to a secondary place. On the contrary, liturgical prayer, as such, derives its efficacy from the union of the faithful with Christ by charity in common worship of the

Father; the Church's mission to the world is only indirectly involved. The sacramentals have a foot in each camp. Like the sacraments, they apply the fruits of Christ's passion to the faithful; but, as in liturgical prayer, instead of Christ's merits alone being called upon, it is the merit of Christ's members in union with the Head which gives value to the sacramentals. Accordingly, the sacramentals stand in the same relation to the prayers and merits of the Church as do the sacraments to the redemptive work of Christ. Just as Christ had authority to institute the sacraments as efficacious signs of his saving action, so the Church, in virtue of her mission, has authority to institute signs giving access to the benefits of the good works of the faithful. Evidently, the Catholic doctrines of merit and of the apostolic ministry form the basis for this practice. The sacramentals are the "sacraments" of the corredemptive function of the Church.

In order to determine the response made by God to the prayer of the Church offered in the ritual of the sacramentals our attention must be directed primarily to the mission given the hierarchy to institute such observances and to use them. It is this mission which makes feasible the Church's directing the prayer of the faithful towards the purpose of the individual sacramentals. The question concerns the Church's mission to exorcise and to bless. Reference has already been made above to the source of the power of exorcism; it remains to consider the mission of blessing.

THE MISSION OF BLESSING

To bless a person means to bring down the favour of God upon him, to win for him the benefits of God's favour. To bless an object means to bring down God's favour upon those who use the thing. The word "grace" that we now use in a technical sense similarly implies both the favour of God and the gifts which He gives to man. Sanctifying grace is indeed the principal blessing bestowed upon creatures by God; but the blessing which the Church calls down upon the faithful is of broader scope, taking in all that can in any way promote the Christian life, not only spiritual gifts, but as well, though in a subordinate place, what is needed for temporal well-being.

God alone is the author of His blessing; the gifts that He gives men flow from His liberality. If men bless, it can only be if they have received a mission from God to do so or if their blessing of another takes the form of private prayer. In the Old Testament we read of God Himself blessing creation (*Gen.*, 1:22, 28) and groups of individuals, Noah and his sons, for example (*ibid.*, 9:1), Abraham, Isaac and Jacob (*ibid.*, 12:2, 3; 22:17; 24:1; 27:16; 35:9) and many others. As well, His representatives bless their fellow-men, but always by calling on His name and praying for His help. The patriarchs bless their sons (*ibid.*, 27; 48:9, 15; 49:28); Moses before his death blesses the tribes of Israel (*ibid.*, 33); and at the dedication of the temple, Solomon speaks a magnificent blessing over the assembled people (3 *Kings*, 8:55-61). Most significant of all, the power of blessing the people is granted by God to the Levitical priesthood and it is God Himself who prescribes the formula, guaranteeing its efficacy: "Thus shall you bless the children of Israel, and you shall say to them: The Lord bless thee, and keep thee. The Lord show his face to thee, and have mercy on thee. The Lord turn his countenance to thee, and give thee peace. And they shall invoke my name upon the children of Israel, and I will bless them" (*Num.*, 6:22-27; cf. *Deut.*, 10:8; *Ecclus.*, 36:19).

In the New Testament it is our Lord first of all who blesses. He lays his hands on the children and blesses them (*Matt.*, 19:13-15; *Mk.*, 10:13-16); before his ascension he raises his hands and blesses the disciples (*Lk.*, 24:50); he blesses the bread, looking up to heaven, before the miracle of the multiplication (*Matt.*, 14:19; 15:36) and before the Eucharist (*Matt.*, 26:27; cf. *Lk.* 24:30-31). This power he passes on to his disciples: "When you come into the house, salute it, saying: Peace be to this house. And if that house be worthy, your peace shall come upon it; but if it be not worthy, your peace shall return to you" (*Matt.*, 10:12-13; *Lk.*, 10:5-6). Linked with the power of blessing is that of curing the sick and exorcising the possessed —"freely have you received, freely give" (*Matt.*, 10:8)—and the power of miracles (*Mk.*, 16:17-18).

The principal indication of the use the apostles made of the power of blessing is found in the introductions of the epistles: "To all that are at Rome the beloved of God, called to be saints:

Grace to you and peace from God our Father and from the Lord Jesus Christ" (*Rom.*, 1:7; cf. *1 Cor.*, 1:7; etc.). In these salutations the theme of grace and peace is repeated; this is the blessing which God has given the Church in Christ (cf. *Eph.*, 1:3). In another place St. Paul condemns those who lay unnecessary restrictions on Christians, "forbidding to marry, (requiring them) to abstain from meats, which God hath created to be received with thanksgiving by the faithful and by them that have known the truth. For every creature of God is good, and nothing to be rejected that is received with thanksgiving. For it is sanctified by the word of God and prayer" (*1 Tim.*, 4:3-5). This blessing of food is the sole reference in the epistles to blessing of objects.

The word of God and prayer, the divine mission and the sanctity of the Church, these are the two streams of life which meet in the sacramentals. In the ordination of a priest the hands are anointed and the bishop transmits the mission: "In thy mercy, o Lord, consecrate and sanctify through this anointing and through our prayer these hands so that whatever they shall bless may be blessed, and whatever they shall consecrate may be consecrated and sanctified." The divine response to the prayer of the Church comes through the hands of the priest so that whatever he blesses becomes a source of God's favour to those who use it with devotion.

CERTAINTY OF EFFECT

With the source of the sacramentals' efficacy established, it is possible to formulate more precisely the degree of certainty they enjoy in producing the effects envisaged by the Church.

DEDICATORY BLESSINGS

Consecrations and verbal dedicatory blessings procure infallibly their immediate effect, granted that the prescribed formula is used and the rubrics observed and that the minister has the required intention. As far as the juridical status of the consecrated person or thing is concerned there is nothing extraordinary about this; in the eyes of Church law the object is set apart for divine worship. But there is a mystery as well, for the divine mission given the Church to bless and consecrate ensures that God accepts the person or object as sacred. We have seen St. Thomas speaking of a supernatural power that is given to a consecrated church by reason of the fact that the act of consecration is the work of God as well as of man. The consecrated object truly becomes a positive source of divine assistance to devout worshippers. Whether the act of consecration achieves its effect of sanctification depends further on the devotion of those who use the object. The effect of the dedicatory blessing is likewise a reality, not a pure juridical fiction. A blessed abbot or virgin, a king, a professed religious—at least one with solemn profession—all of these are placed in a special relationship with God, founded on their acceptance of certain obligations according to the law of the Church. This privileged status is the source of special graces of state granted by God to those who fulfill sincerely the obligations they have undertaken.

EXORCISMS AND SIMPLE BLESSINGS

Exorcisms and simple or prayer-blessings, on the contrary, while they infallibly call upon the intercession of the whole Church, have no specific guaranteed result. Though the bishop or priest acts in virtue of the mission of the Church, there are other considerations to be taken into account, principal among them the dispositions of the faithful.

This is particularly stressed in the case of exorcisms. "Why could not we cast him out?" the disciples ask our Lord after their unsuccessful attempts to expel a demon. "Because of your unbelief," is the reply. "This kind is not cast out but by prayer and fasting" (*Matt.*, 17:18, 20). This restriction applies to exorcisms of the possessed and not to those incorporated into the ritual of the sacraments and of other sacramentals. When the Church permits the more extraordinary form she acts with prudence by adding to the formula of exorcism other good works such as the use of holy water, fasting, adjuration in the name of God; and, in addition, she looks for an outstanding degree of holiness in the minister she entrusts with the act of exorcism.

Similarly, the effect achieved by simple blessings, whether

of persons or of religious objects, depends on the dispositions of the persons who receive the blessing or use the objects. When one of the faithful prays before a blessed statue, quite apart from the psychological assistance given by the image,[3] there is the opportunity, given as a result of the prayers of the whole body of the Church, to receive from God the actual graces needed for devout prayer; here the individual's readiness to cooperate is essential. The like is to be said of blessings directly concerning the moral life of Christians, such as the nuptial blessing or benediction of the Blessed Sacrament.

More complicated is the question of objects used by the faithful in their ordinary occupations. Whether a car blessed according to the formula in the Ritual will escape accident depends on several factors of which the blessing is only one; as far as the driver is concerned it depends on his own driving. It does not at all follow that it is all the same whether his car is blessed or not; the blessing retains its own validity; but it must be remembered that it is a limited validity and that it does not dispense the driver in the slightest degree from normal caution. We are involved here in the mystery of divine Providence; God calls into play a whole network of created causes to bring about any particular effect. The prayer of the Church expressed in her blessing is a strand in the divine pattern for the world; without it the pattern would be different, yet there are many other strands in the design. It may be mentioned in passing that the images of St. Cristopher carried in cars are not sacramentals. While devotion to the saint of travellers is traditional in the Church, one suspects that his present popularity as a driving companion owes more to commercial propaganda than to the preaching of the Gospel. The Church would clearly prefer motorists to have their cars blessed.

Blessings of the tools of trade and of the other material necessities of human life bear out the attribution to sacramentals of temporal benefits, though these are not primarily envisaged. Temporal goods—health, fruitful crops, rain, fair weather and so on—are granted to the prayer of the Church only condition-

---

3. Cf. **The cult of images and sacred art,** "Irish Rosary," 64 (1960), pp. pp. 234-241.

ally, that is to say, only if they are not an obstacle to spiritual good or, to put the same thing more positively, only in so far as they help Christian life. Here again, sacramentals conform to the rule which governs prayer of any kind and it is useless to attempt to decide on general principles whether a man might not be a better Christian if he were assured of a good harvest.

There is some discussion among theologians as to whether sacramentals can win remission of temporal punishment due for sins. Since the whole liturgy of the dead, in particular the funeral rite, is directed towards this purpose it seems clear that they can; but in fact the Church does not appear to have instituted any corresponding sacramental in favour of the living. What the Church does do is attach an indulgence to certain sacramentals; and in virtue of the indulgence, not of the sacramental as such, temporal punishment may be remitted. The apostolic blessing for the hour of death, for example, brings a plenary indulgence and there is a long list of indulgences attached to the papal blessing of religious objects.[4] It would, however, be a mistake to envisage blessings and indulgences as two quite unrelated things. The distinction is somewhat artificial except for lawyers who draw up one document dealing with blessings, another dealing with indulgences. There is a clear distinction between the effects procured by each—the favour of God and remission of temporal punishment—but both are a manifestation of the community of life in the mystical body; and the life of an organism does not conform in its operation to the abstract formulas which express, however accurately, certain aspects of it.

SACRAMENTALS AND LITURGY

If Christians who attribute exaggerated powers to the sacramentals are suspect of superstition, those who deride them as spiritual placebos which cheapen Christianity are at fault in

---

4. The indulgences attached to the papal blessing of religious objects are determined by each pope. For Paul VI's blessing, cf. **Acta Apostolicae Sedis**, 55 (1963), pp. 657-659. This is identical with that of John XXIII (cf. ibid., 51 (1959), pp. 48-50), apart from the addition by Paul VI of the Feast of Our Lady of the Rosary to the feasts on which a plenary indulgence may be gained under prescribed conditions.

their understanding of the deeply human shape that the mystery of salvation takes on in the Church of the Incarnate Word. As developments of the sacramental idea on which Christianity is based, the sacramentals form an integral and typical element of the mystical body.

It is the genius of sacramentalism that it provides fallen man with a connatural vehicle for expressing his religious belief at the same time as it plots his way to the source of holiness, the Blessed Trinity, active in Christ and in the Church. But the full significance of this consecration of material things is not always apparent in the seven sacraments, particularly at a time like the present when the value of symbolism is only obscurely recognized. It is possible to accept the activity and materiality of the central liturgical ritual as a perfectly adapted mode of worship and sanctification for human beings without realizing that one of its principal lessons points to the constant immersion of a holy life in the created world. The sacraments are not escape-hatches through which to abandon the material world and flee to the world of the spirit. They are points of insertion of the Holy Spirit into matter as it falls under the dominion of the human spirit. They are centres of incarnation where vague ideas about Christian virtue should take shape in concrete action directed towards the sanctification of human affairs and of the material world. We are apt to miss the point in the sacraments themselves because we call them "religious ceremonies" and, because of the unfortunate connotations which that phrase has acquired in a secular culture, we are tempted to set them apart from everyday living as though religion had no immediate significance for farming or driving a car or putting out fires or measuring earthquakes. The sacramentals spell out the connection for us. Through the "liturgy of the sacraments and the sacramentals," states the Second Vatican Council, "there is hardly any proper use of material things which cannot be directed towards man's sanctification and God's praise" (Vat. II Const., ch. 3, art. 61).

The medieval view, typified in St. Thomas, only begins to grasp this pedagogy of the sacramentals. It is a centripetal view that the medievals adopted, according to which the ceremonial of the liturgy leads the faithful into fuller appreciation and more fruitful use of the major sacraments, above all the Eucharist. The later development of practice and theology complements this inward-turned contemplative tendency. For the Church as a whole—individuals may be exceptions—withdrawal to the Eucharist must be accompanied by active realization of the eucharistic mystery in the world where men move in a climate of thought foreign to Christianity and where material progress represents the primary objective of the human spirit.

The sacramentals mark the advance of the Church into this outside world, beginning with the private devotions of the faithful, where eccentricity is already a threat to the incarnational mission of Christ, and going on to incorporate into Christ the tools with which man earns his living and the instruments with which he strives to dominate nature. The sacramentals take on endless forms as the Church attempts to expound through their symbolism the implications of the Eucharist and to nudge the faithful into awareness of the fact that being a Christian is a full-time occupation. To this task the sacramentals bring much more than visual aid to education; they carry with them the prayers of the Church, the bride of Christ, whose requests he cannot fail to hear and for whom he intercedes with the Father; they form a line of defence raised by the Church to protect the faithful from evil; they are at the same time the leading edge of the Church's advance into the daily life of the world. The sacramentals are at the service of the priesthood of the faithful. For those who bear the priestly and baptismal characters they lead to the sacraments. For those who bear the characters of orders or confirmation they are efficacious signs of union with the Church in the apostolate.

Because they derive from the sacraments, the sacramentals provide an obvious introduction to the heart of the liturgy and a method of training in putting the lessons of the liturgy into practice. It would be regrettable if the faithful were to give more appreciation to the perimeter of the sacramental system than to its heart; but equally to be deplored would be any attempt on the part of misguided liturgical enthusiasts to pass over as insignificant the Church's ready-made system of liturgical initiation. The liturgical movement will never succeed if its promoters do not learn to respect the spontaneous devotions of the faithful. The task of the pastor is one, not of conversion, but of fuller initiation. This leads to our final chapter.

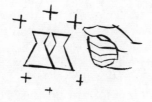

14 Sacramental Piety: Finding Christ

Is it possible to sum up in a few words the central idea which has been put forward in many guises throughout the preceding chapters? Though the discussion has ranged over many subjects there has in fact always been present one dominating problem and theme.

THE BASIC INSIGHT

CHRIST IN THE CHURCH

The sacraments, the Mass, the sacramental roles of Christ and the faithful, the relation between moral effort and liturgical practice—the questions which arise about each of these are various formulations of one basic question concerning the structure of the Church. Sacraments and our part in their celebration, these are activities of the Church and can be understood only when we understand what the Church is. And, to put it in its simplest form, the Church is the place where we must seek for and unite ourselves to Christ our Saviour. "That divine and human institution," Pope John XXIII called it in his address at the opening of the General Council, "the Church of Christ which from Jesus takes its name, its grace and its meaning." For the Church is the body of Christ; and this means not only that its members, through grace, constitute the fullness of that Person in whom God and man are united as Son of the Father, but also that the Church is in intimate contact with the life-giving humanity of the risen Christ so that the Spirit, sent down from heaven by the Redeemer to raise men up as sons of God, is transmitted to individual men through the body of Christ on earth.

Here is the ground-structure, the essential nature of the Church; when we have grasped this we have the fundamental insight from which appreciation of sacramental life derives. That any sort of adequate appreciation demands as well a detailed analysis of a whole series of specific manifestations of the life of the Church will have emerged from the development of our chapters. But the original insight must not be lost through close-up examination of the details. There should be mutual illumination, study of the details lending depth and width to the basic insight, while the insight reveals the harmonious pattern and unity of purpose of the details.

To see Christ in the Church, personally acting through the organs of her visible, earthly structure, so as to build up his own body, this is the key concept of sacramental theology. To seek consciously to discern the features of Christ in the doctrinal, juridical and liturgical organs of the Church and to go forward to live in union with him as he exists and acts through these organs, this is the distinctive characteristic of sacramental piety.

THE CHRIST OF THE SACRAMENTS

This seeking for the Christ of the Church in the Church imparts a colour all its own to the whole life of the Christian. It is not a Christ of our own making that we are looking for, not a Christ fashioned after the image of our own selfish desires. We can be as far off in our personal evaluation of Christ as were the disciples who halted him even as he was about to ascend to the Father and release the Spirit upon the Church: "Lord, wilt thou at this time restore again the kingdom to

Israel?" (*Acts*, 1:6). Not only his patient teaching but the shattering significance of his death and resurrection were passed over in their excitement at the prospect of earthly ambitions fulfilled. Christ living on in the Church is not some kind of superhuman philanthropist, an everyman's millionaire, who can be reckoned on to set to rights economic injustice or mismanagement, or to whom appeal can be made against the consequences of irresponsibility or inefficiency in the conduct of affairs that fall within the competence of earthly society or of individuals.

He is the Christ of revelation, the Word made flesh, in whose person the world-central Alliance between God and man is brought to the peak of realization. He is the Son of God come into the world to restore to humanity the divine sonship which it had rejected. He is the unique Priest of the human race who invites all men to fellowship in his all-embracing act of divine worship. He is the supreme manifestation of the love of God for His children; and at the same time, in him, through his one acceptable sacrifice, all mankind makes its whole-hearted response to divine love. The Christ of the Church is the mediator of the Alliance; to find him in the Church and to accept him is to become a son of God, sharing in his sonship, and to ratify by a life of filial devotion the sacrifice which he offered. The Christ of the Church is the risen Christ who has passed through death to eternal glory; to be united with him through the Church is to enter upon a course of progressive conformation, beginning with resurrection from sin and brought to fulfillment in the vision of God and bodily resurrection.

Christ himself could describe in simple words the object of our search: "Seek first the kingdom of God"; the rest will be given in the measure useful for one who has found the kingdom (cf. *Matt.*, 6:33). This is what liturgical participation is about.

THE CHRIST OF THE EUCHARIST

If sacramental piety derives its basic attitude from contemplation of the authentic Christ of revelation who appears in the Church, it finds the natural focus for its activity in the Blessed Eucharist "the source and centre of true Christian devotion"

(Pius XII, Encyc. *Mediator Dei*, CTSE ed.,[1] §§ 5, 214). The Eucharist is not simply a most perfect way of coming face to face with Christ in the Church; it is the key-stone of the temple of the Spirit which is being built in the world. To be saved is to have fellowship with Christ in and through the Church; and all that is in the Church is directed towards the Eucharist. This idea has already been developed at length in the chapters on the Eucharist; here it must be repeated, for piety is truly sacramental only when there is vivid realization of the supreme dominion of the Eucharist over all men and all things belonging to Christ on earth.

In this sacrament we find our Priest offering the sacrifice which we must offer if we are to please God. Since it is the body of Christ, symbol and source of the mystical body, which is offered, there is no good action of the Christian community which is not drawn into the sacrifice. In this sacrament we eat our sacrificed Saviour, sharing in that union with God in charity which is the fruit of the sacrifice. Unless we eat this sacramental bread we cannot have life in Christ; wherever there is life in Christ the body has been eaten, either actually or in desire. Sacramental piety—which is simply Christian piety fully conscious of itself—is wholly directed to the Eucharist and through it to the Blessed Trinity to whom our sacrifice is offered and in whom we have life.

CHRIST IN OUR LIVES

The broad lines have now been drawn, sketching out the theme which lends unity to the whole Christian life: union with the risen Christ, our Priest, in the Church. But this is nothing more than a schematic presentation of what it means to be a Christian. The life must be lived by individual men through all the changing circumstances of their earthly existence. Here the richness implicit in the theme and the infinite variety of the forms in which it is realized in individuals come to light. To understand sacramental piety adequately it is imperative that these ramifications of the central idea be explored. If they are neglected, as

---

1. Referred to below as: MD.

they have been neglected, at least in part, by many of our contemporaries who have grasped the basic concept, the result is a more or less superficial enthusiasm for things liturgical which is lacking in the subtlety and the flexibility indispensable for dealing with so intimate and personal a matter as union with God.

The liturgy itself, with its system of sacraments radiating from the Eucharist, gives the first indication of the complexity inherent in the unity of the central theme. The sacramental means of union with Christ the Priest are multiplied to accommodate the varied requirements of Christian life. It is a life which must be led in a visible society, in obedience to laws and to a hierarchy; a sacrament of entry with juridical consequences and obligations must be received (baptism). It is a life which imposes apostolic and pastoral duties (accepted in confirmation and orders). It is a life which must transform human nature down to its material roots; marriage consecrates human reproduction and family life. It is a life which must recognize human frailty and man's inability to give himself wholly and constantly to the mystery of love revealed in Christ; confession and anointing are a constant warning against superficial optimism. It is a life which must be sustained by innumerable tiny props, the sacramentals, acting as reminders that union with Christ is something more than a dramatic decision, taken once for all, that it is something which demands generous but painstaking attention to the details of eating and working, learning and praying, suffering and taking one's ease, and doing whatever else belongs to the business of being human.

CHRIST IN THE COMMUNITY

There is another dimension to be discovered in the Christ of the Church. Union with God, while utterly personal, is at the same time achieved only as a member of a community bound together by a common fellowship in the sacrifice of Calvary and the Eucharist. There is one High Priest whose charity is such that it makes the sacrifice of himself valid and saving for all mankind. All those who belong to Christ are united in him to one another, sharing in his universal charity. Ideally this should mean that all the members, and indeed all the redeemed, should live in charity; but even where sin still reigns the charity of Christ is an active force working for full union.

Once again, the Eucharist is central. It symbolizes the fellow-ship of Christians in Christ. To eat the Eucharist is to proclaim one's union, almost one's identity, with one's fellow-members of Christ. Nor may we interpret this in the narrow sense of union with those who join with us in open submission to the vicar of Christ. We proclaim our union in Christ with those also who eat the Eucharist in good faith in the schismatic churches where the sacrament is preserved. We proclaim our union with those whose good will hides an unconscious longing to receive the sacra-ment, and even with those who, though separated from Christ by sin, are numbered among the redeemed; for Christ died for all men and all are called by him to share in his body. It is, in a word, our union with the whole of humanity, our common destiny in Christ, that we proclaim when we receive the Eucharist. Though at present this union is in varying degree imperfect in respect of those who are not in open union with the one, un-divided Church of Christ, nevertheless the obligations which it imposes on us are uniformly exacting.

If the nature of this supernatural union of all men in Christ is mysterious, there is nothing difficult to understand about its practical consequences. The unselfishness of sacramental piety is not confined to submitting our personal ideas and desires to the design of Christ our Priest; it extends our interests and our prayers to the whole human race. It enshrines the true motive for justice and even more for charity in our social contacts: these other persons we are dealing with in the coin of the earthly city are one with us in Christ. It imposes on us the duty of working for the kingdom of God, of preparing the world for the full expansion of the saving power pent up in the sacrifice of Christ. In all his members Christ the Priest is present in human society; his redemptive work must be continued in and through each one of them. Redemption is not brought about exclusively by divine intervention in human affairs; it calls too for specifically human activity directed not only to the explicit proclamation of the Gospel but also towards the full develop-ment of the potentialities of the created world in a fashion harmonious with man's rational nature and divine destiny. Technical progress, above all—since it represents the most dangerous threat of materialism—must be humanized, made to serve, not dominate, human development. Only if this is done will the way be open for the blood of Christ to save, not just individuals, but human society as such. Perhaps this is never to be completely achieved on earth; it still remains a goal to be striven for by every Christian, working at home, at his desk, in his factory or shop, on his fields. Progress in human skills, governed by justice and charity; this is the programme implicitly accepted by the liturgical participation of the adult, confirmed Christian.

THE ROOTS OF SACRAMENTAL PIETY

TRADITIONAL SPIRITUALITY

So far we have been speaking of the dimensions of sacramental piety as they appear from a consideration of the sacraments, especially the Eucharist. But it is vitally important for practice to understand that piety is piety before it is sacramental. It is undoubtedly true that in redeemed man there is no such thing as sanctifying grace, pure and simple; all grace is sacramental in one way or another because given in virtue of a sacrament received either actually or in desire. This fact—which provides yet another insight into the structure of the Church—does not take away in the slightest from another fact, namely, that sacramental grace is in essence sanctifying grace, even though adapted to the conditions of life in the Church, and that, consequently it subjects the person whom it makes a son of God to the norms which govern the activity and development of a free person. The Christian life, sacramental piety, must spring up from the deep centre of human nature; it cannot be imposed from outside; it cannot flourish if participation in the liturgy or in the apostolate is something accepted only on the surface of consciousness and is not the natural, spontaneous flowering of a root planted deep in the individual Christian.

Here is where vision of the central theme of sacramental piety fails unless it is accompanied by appreciation for the normal demands of traditional spirituality. God is not honoured by "fine words and theatrical gestures" if sin has not been uprooted (MD § 25). The sacraments are certainly the dominant means given for progress in Christian virtue; but they do not provide an alternative route. Man has a certain kind of nature and one which is injured by sin; he can make himself a better man, he can intensify his union with Christ, only if he is prepared to undertake the painful task of ridding himself of bad habits and cultivating good ones. The grace of the sacraments enables the Christian to carry out this task. Conversion from sin and progress in virtue is the work of the Blessed Trinity in man. Yet this mystery of salvation takes effect in terms of human resolution and self-discipline with all the difficulties that these entail.

There is, however, this to be said. If by sacramental piety we mean a service of God which is consciously based on what we have called an insight into the central theme of Redemption and of the liturgy, then this kind of piety will eliminate from the Christian life a great deal of the unattractiveness, the sense of deliberate rejection of human nature, that appears in some of the classic texts of spirituality. This inhuman rationalization of the Christian life has no place in the authentic tradition of the Church. It harks back to a strain in St. Augustine's writings where, however, in the context of the contrasts and paradoxes characteristic of the great doctor of grace, it loses its harshness in the light of the mystery of Christ. But a current of theology, exaggerating St. Augustine's "pessimism," began to gather strength in the fourteenth century. It swept aside the splendour of St. Thomas's synthesis of reason and faith, nature and grace, in which each order receives its due respect and the two are coordinated in a harmonious Christian whole. It found its greatest exponent in Luther who could exalt the salvation of Christ only at the expense of human nature. Its influence remained at work within the Church where its greatest triumph was Jansenism, a heresy that still taints the outlook of many whose orthodoxy in matters of faith cannot be called in doubt.

As St. Pius X so well understood when he issued his decree on frequent communion, the liturgy has its own methods of forming an authentic Christian mentality. The spirit of pharisaical narrowness must struggle hard to resist the serenity and breadth of vision with which the liturgy contemplates the Blessed Trinity,

Creator of the world no less than Author of salvation. The reality of the Christian life remains the same; what is changed is our attitude to it. In place of a lonely struggle against self, which if not exactly joyless is saved from this only grudgingly, there is an awareness of the full meaning of what one is about, a realization that one is involved in the great mystery of love that took shape in Christ, the purpose of which is to bring to perfection all that is human, rejecting only sin.

TRUE PIETY

The dangers of a too superficial view of the liturgy which would neglect the solid spadework of Christian conversion have been carefully charted by Pius XII. With deliberate intent he reverts to the undecorated language of Scholasticism when he wants to make it quite clear that liturgical participation is not a discovery of the twentieth century which permits us to dispense with old-fashioned methods of spirituality or apostolate. He writes:

> True piety, or "devotion" as St. Thomas calls it, is the chief act of the virtue of religion; it is the act by which a man is set in his right relation to God, properly directed to Him, by which he promptly and willingly devotes himself to all that concerns the worship of God (*Summa theol.*, II-II, q. 82, a. 1). Now if such devotion is to be nourished, if it is to be vigorously alive, if it is to impel us to lead a more perfect life, we need meditation on heavenly things and we need spiritual exercises. If the Christian religion is to be practised as it should, the will must in the first place dedicate itself to God and by its influence control the other faculties of the soul. Now any act of will presupposes an act of intelligence; and therefore before there can be any resolution to consecrate oneself to Almighty God by an act of sacrifice, there must be a knowledge of the facts and reasons upon which the obligation of religion is based.... And because motives of love do not always appeal to the soul, which is sometimes under the stress of evil desires, it is also most oppor-

tune that we should be moved to salutary compunction by the consideration of the divine justice, and so be brought to a sense of Christian humility, and to repentance and amendment (MD § 35).

"Everything," adds Pius XII later, "must be disposed in its proper order, 'theocentrically' as one might say, if we sincerely want everything to be dedicated to God's glory by means of the life and power that flow into us from the divine Head" (MD § 37).

To expect external or ceremonial liturgical participation of itself to reanimate the Christian community is like thinking that a prize rose can be produced by binding together fallen petals. Admitting all that can be said about the educative value of the Church's prayer and ceremonial, it still remains true that external participation is more an effect than a cause of genuine devotion.

VERNACULAR LITURGY

This last consideration helps us to put in its proper perspective the question of a vernacular liturgy. We are of course meant to understand the prayers and readings; but such understanding is not so desirable that to it should be sacrificed other secondary benefits of the liturgy. The fact that the principal parts of the Roman rite are conducted in Latin—and, by decision of the Second Vatican Council, will as a rule continue so—need present no obstacle to the Christian whose attachment to the liturgy springs from a deeply-felt desire for union with Christ in the Church. We must never allow ourselves to forget that far more is hidden in the liturgy than can be seen or heard. The problem of communication with Christ and with one's fellow-worshippers is to be solved primarily on the level, not of words, but of interior dispositions. While words and understanding them are important, this is not so crucial an issue in community worship as in private prayer; and consequently, if a choice has to be made in the liturgy, verbal understanding may be more easily renounced. It is not being suggested that this is an ideal solution; it is simply making the best of an unsatisfactory situation in which a language which in itself has everything to recommend it as a liturgical medium is no longer widely understood. As a result of the Council certain faculties will be extended to regional conferences of bishops so that modifications may be made regarding the use of the vernacular in the specifically instructional parts of the Mass, in the restored "Prayer of the Faithful," and in other parts of the liturgy; but there is no justification for dissatisfaction because in the present circumstances Latin is preserved as the first language of the Roman liturgy (cf. Vat. II Const., ch. 1, art. 36; ch. 2. arts. 54, 63, 76, 78, 101). A readiness to submerge oneself in the worship of the universal Church implies a deeper understanding of the reality of what is being done by the community than does facility in reading the texts. If we cannot have both of these together without thereby forfeiting other benefits, then we will lose nothing essential by renouncing the second.

REVISION, NOT REVOLUTION

What all this discussion of the roots of sacramental piety comes to is that those who form the serious core of the liturgical movement are seeking, not for a revolution in Christian spirituality, but for a revision of attitude. They want to see the restoration to Christian consciousness of a unified master-concept which will give meaning and proportion to the multiplicity of details which go to make up the pattern of a life dedicated to Christ the Priest. "The society founded by the divine Redeemer," Pius XII puts it, "has only one aim, whether in her doctrine and government, whether in the sacrifice and sacraments which he instituted, whether in the ministry which he entrusted to her, or in the prayers she offers and the blood she sheds: to grow and become more closely knit as one body. And this happens when Christ is, after a manner, built into the souls of men and grows in them, and when souls also are built into Christ and grow in him" (MD § 18; cf. §§ 38-41).

THE PRACTICAL APPROACH

OUT-OF-TOUCH LITURGISM

There is an important practical consequence to be drawn from what has gone before. Genuine liturgical participation is not something that can be procured by clerical ukase or hastened by

impatience, clerical or lay. Confusion and irritation will be the
only result of imposing prematurely a form of external worship
which is neither familiar nor welcome. Nor does it appear that
instruction, however necessary this may be, is enough to make
participation whole-hearted, at least for the majority of the
faithful. It is all very well for Benedictines to enthuse about the
hieratic perfection of liturgical ceremony and prayer, or for
Dominicans to analyse the theological significance of lay participation; both—and any others who join them—ought to be aware
that what they are talking about can have direct appeal only to
a minority. Minorities are of course vitally important and, it is
to be hoped, can influence others; but the liturgy is meant for all.

We are touching here upon a symptom of a malaise that can
be discovered in more than one of the vital movements of renewal
which are sweeping through the Church. We could perhaps
characterize the spirit of all these movements as a search for
wholeness. In theology an attempt is being made to exploit the
richness of the sources so as to give new authority, freshness and
depth to the science. Our view of the Church is being broadened
as we attempt to establish the role of the layman and the position
of the non-Catholic. The liturgical movement seeks to give a
broader, more authentic base to the devotion of the faithful. But
the result of all this in practice is too often, not wholeness of
outlook, but a new exclusiveness. Too many of those who are
attempting to find a new approach in catechetics, for example,
interpret the biblical revival as a rejection of traditional theology.
Theologians, an influential few, appeal to the charismatic and
prophetic function of the Church against the central teaching
authority which is described as infallible—of course—but ultra-
conservative. Laymen produce magazines notable more for enthusiasm for the latest piece of theological journalism than for awareness of what theology is. Those who have discovered, but not
meditated upon, the liturgy are not content unless everybody
has a missal in hand and novenas are suppressed. Theological
fantasies, such as the suggested abolition of Masses where no
congregation is present, are put forward as self-evident reforms.
A great deal of this, probably all of it, is well-intentioned; but
what it amounts to is a blind rejection of all that is "old," "post-
Reformation," even, in more daring circles, "Tridentine." Noth-

ing, of course, breeds enthusiasm so much as the simplicity of a single, half-formed idea.

Extremism of this kind defeats its own purpose; it inevitably provokes reaction. The new movements are deformed by their publicists, the parasites of modern theology, and opposed by those who recognize the lack of balance in the movement's most articulate supporters. Instead of wholesale rejection of what is "new" or "old," what is required is a cautious process of assimilation, an acceptance of what good there is in new approaches, integrating it into the traditional wisdom of the Church. This will involve change in ways of thinking and behaving, a weeding out of foreign growths that have sprung up on the authentic tree of tradition, a reformation of whatever is of only passing value and has now lost its significance. But what has been proved by the test of time, the system of thought which has won the approval of the Church, practices that have brought men to God, devotions that touch the heart of the faithful, these cannot—and, though lacking the charism of prophecy, we may add, will not—be surrendered. If the liturgy—to restrict a much wider problem to the field which interests us here—is to be restored to its place in the affections of the faithful, then liturgists must learn to be prudent and, above all, to be sympathetic to the natural instinct of the Christian.

POPULAR LITURGY

Is it not time for liturgists to ask themselves why popular devotions are popular and whether the liturgy could not be made popular too? If derivation of words has any significance, "popular" and "liturgical" should mean the same thing. It is too easy to dismiss novenas and triduums as appealing to selfish motives; it is indicative too of selective reading of *Mediator Dei* which speaks of "pious practices which, though not belonging strictly to the liturgy, nevertheless enjoy a special importance and dignity, such that they are regarded as raised to liturgical rank, and have received repeated approval from this Apostolic See and the episcopate" (MD § 194; cf. Vat. II Const., ch. 1, arts. 12, 13). As examples, the encyclical goes on to list May devotions, devotions to the Sacred Heart in June, novenas, triduums, the Stations of the Cross, "and other devotional exercises." Their value lies in the fact that they bring people to the sacraments and incite them to meditate on the mysteries of Redemption and to imitate the example of the saints; "they therefore cause us to take part in the liturgy with greater spiritual profit" (MD § 195). The rosary is given special commendation (MD § 186). It would be "damaging as well as erroneous" to attempt to change all these practices and to fit them into the framework of the liturgy (MD § 196).

That non-liturgical devotions can be abused, that they can give the impression that the Christian life consists in "a multiplicity of different prayers and devotional practices," Pius XII is quick to point out (MD §§ 196, 197). They "must be influenced by the spirit and principles of the liturgy" (MD § 196); they should have in view the end proposed by the Eternal Father who "has chosen us out, in Christ, before the foundation of the world, to be saints, to be blameless in his sight" (Eph., 1:4; cf. MD § 197). "These devotions," says the Second Vatican Council, "should be so arranged, with a view to the liturgical seasons, that they harmonize with the sacred liturgy, are in some fashion derived from it, and lead the people to it; for the liturgy, by its very nature, far surpasses them all." There is a positive suggestion here that liturgists cannot afford to ignore. The enthusiasm and spontaneity which inspire popular devotions must be directed towards the liturgy, led to find in it a connatural mode of expression. Sympathy is the watchword here, sympathy for the feelings of ordinary people who do not feel at home with a form of worship which appears out of touch with the human problems that they want to bring before God.

THE SYMPATHY OF CHRIST

Less often quoted than *Mediator Dei*, another encyclical of Pius XII explains the doctrine of the Sacred Heart (*Haurietis aquas*, 1956). It should be made required reading for everybody who feels enthusiasm for the liturgy for it is an example of translating a popular devotion into terms of integral Christian piety.

This is authentic liturgical training which develops what the faithful already possess and treasure, and is not simply an arbitrary introduction of unfamiliar formulas.

Pius XII distinguishes between "the essential nature" of devotion to the Sacred Heart and "the various forms in which it finds expression." The latter "the Church encourages and fosters, but does not impose them as of obligation"; but this does not mean that the cult itself is something "non-essential and added, which the individual may adopt, or not, as he pleases" (*Haurietis Aquas*, CTSE ed.[2], § 6). In its essential nature this cult:

> is a most excellent act of religion; since it involves on our part a total and unreserved intention of giving and consecrating ourselves to the divine Redeemer's love, to which love his wounded Heart is a living pointer and symbol. It is equally, if not more clear, that the principal idea of this cult or devotion is that we should ourselves make a return of love to the divine love (HA § 4).

This is, of course, almost exactly the same language as that used by liturgists. But there is this difference: in the cult of the Sacred Heart a direct appeal is made to the fullness of human love in both Christ and the faithful. By that is meant that this devotion does not neglect the emotional factor in human love. Theologians sometimes overtrain their intelligences at the expense of their emotions and forget that the people they are writing about, if not as learned as themselves, may well have preserved a more perfect human balance in their own lives and may, consequently, be able to react to contact with other persons in a more fully human fashion, emotionally as well as intellectually. The faithful are meant to do this when they encounter the person of Christ; for he comes into the world with a full and perfectly-balanced human nature and appeals to mankind with his whole being. "For we have not a high priest who cannot have compassion on our infirmities; but one tempted in all things like as we are, without sin" (Heb., 4:15). Pius XII writes:

---

2. Referred to below as: **HA**.

It is St. Augustine who in a special way draws our attention to the connection between the emotions of the Incarnate Word and the purpose of man's Redemption. "These emotions of our human weakness, together with the very flesh of our human weakness, and death of our human flesh, the Lord Jesus did assume, not indeed through any compulsion in which he was placed, but of his free-will, impelled by pity. For he wished to transform into himself his body, even the Church whose Head he has deigned to be; to transform, in other words, his members, that is his saints and faithful ones, so that, if any of them should happen to grieve and sorrow in the midst of human temptations, such a one should not for that reason think himself to be out of his grace, and, like a choir coming in on the opening notes of its leader, so the body should learn from its own Head that these things are not sins, but merely concomitants of our human weakness" (Comm. on Ps. 87:3; HA § 25).

And then, quoting St. John Damascene, *The orthodox faith*, III, 6:

He wholly assumed me wholly; and Whole was made one with whole, that he might bring salvation to whole. For otherwise what had not been assumed, could not be healed (HA § 25).

The Sacred Heart, united hypostatically to the divine Word, is the symbol of three loves: the love of God for man, the charity of Christ's human soul, and Christ's emotional affection (HA § 27). The faithful recognize the human appeal of this Heart, the sympathy of Christ for their human problems, felt in every part of his human nature. He, by his Incarnation, has brought salvation to all that is in man; he draws men to himself through every particle of their being.

THE TWO HEARTS

The liturgy, since it is the place of meeting between men and Christ, true man as well as true God, must not be over-intellectualized. Its symbolism must not be explained away in terms of mind and will exclusively. Our offering to be reasonable—in the magnificent phrase of the Litany of the Saints—does not have to be superhuman. The human appeal of the Sacred Heart must be preserved. What is called for is an exploitation of the full significance of this devotion. The Sacred Heart must be seen to be the heart of Christ's priesthood. The faithful must be led to understand and to feel that no more intimate contact can be achieved with the Sacred Heart than in the Mass and the sacraments. The responses of the dialogue Mass must be interpreted in terms of the spontaneous religious feeling of the faithful, while at the same time the call to lofty Christian endeavour which these responses enshrine should be made clear. "Without any doubt," says Pius XII, "a burning devotion to the Heart of Jesus will cherish and advance our reverence for the holy cross especially, and our love for the august sacrament of the altar" (HA § 71).

The supreme example of liturgical participation is to be found in the Immaculate Heart of Mary, standing at the foot of the cross. The perfect harmony of these two Hearts, Christ's and Mary's, is the ideal pursued by the Church in the liturgy.

Index

See also Contents